2945

D0817871

Essential Blogging

Essential Blogging

Cory Doctorow, Rael Dornfest, J. Scott Johnson,
Shelley Powers, Benjamin Trott, and Mena G. Trott

O'REILLY®

Beijing · Cambridge · Farnham · Köln · Paris · Sebastopol · Taipei · Tokyo

Essential Blogging

by Cory Doctorow, Rael Dornfest, J. Scott Johnson, Shelley Powers, Benjamin Trott, and Mena G. Trott

Copyright © 2002 O'Reilly & Associates, Inc. All rights reserved.
Printed in the United States of America.

Published by O'Reilly & Associates, Inc., 1005 Gravenstein Highway North, Sebastopol, CA 95472.

O'Reilly & Associates books may be purchased for educational, business, or sales promotional use. Online editions are also available for most titles (*safari.oreilly.com*). For more information, contact our corporate/institutional sales department: (800) 998-9938 or *corporate@oreilly.com*.

Editor:	Nathan Torkington
Production Editor:	Sarah Sherman
Cover Designer:	Ellie Volckhausen
Interior Designer:	Melanie Wang

Printing History:

September 2002:   First Edition.

ISBN: 0-596-00388-9   [10/02]
[M]

Table of Contents

Preface

Blogging has exploded. Every day 1,500–3,000 new bloggers join the Internet. That's a staggering number of new voices, new opinions, and new experiences. You can join these bloggers—all it takes is some software and something to say. We've written this book to help you quickly get up and running with the software.

There are many different choices for blogging software, with names running the gamut from the obvious (Blogger) to the literary (Movable Type) to the bizarre (Blosxom). Everyone who blogs has an opinion about the software they use and often about software they don't use. This book tries to take a balanced look at some representative blogging tools and to show you how to use them to produce a unique blog worthy of your thoughts.

We start by defining a blog and how the various blogging tools differ in features, price, and ease of use. The first chapter will help you find a blogging system. The second chapter surveys some programs that can make posting and maintaining a blog easier, regardless of which tool you choose.

The rest of the book is devoted to the tools. For each tool, we show you how to install and configure it, post to and maintain your blog, customize your blog's appearance, syndicate stories with other blogs, and customize and manage your archive of old posts.

Generally, it takes two chapters to explain all the functions of each tool. Some products might have very simple posting maintenance but complex templates, or have simple installation but complex syndication. For this reason, the division of material between the introductory and the advanced chapters isn't consistent from product to product.

Finally, we end with advice from experienced bloggers; what to do, what not to do, and how blogging has changed people. We don't provide much information on the philosophy and sociology of blogging—we don't address the question "Is Blogging Journalism?", nor do we try to define just what a *warblogger* is. Our main objective is to help you select a blog system and get it up and running as soon as possible.

Audience for This Book

If you want to know how to start and run a blog, this book is for you. You can quickly learn which blogging system is right for you, and then you can soon run your first blog.

If you already run a blog, you may still be able to learn about desktop clients in Chapter 2 or learn more about your chosen blogging system from the later chapters. We've tried to provide you with the information you'd have otherwise spent a year learning. We do not cover every feature of every blogging tool exhaustively, so if you've been using and customizing your blogging environment for a long time, you probably know everything we say and more.

You don't have to be a power user to run your own blog. The software described in this book runs the gamut of complexity, from Blogger (no deep computer knowledge required) to Blosxom (designed for Unix tinkerers and experimenters).

You don't have to be a Unix guru or own a PC. There are blogging systems that run on Windows, Macintosh, and Unix machines. None of the systems we describe in this book require guru-level knowledge of the operating system to install, configure, or use.

Although some systems attempt to hide it from you, blog posts are eventually turned into HTML. Most blogs let you write and edit HTML. However, this book doesn't cover how to design in HTML. For more information on HTML, we recommend *Learning Web Design*, by Jennifer Niedherst (O'Reilly).

To benefit from this book, all you need is interest, enthusiasm, and some basic technical know-how.

Structure of This Book

We've arranged the material in this book so that you learn about blog systems, acquiring the knowledge to select one that's right for your needs, then jump straight to the chapters that address those needs.

Chapter 1, *Introduction to Blogging*, talks about the different types of blogs, their basic structure, and the different features of the various blog management systems.

Chapter 2, *Desktop Clients*, shows you several programs that run on your PC or Macintosh and lets you post to your blog more easily than your blogging system may otherwise allow.

Chapter 3, *Hosted Blogging with Blogger*, shows you how to create a Blogger blog, create and manage posts, change your archives, adjust the look of your blog, and start a group blog, as well as show to use Blogger to create a blog on your own web site.

Chapter 4, *Desktop Blogging with Radio UserLand*, covers downloading and installing Radio UserLand, creating posts and stories, adding titles and images to posts, and adjusting your preferences.

Chapter 5, *Server Blogging with Movable Type*, shows you how to install and configure Movable Type, configure your blog, add authors and entries, and add images and comments.

Chapter 6, *Advanced Blogger*, discusses the advanced features of subscription-based Blogger Pro, as well as Blogger template and archive customization, blogrolls, statistics, syndication, and more.

Chapter 7, *Advanced Radio UserLand*, covers shortcuts and categories, backing up Radio, customizing the appearance with Themes and Macros, Upstreaming, and explains a little about the software behind Radio UserLand.

Chapter 8, *Advanced Movable Type*, goes into detail on templates, archives, security, and gives a cookbook of such tricks as displaying random entries.

Chapter 9, *Minimalist Blogging with Blosxom*, shows you how to install, configure, and use the Blosxom blogging system, including the Blagg RSS aggregator.

Chapter 10, *Blogging Voices*, is a collection of advice and experience from seasoned bloggers.

Conventions Used in This Book

The following typographic conventions are used in this book:

Italic
> Used for file and directory names, email addresses, Unix commands, and URLs, as well as for new terms where they are defined.

Constant Width
> Used for code listings and for keywords, variables, tags, functions, command options, and strings where they appear in the text.

Constant Width Bold
> Used to mark lines of output in examples.

Constant Width Italic
> Used as a general placeholder to indicate items that should be replaced by actual values.

This icon designates a note, which is an important aside to the nearby text.

 This icon designates a warning relating to the nearby text.

Comments and Questions

Please address comments and questions concerning this book to the publisher:

O'Reilly & Associates, Inc.
1005 Gravenstein Highway North
Sebastopol, CA 95472
(800) 998-9938 (in the United States or Canada)
(707) 829-0515 (international/local)
(707) 829-0104 (fax)

There is a web page for this book that lists errata, examples, or any additional information. You can access this page at:

http://www.oreilly.com/catalog/essblogging

To comment or ask technical questions about this book, send email to:

bookquestions@oreilly.com

For more information about books, conferences, Resource Centers, and the O'Reilly Network, see the O'Reilly web site at:

http://www.oreilly.com

Acknowledgments

We would like to thank the following people for their generous contributions to this book: DJ Adams, Aherdofturtles, Amber, Timothy Appnel, Brent Ashley, Elaine Ashton, Ali Baitam, Robert Barksdale, Craig Barratt, Paul Beard, Kristine Beeson, Jenny Berger, Thomas Beutel, David Bigwood, Michelle Billies, Tim Bishop, Laura Blalock, Bryce Bounds, Ralph Brandi, Rowan Brewer, Dan Bricklin, Paul Brown, Buzz Bruggeman, Leslie Camacho, Shannon Campbell, Chris Carline, Todd Chapman, Chewybrain, Tom Coates, Mike Coen, Jay Cross, Christian Crumlish, David Davies, Joey deVilla, Hernani Dimantas, Eric Dolecki, K. Dadamo, Meryl K. Evans, Faust, Shawn FitzGerald, Jane Fothergill, Andy Fragan, Elaine Frankonis, Richard Giles, Dan Gilmor, Danny Glassmann, Ewan R. Grantham, Joyce Guan, Mike Gunderloy, Jimmy Guterman, Guy K. Hass, Greg Hard, Eszter Hargittai, Guy Haas, Patrick

Nielsen Hayden, Andrew Helsby, Dan Hersam, Morbus Iff, Chris Janton, Justin Klubnik, Mark Kraft, Mike Krus, Greg, Kucharo, Andrew Kueneman, Ehud, Lamm, Fred Lapides, Ilya Eric Lee, Lawrence Lee, Greg Leffler, William Leshner, Russ Lipton, Victor, Lombardi, Erwin Lyndon J. Lomibao, lyndy, Ryan A. MacMichael, Tim Maloney, Kevin Marks, Lindsay Marshall, Gordon McLean, Allan Moult, Lauri Mueller, Ed Murray, Robert Occhialini, Debbi Ridpath Ohi, Teresa Ortega, Jorge Otero, Abigail Leah Plumb, Derek Powazek, Mike Riley, Phil Ringnalda, Guido van Rossum, Allan Rousselle, Victor R. Ruiz, Jake Savin, Doc Searls, Bill Seitz, Kaiser Shahid, Ed Silva, Alison Sirota, Lisa L. Spangenberg, Frank Steele, Mike Stevenson, SubAverage, Andrew Sylvestor, ThatGrrl, Gasper Torriero, Roger Turner, Jon Udell, Benjamin Vierck, Donald Weightman, Tyler Weir, Robert Williams, Evan Williams, Dave Winer, Peter Wolf, Phil Wolff, Matt Yarbrough, Mark Yeager, Sie Yin, Jason Zada, Steve Zellers, Judith Zissman.

Cory

I'd like to thank Tom Coates, Joey DeVilla, Meryl K. Evans, Dan Gilmor, Patrick Nielsen Hayden, Mark Frauenfelder, Debbi Ridpath Ohi, Teresa Ortega, Derek Powazek, Dave Winer, Judith Zissman, Rael Dornfest, and Nat Torkington.

Rael

To Asha and Sam, my inspiration and support, I dedicate my work on Blosxom and this book.

And, of course, many thanks to my gentle readers and dedicated contributors, without whom this would all be just so much software.

Scott

I'd like to thank Guy K. Haas, Lawrence Lee, Jake Savin, Andrew Sylvester, Russ Lipton, Eszter Hargittai, and Buzzy Bruggeman.

Shelley

I'd like to thank Laurie Petrycki and Simon St. Laurent for allowing me time off from the *Unix Power Tools* and *Practical RDF* books in order to work on the *Essential Blogging* book.

I'd also like to thank my weblogging virtual neighborhood for making weblogging much more interesting.

CHAPTER 1

Introduction to Blogging

Here's a dry definition of a blog:

> A *blog* is a web page that contains brief, discrete hunks of information called *posts*. These posts are arranged in reverse-chronological order (the most recent posts come first). Each post is uniquely identified by an anchor tag, and it is marked with a permanent link that can be referred to by others who wish to link to it.

That's what a blog *is*, but not what it's *for*. A blog is a means of communication, and there are many different types of messages carried by blogs. Some are nothing but pointers to other web sites, while others run long essays; some are personal diaries, others feature technology; some are edited by one person, others by teams.

This chapter is an introduction to the world of blogging. You'll learn key terms such as *blog* and *syndication*, see the different types of blog, analyze the ingredients of a blog, and compare and contrast the different ways you can run your own blog. After reading this chapter, you can make an intelligent decision on which blogging system to use and will know which of the later technology-specific chapters are for you.

The World of Blogging

There are hundreds of thousands of blogs on the Internet, and new blogs are created every day. Originally, they were known as *weblogs*, a term coined by Jorn Barger. The word implies that it might be a record of where some editor has been that day and what she has seen along the way. Now they're *blogs* (as in "we blog"), a term coined in jest by Peter Merholz (*http://www.peterme.com*), and contain everything from political commentary to private journals.

The word *blog* is also a verb meaning to maintain a blog ("Yah, I blog from time to time.") or to post something to a blog ("Oh, that is *so cool*, I'm gonna blog it as soon as I get home."). Most people use software to automate the maintenance of their blogs, rather than edit the raw HTML themselves. Chapters 2 through 9 explore some of the most popular blogging tools.

Can I Blog?

Short answer: yes. There are bloggers of all types, equipped with all levels of technical skill. From Octavia Philips's personal blog at *http://www.tavie.com* to Charlie Stross's auctorial blog at *http://www.antipope.org/charlie/blosxom.cgi*, bloggers approach their sites with as much variety and passion as the general Net public approaches the Web itself.

What Would I Talk About?

Creating a taxonomy of the blogiverse is a fruitless task. There's no good, central directory of blogs that puts each one in its own pigeonhole, because even the most topical blogger will stray from the subject from time to time to celebrate some personal victory or warn his readers off a terrible movie.

Blogs are rich tapestries of something-or-other, mind-croggling crazy quilts of opinion, fact, community, humor, bile, and lust.

Cult figures such as Neil Gaiman, an award-winning writer best known for the *Sandman* comics (*http://www.neilgaiman.com/journal/journal.asp*), and Wil Wheaton, geek hero best known for his role as Ensign Wesley Crusher on *Star Trek: The Next Generation* (*http://www.wilwheaton.net*), blog, holding forth on the subjects that have wandered over their personal and creative transoms that day.

Amateur pundits such as Jorn Barger (*http://www.robotwisdom.com*) and pros such as Andrew Sullivan (*http://www.andrewsullivan.com*) comment on current affairs and make political points.

People from all walks of life maintain personal diaries, from Scraps deSelby's Live-Journal (*http://baldanders.livejournal.com*), which chronicles his obsession with music and his struggle to stay employed in New York City to Punk Rock Girl (*http://www.mokuzen.net/journal/*), the caffeinated rantings of its eponymous author. Journalists, such as the *San Jose Mercury*'s Dan Gillmor, keep blogs (*http://www.dangillmor.com*) where they engage in "Journalism 3.0," interacting with the subjects of and audiences for their articles in real time; Paul Boutin, former senior editor of *Wired* magazine, does much the same on his blog (*http://paulboutin.weblogger.com*), where he has taken to drumming up scientists to debunk the claims of conspiracy nuts who say the Pentagon bombing was faked.

Freelance analyst George Scriban (*http://www.scriban.com*) keeps a blog where he dissects the "piracy" claims of the entertainment industry by gathering (and linking to) data from sources all over the Web, taking investigative journalism to the next level. Jason Lubyk of New World Disorder (*http://www.drmenlo.com/nwd/*) posts a half-dozen news-of-the-weird stories every day, while Gary Farber's Amygdala (*http://amygdalagf.blogspot.com*) does much the same with lengthy commentary and analysis.

Glenn Fleishman's 802.11b Networking News (*http://80211b.weblogger.com*) is *the* place for news and analysis of new wireless networking technology. He's not the only one—bloggers cover technology like no other subject. Wes Felter's pithy notes on Hack The Planet (*http://wmf.editthispage.com*) provide razor-sharp point-form commentary on important tech news.

The author of this chapter is Cory Doctorow, a coeditor of a blog called *Boing Boing: A Directory of Wonderful Things.* Boing Boing (*http://www.boingboing.net*) originated as a paper "cyberculture" zine, and while the medium has changed, the content is much the same: snide and impassioned commentary on technology, civil liberties, Disney theme parks, community wireless networks, science fiction, natural oddities, and Fortean phenomena, *und zo wieter.* While all three contributors to Boing Boing earn parts of their living as professional journalists, the blog is a wonderful opportunity for us to spout off on the subjects we're excited about, without having to duke it out with an editor over subject and word choice.

Anatomy of a Blog

Figure 1-1 shows Kottke.org, while Figure 1-2 shows Calamondin (*http://www.calamondin.com*).

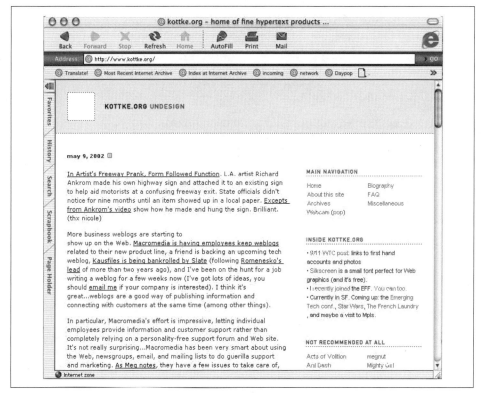

Figure 1-1. Kottke.org

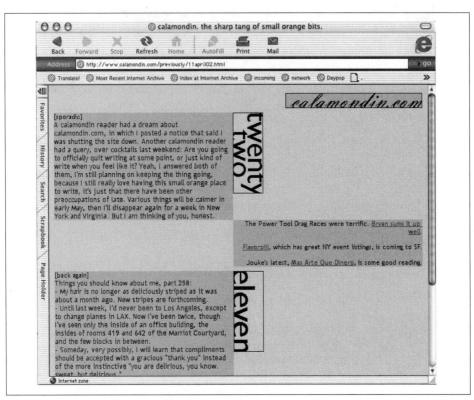

Figure 1-2. Calamondin

Figure 1-3 shows Camworld (*http://www.camworld.com*).

Figures 1-1, 1-2, and 1-3 are all distinctive in look and content, but they share a similar structure. A title, a logo, suggested links, and a list of current entries are all standard components of a modern blog.

Here and in the next section, we'll look at these elements, drawing our examples from Boing Boing (Figure 1-4).

Title

Titles are pretty self-explanatory. As with any project name, your blog's title should be easy to remember, catchy, easy to spell, and distinctive. My favorite blog title of all time is "Insolvent Republic of Blogistan" (*http://slotman.blogspot.com*). A good, distinctive title helps people find your blog easily on Google if they lose the address (so think twice before naming your blog after the English rock band "The The").

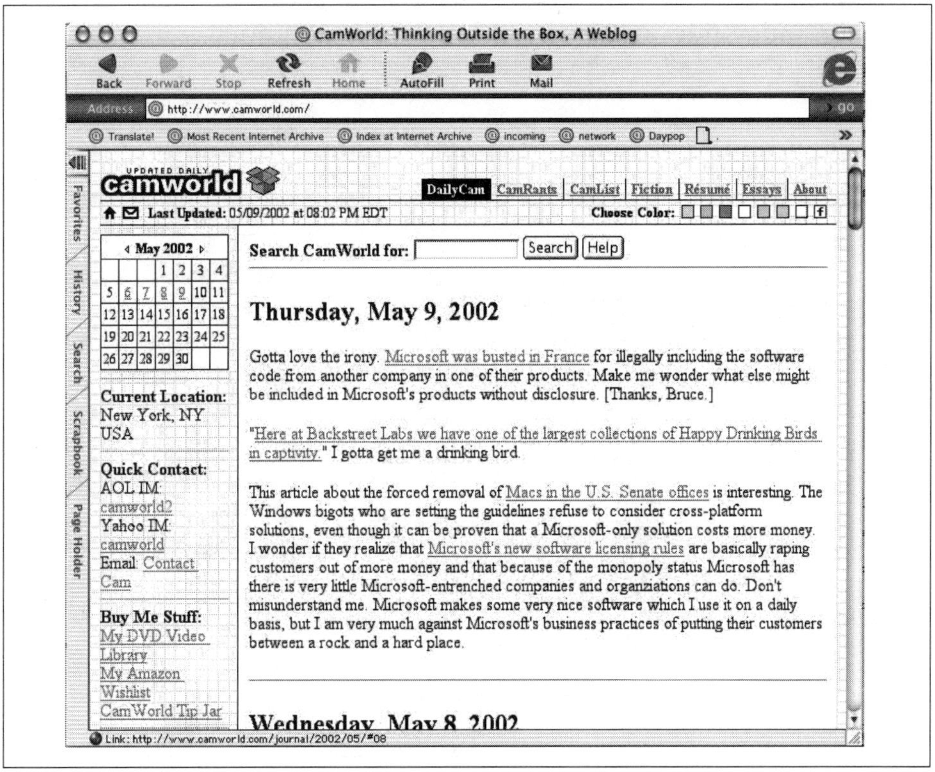

Figure 1-3. Camworld

Subtitle

A subtitle is an opportunity to further explain the raison d'etre of your blog or to indulge in a bit of wit. Here are some examples:

Kottke.org (http://www.kottke.org)
 "Home of Fine Hypertext Products"

Electrolite (http://nielsenhayden.com/electrolite/)
 "Growing Luminous by Eating Light"

Scripting News (http://www.scripting.com)
 "It's a weblog about scripting and stuff like that"

While not obligatory, subtitles are a widely used convention in blogging. Figure 1-4 shows Boing Boing's subtitle.

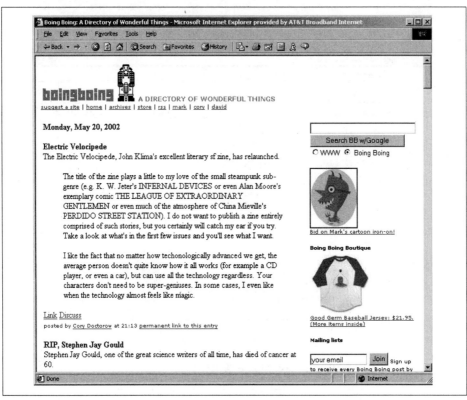

Figure 1-4. Boing Boing

Suggest Link

Blogging is a collaboration between readers and writers. As people become familiar with your blog, they may stumble upon interesting material that they think might interest you. A suggest link gives your readers an easy way to send suggestions. Figure 1-5 shows Boing Boing's suggest link. Some advice on handling suggestions:

- You don't need to follow every suggestion you get—it's your blog.
- You don't need to explain why you're not following any given suggestion—it's your blog.
- If someone pesters you about your rejection of his suggestion, try a response like "Sorry, it just didn't tickle my bloggerbone," which is, of course, another way of saying, "It's my blog."
- Be sure to attribute suggested links that you include in your blog ("Thanks, John!").

We used to thank every person who sent in a suggestion, but we get lots and lots of suggestions on Boing Boing (over 30 suggestions per day), and it became impractical. This Boing Boing form is shown in Figure 1-5.

Your suggestion link can be a simple `mailto` link that sends you a message by email. On Boing Boing, we use a form with a script that my pal Chris Smith wrote and hosts for us. You could use a script like Formmail from *http://nms-cgi.sourceforge.net*. The Boing Boing form is shown in Figure 1-5.

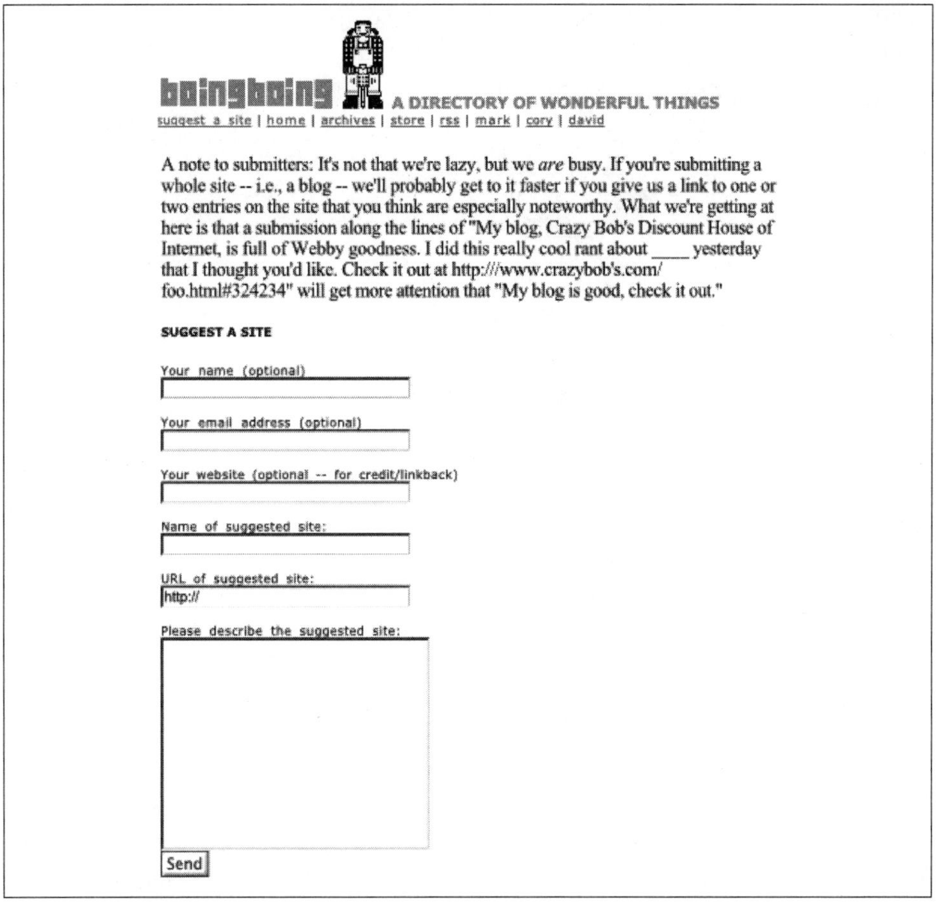

Figure 1-5. Suggestion form

There are some advantages to using a script instead of a `mailto` link:

- All the information we use for a post is included—no going back to the submitter if she forgot to include the URL.

- The format is normalized, so we can reliably find the URL and the description without having to dig through the message.

- The messages are easy to write mailer rules for—we have a different mail-chime that goes off when we get a link suggestion, and suggestions are automatically filed in a separate mail folder.

Blogroll

A *blogroll* is a list of blogs that you visit frequently and want to call others' attention to. This is more than free advertising for your friends and inspiration; it's also an easy way to keep track of sites that you want to revisit frequently. This is especially handy when you're traveling from computer to computer and don't have access to your bookmarks.

Figure 1-6 shows Boing Boing's blogroll.

BEST BLOGS
Weblogsky
Atom Grid
Electrolite
Making Light
Scrubbles.net
Mooselessness
Follow Me Here
Jimwich
Kottke.org
Blather
The Null Device
Pigs & Fishes
Factovision
randomWalks
Subterranean Notes Oddball
Comic Book of the Day

Figure 1-6. A blogroll

Mailing Lists

We have two mailing lists for Boing Boing. One is a general-purpose announcement and discussion list, usually used to pass the word that our server has gone down and when we expect it to come back up. The other is a moderated list that gets a copy of every entry we post to the blog. It's a convenient way for our readers to get new items without having to check back several times a day to see what's been posted. This is a feature that's new with Blogger Pro, the for-pay version of the Blogger blogging tool (see Chapter 6).

There are any number of free mailing list services online, including the popular Yahoo! Groups service (*http://www.yahoogroups.com*). In five minutes, you can create a moderated (or unmoderated) mailing list and away you go. Yahoo! Groups even generates HTML for a sign-up form that you can paste into your blog template.

Figure 1-7 shows what an emailed post looks like.

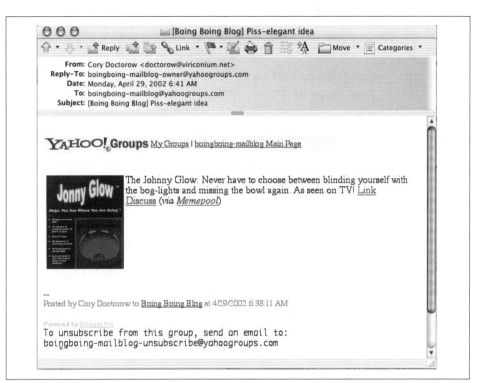

Figure 1-7. A post by email using Yahoo! Groups

Counters

People who manage their own web servers have access to powerful auditing tools that will analyze their server logs (confusingly, these are also called weblogs), telling them how many visitors have been to the site, what page visitors were at last, what operating system and browser they were using, and even what times of day and days of the week are most popular with visitors.

Bloggers are more likely to be tech-civilians, hosting their blogs with commercial or free hosting companies that don't provide access to the server logs.

Free tracking systems such as Extreme Tracking (*http://extremetracking.com*) fill the void, providing statistics and analysis for personal web sites. These trackers require that you put a small graphic somewhere on your blog. Every time this graphic is loaded from the tracking service's server, statistics about the visitor whose client loaded it are gathered (see Figure 1-8).

Frequently, these trackers have a pay version that includes better and deeper reporting, as well as privacy—the free versions let anyone examine your site statistics. Publicly available statistics are an interesting phenomenon, as they make it possible for you to compare how much traffic your favorite bloggers enjoy and where these visitors come from.

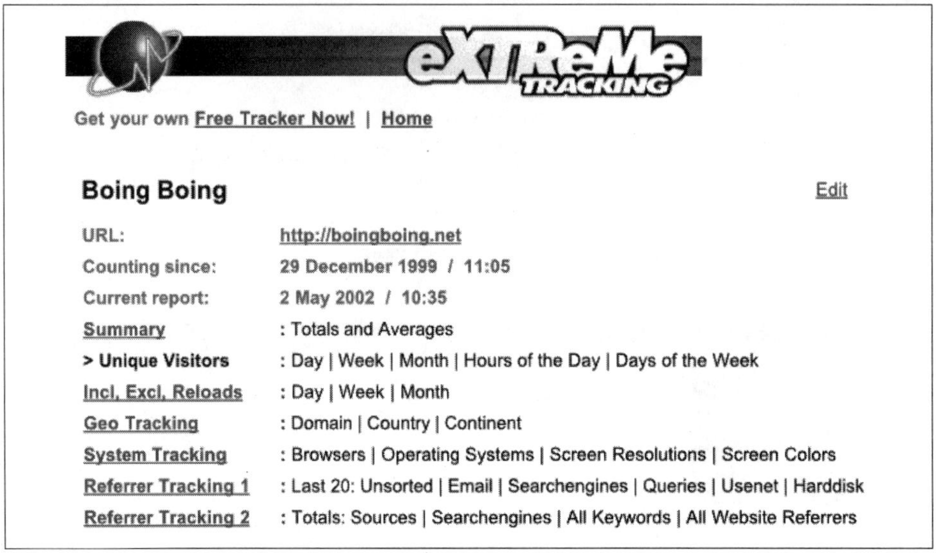

Figure 1-8. Extreme Tracking statistics overview

Watching your statistics can be addictive. In particular, the lists of URLs from which your visitors linked (called Referrer logs) are the best way to discover who's been linking to your blog, as shown in Figure 1-9.

Radio UserLand, a popular blogging tool covered later in this book, includes its own log-analysis tool, whose statistics can be made public or kept private.

Anatomy of a Blog Post

The *blog post* is the atomic unit of a blog. Blogs are made of successive postings. Some blogs are updated only once a week, others get updated 30 or more times per day (the record for Boing Boing is 27 posts in one day).

Everything about a blog post is optional. There are no rules for blogging. That said, Figure 1-10 shows what a post on Boing Boing looks like. Many weblogs follow a similar format. Some of the salient features of that post follow.

Title

A post's title (see Figure 1-11) serves much the same role as a newspaper headline: to sum up the post in a few words that are meant to intrigue the reader and highlight some aspect of the story. A title visually separates your posting from the one above it. Usability guru Jakob Nielsen, in his essay on "Microcontent" (*http://www.useit.com/alertbox/980906.html*), warns headline writers to be aware that headlines are often viewed out of context, on search-engine result pages, in alphabetical listings (he advises leaving off leading "The"s and "A"s for this reason), and as subject-headers for email and titles for web pages.

Last 20 Referrers	Unique Visitors
02 May, Thu, 10:27:40	http://www.google.com/search?hl=en&q=blog+directory
02 May, Thu, 10:28:36	http://my.yahoo.com/
02 May, Thu, 10:28:55	http://quicklikeabunny.net/
02 May, Thu, 10:30:02	bookmarks
02 May, Thu, 10:30:40	http://gilbert.pitas.com/
02 May, Thu, 10:31:34	http://www.scripting.com/
02 May, Thu, 10:31:39	http://www.scripting.com/weblogs/
02 May, Thu, 10:32:13	http://www.timtate.org/
02 May, Thu, 10:32:27	http://www.fluffybunny.com/links.html
02 May, Thu, 10:32:55	http://www.dansanderson.com/blogtracker/tiny.php
02 May, Thu, 10:33:11	http://www.scripting.com/
02 May, Thu, 10:33:43	http://www.centrs.com/
02 May, Thu, 10:34:32	bookmarks
02 May, Thu, 10:34:33	http://www.akula.com/~mbrose/cgi-bin/start.cgi
02 May, Thu, 10:35:05	bookmarks
02 May, Thu, 10:36:16	http://www.geocities.com/faunafrailty/blog.html
02 May, Thu, 10:36:27	http://www.timtate.org/
02 May, Thu, 10:37:48	http://www.camworld.com/
02 May, Thu, 10:37:48	http://www.blackbeltjones.com/work/index.html
02 May, Thu, 10:39:11	[unknown origin]

Figure 1-9. Referrer log

As you'll see later, titles are also used when blogs are syndicated using a technology called RSS, in which they may appear in a list of hundreds or even thousands of other blog headlines. The point is that your title should be separable from the posting below it—informative even when taken out of context.

The Picture

There are, of course, copyright issues when posting an image to your blog such as the one in Figure 1-12, and technically it can be a little harder to post an image than it is post plain text (though increasingly blogging engines make this simpler). Here are some tips for posting images:

- Make a local copy of the image on your own server. Don't "inline" someone else's images by linking directly to the other person's server, because this uses their bandwidth and server cycles to serve images on your blog. This is rude.
- Crop and resize images to small thumbnails, sufficient to give your readers an idea of what they'll see if they follow the link. This is both a principle of fair use of others' copyrighted works and a means of reducing the load time for your page.

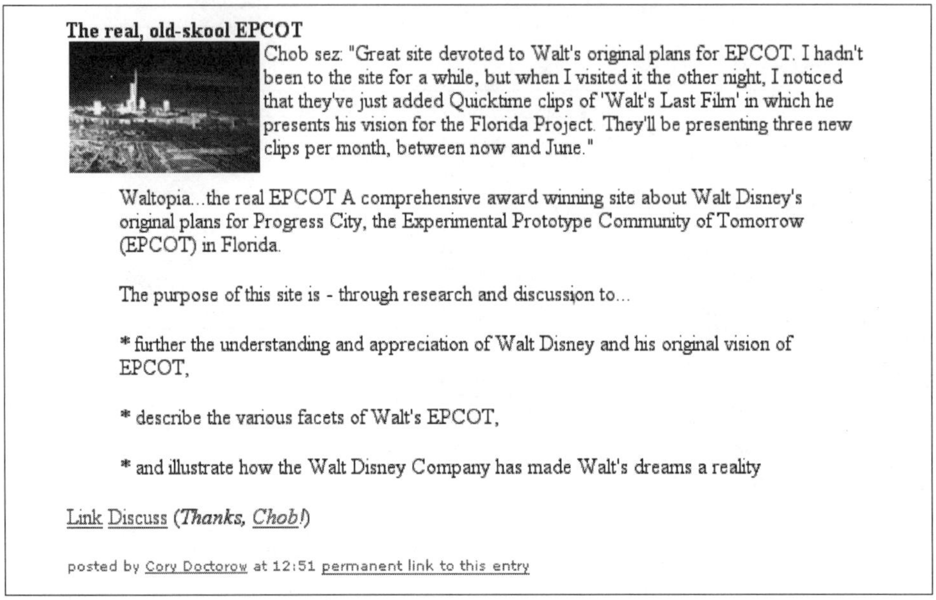

The real, old-skool EPCOT

Chob sez: "Great site devoted to Walt's original plans for EPCOT. I hadn't been to the site for a while, but when I visited it the other night, I noticed that they've just added Quicktime clips of 'Walt's Last Film' in which he presents his vision for the Florida Project. They'll be presenting three new clips per month, between now and June."

Waltopia...the real EPCOT A comprehensive award winning site about Walt Disney's original plans for Progress City, the Experimental Prototype Community of Tomorrow (EPCOT) in Florida.

The purpose of this site is - through research and discussion to...

* further the understanding and appreciation of Walt Disney and his original vision of EPCOT,

* describe the various facets of Walt's EPCOT,

* and illustrate how the Walt Disney Company has made Walt's dreams a reality

Link Discuss (*Thanks, Chob!*)

posted by Cory Doctorow at 12:51 permanent link to this entry

Figure 1-10. A sample post from Boing Boing

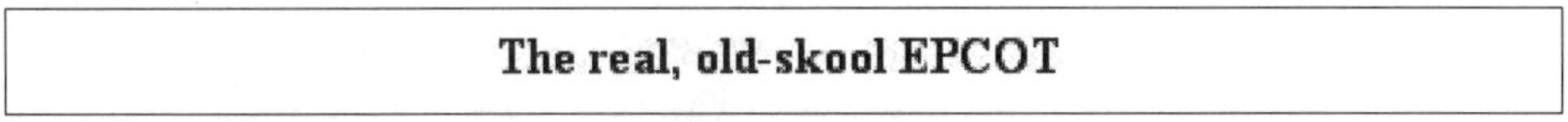

The real, old-skool EPCOT

Figure 1-11. The post title

Figure 1-12. The post picture

- Use the `height`, `width` and `alt` attributes in your image tags, which reduce load times for your readers.
- If you're worried about copyright, send a note to the image's author asking for permission before posting.

The Posting

The nice thing about blogs is that they're infinite. There's no word limit, no copy fit, no sense of filling up all the space you have. If you want to write a 10,000-word polemic about your subject, go ahead and pound on the keyboard like a Fox celebrity boxer.

That said, blog entries typically come in packs—you hardly ever get a blog entry all on its lonesome. So the tradition is to keep blog entries short—a screenful or less. Postings to Jorn Barger's Robot Wisdom weblog are a single, punchy sentences. Movable Type and some other blogging engines allow you to create a "preview" block of text that links to a "full text" block for longer entries.

Infinite space aside, as with all writing, your blog entry should take exactly as many words as it needs to make its point, and not one word more.

Chob sez: "Great site devoted to Walt's original plans for EPCOT. I hadn't been to the site for a while, but when I visited it the other night, I noticed that they've just added Quicktime clips of 'Walt's Last Film' in which he presents his vision for the Florida Project. They'll be presenting three new clips per month, between now and June."

Figure 1-13. The post body

Some blog authors play at mystery in their postings, writing deliberately obscure things like "Boy, this sure must have hurt!" and nothing else. The idea is to pique the reader's interest with your pith and jocularity, so that he follows the link to find out what it is that hurt so much. I try never to do this, operating on the principle that the best way to get someone to follow a link is to describe what's on the other end of it and why it's interesting, as in Figure 1-13.

The Quote

Sometimes, the best way to explain why a page is blogworthy is to include a brief quote or two. As with pictures, there are copyright issues associated with this, because fair use is generally held to include only excerpts, not the whole text (though some would argue that the standard for fair use is the minimum amount necessary to make the point, which could, conceivably, be the whole thing).

It's traditional to set off quotes from the main body of a blog post (see Figure 1-14) with some combination of blockquote tags and stylistic changes, such as italicizing. Long blocks of *italic* text are difficult to read, though.

The Link

There are a lot of little niceties that comprise many blog entries. On Boing Boing, the convention is to limit the number of links per entry to one, at the very end of the entry, with the hot-text being "Link" (see Figure 1-15). We do it this way for a couple of reasons, which we've listed here.

> Waltopia...the real EPCOT A comprehensive award winning site about Walt Disney's original plans for Progress City, the Experimental Prototype Community of Tomorrow (EPCOT) in Florida.
>
> The purpose of this site is - through research and discussion to...
>
> * further the understanding and appreciation of Walt Disney and his original vision of EPCOT,
>
> * describe the various facets of Walt's EPCOT,
>
> * and illustrate how the Walt Disney Company has made Walt's dreams a reality

Figure 1-14. A quote from a referenced page

- We want our readers to get our context on a story before following the link. We hope that people come to our blog to get information about the links we post, not just links. Putting the link at the end of the post encourages readers to go through the context before moving on.

- Multiple inline links can be confusing. Setting the link off on its own and limiting ourselves to one link per post makes the link itself unambiguous.

Compare the Boing Boing approach to that of Memepool (*http://www.memepool.org*), with sentences such as "Professional wrestlers are bigger than ever" where every word is a link to a different page related to the blog entry. The Memepool style has its followers. There is no right answer here.

Link

Figure 1-15. A link

Discuss Link

Discussion links (see Figure 1-16) are links to web-based message boards where your readers can talk about your entries. Some blogs don't bother with discussions, while others are defined by the communities in their discussion areas. Some blogs have a different discussion area for each post, others have a single Ür-message-board with a long running discussion about the posts on the front page.

Discuss

Figure 1-16. A discuss link

Depending on which blog tool you use to maintain your blog, you may have to use a third-party service to host your discussions. On Boing Boing, we use QuickTopic (*http://www.quicktopic.com*), creating a new topic for each post.

Some blogging tools have message boards built in. With Movable Type, for example, you just check a box labeled Allow Comments when you're creating your post, and Movable Type automatically generates a new discussion board and puts a link to it on your post. Likewise, Radio UserLand has an automated facility for adding discussion boards to blog entries.

Discussion boards can be a vital part of a healthy blog. They transform your blog from a broadcast into a conversation, where you and your readers can discuss the items you post. Be warned, though: message boards abstract discussion away from the social cues that we use when we talk face-to-face. Decent people can be breathtakingly abusive on a message board. A single jerk can ruin a fruitful discussion with persistent bile. If you run a blog, you will eventually attract such a jerk (a "troll" in Internet parlance), and he will make your life absolutely miserable.

When confronted with a troll, you have three immediate temptations:

- To argue back, meeting fire with fire
- To delete the offending post
- To shut down the message board entirely

Resist these temptations. Arguing back is fruitless. Internet trolls live to engage otherwise sane people in pointless, heated debate. Deleting the post sets up an arms race, where your troll returns again and again, assuming new identities, until you find yourself spending all your time hunting down and eliminating offensive posts, while your blog idles away, untended and static. Deleting the message board altogether satisfies the troll's victory condition: he has silenced your readers with his vitriol.

Take a lesson from free speech advocates: the answer to bad speech is more speech. Ignore your troll (and encourage your readers to do the same), while you continue to have your discussion. Trolls really *do* disappear if no one pays them any attention. Some message boards have email gateways, allowing you to read and post from your mail client. If your message board has this option, use it and avail yourself to your mailer's filters and delete the troll's posts unread.

Matt Haughey runs a sprawling and excellent group blog called Metafilter (*http:// www.metafilter.com*), where heated debate often flares. Matt jokes about installing the ultimate anti-troll measure: a filter that makes it appear to the troll as though his posts are being sent to the Metafilter message boards but makes those posts invisible to all other users, removing the temptation to encourage the troll by responding to him.

Attribution

The currency of the Distributed Republic of Blogistan is the link. One link equals approximately $0.00. Even so, links aren't worthless. There is no shame in getting links for your blog from other bloggers—indeed, one of the blogiverse's finest characteristics is its ability to examine a single story from a thousand angles, wearing it as smooth as a riverstone as it is handled by a horde of self-appointed analysts.

So no blogger will complain that you are stealing from her if you reproduce her links on your site, but woe to the blogger who does so without attribution (see Figure 1-17). If we find a link on your blog, we don't need to ask your permission to post it on ours, but we'd be very rude indeed if we didn't link back to your site.

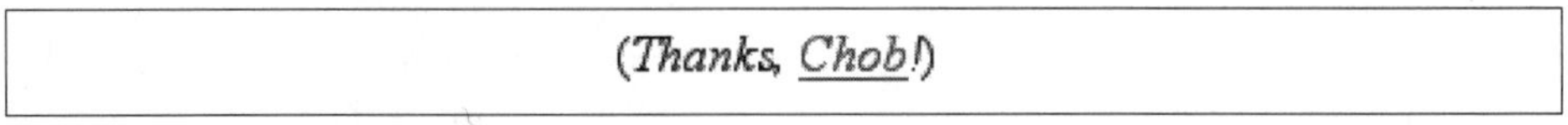

> *(Thanks, Chob!)*

Figure 1-17. Attribution with link

Attributing links establish the chain of authorship. They drive your readers to the sites that you read. They are the invaluable payback from one blogger to another, the indispensable, virtual high-five.

On Boing Boing, we attribute in two ways:

- For suggestions sent by email, we add (*Thanks, <first name of sender, with link>!*) to the end of the post.
- For items found elsewhere, we add (*via <name of site link was found on>*) to the end of the post.

Other blogs handle attribution in their own way. Some do it inline ("Found on Metafilter: Yet another domain hijacking"). Some do it very briefly, at the beginning or the end of the post ("Check out this amazing Flash animation. [slashdot]", "*Scripting News*: More cease and desist letters from the Church of Scientology").

By-Line

Blogs are written by people, not PR departments or staff writers. Blog entries are almost always signed by their authors (see Figure 1-18), even if the author uses a pseudonym. On Boing Boing, we link the by-lines to the author's email address, so readers can respond personally to a story with one click. Some sites use feedback forms to avoid putting their email addresses on the Web where they can be harvested by spammers.

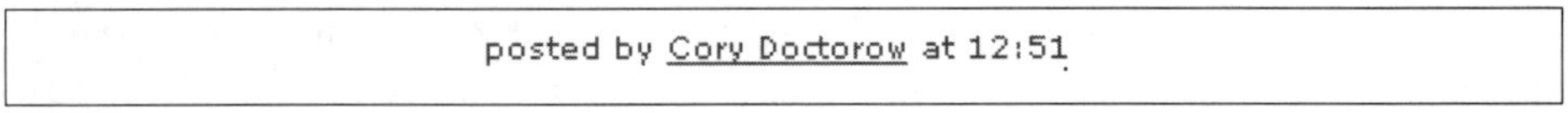

> posted by Cory Doctorow at 12:51

Figure 1-18. By-line

The by-line is part of the Internet personal publishing revolution. Before the rise of online publishing, the average person's only chance to write something for public consumption that carried her name was a letter to the editor. The real world is thick with unattributed, seemingly authorless material—who wrote that Associated Press story on page two of your morning paper, or the newscast that you heard at the top of the hour? Who wrote the instructions that came with your VCR or the warning label on your gas cap?

Blogs are covered with by-lines. Bloggers gleefully lay claim to their words and bear blame when those words arouse ire in their readers.

Permanent Link

The front page of a blog is a book written on water. A busy blog rotates its entire front page every day or two. Links to items on the front page of a blog are only good until sufficient new material is added to the page to push the items off into oblivion.

The solution is permanent links (see Figure 1-19). Most blogging tools generate two copies of every post you create: one on the front page and one on a permanent, sequential archive page. It's up to you how much material you want on each archive page. At Boing Boing, we put a month's worth of links (300–400) on each archive page. This keeps the number of archive pages to a minimum, but it does mean that digging through the archives can take a long time, as each archive page has to load and render in your browser. Some bloggers archive a week at a time; especially wordy bloggers may opt to generate a new archive for every day.

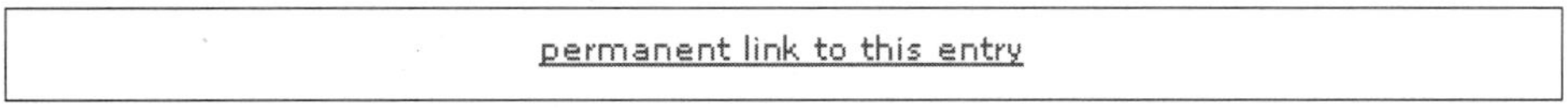

```
permanent link to this entry
```

Figure 1-19. Permanent link

Your blogging tool will generate a permanent link to the archive copy of each new post automatically. It's up to you to choose where that link goes and what it looks like. As you can see on Boing Boing, we put permanent links underneath each post. Some other suggestions:

- A small icon next to the title (see Figure 1-20)
- A special typographic character (#, Ω, ∞) at the end of the post (see Figure 1-21)
- An abbreviation ("permalink") at the end of the post (see Figure 1-22)

We like the Boing Boing approach because it makes it very clear where the permanent link is. Other bloggers who want to link to my posts can quickly and easily locate our permalinks, even if they've never been to Boing Boing before.

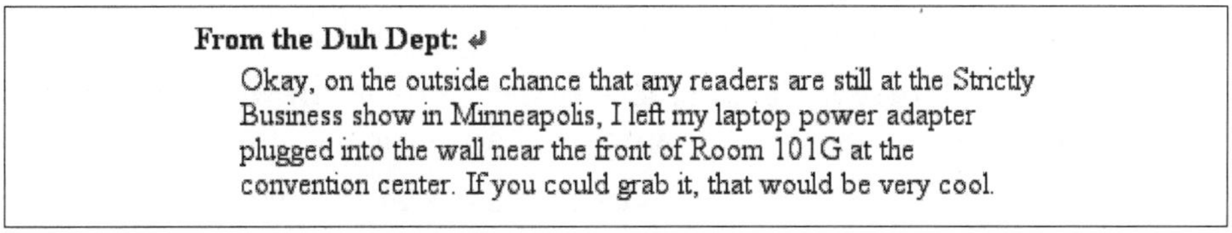

> **From the Duh Dept:** ↵
> Okay, on the outside chance that any readers are still at the Strictly Business show in Minneapolis, I left my laptop power adapter plugged into the wall near the front of Room 101G at the convention center. If you could grab it, that would be very cool.

Figure 1-20. An icon used to indicate a permanent link in Doc Searls's Radio blog

Syndication

Rich Site Summary (RSS) is a data format that allows computers to exchange files containing summaries of stories. Each story typically has a title, location, and

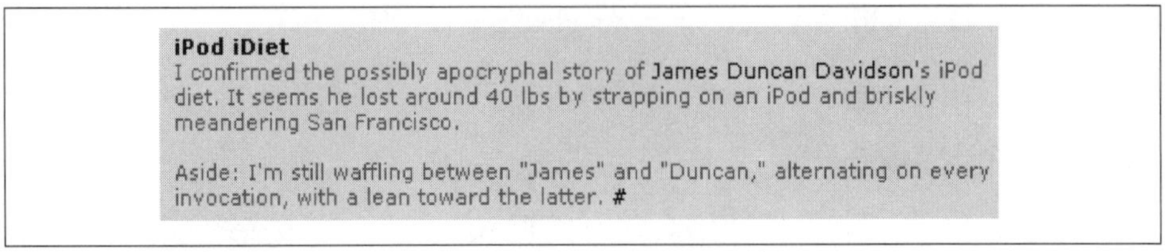

> **iPod iDiet**
> I confirmed the possibly apocryphal story of **James Duncan Davidson's** iPod diet. It seems he lost around 40 lbs by strapping on an iPod and briskly meandering San Francisco.
>
> Aside: I'm still waffling between "James" and "Duncan," alternating on every invocation, with a lean toward the latter. #

Figure 1-21. A special typographic character (#) used to indicate a permanent link on Rael Dornfest's Blosxom blog

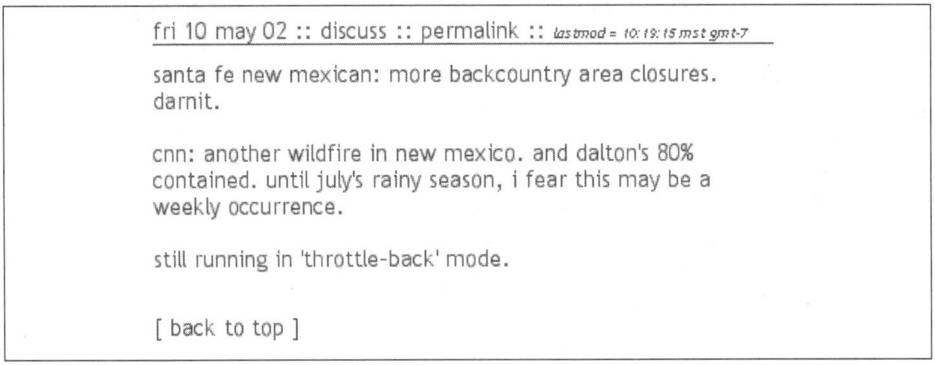

> fri 10 may 02 :: discuss :: permalink :: *last mod = 10:19:15 mst gmt-7*
>
> santa fe new mexican: more backcountry area closures. darnit.
>
> cnn: another wildfire in new mexico. and dalton's 80% contained. until july's rainy season, i fear this may be a weekly occurrence.
>
> still running in 'throttle-back' mode.
>
> [back to top]

Figure 1-22. An abbreviation ("permalink") used to indicate a permanent link on Dangerous Meta

possibly a brief synopsis. RSS is extremely simple, and is expressed using standards-defined Extensible Markup Language (XML). Thousands of blogs and other web sites all over the Net produce RSS files describing their content.

The cool thing about RSS is that it's easy to write a program to produce or manipulate the data in an RSS document. RSS is so simple to generate and manipulate that hundreds of programmers have written tools to exploit the thousands of RSS feeds on the Internet.

For example, the Mac OS X toolbar application called MacReporter (*http://www.inferiis.com/mac/macreporter/*) can regularly fetch headlines from news sites and blogs. You can then scan the headlines looking for interesting news to blog or simply read. Meerkat (*http://meerkat.oreillynet.com*) is an excellent web-based RSS reader that allows you to filter the feeds you receive by keyword, time, and origin.

Some bloggers have coded custom RSS tools that integrate tightly with their blogs, so that filtered headlines from other sites appear in sidebars on their front pages.

Dave Winer's *Weblogs.com* is a list of blogs that have sent an "updated" notice over the Internet to the service. If you're looking for a list of recently updated weblogs, you can visit *http://www.weblogs.com* and browse the list; but if you're a programmer, you can fetch the *Weblogs.com* RSS feed and get an easy-to-manipulate list of recently updated sites to feed to a search engine or RSS reader.

RSS is a powerful way of spreading your blog entries far and wide.

Publishing a Feed

Some blogging tools, such as Radio and Movable Type, publish RSS feeds by default. Others have options to enable feeds. If your blogging tool doesn't generate its own feed, you can still publish blogs by using Julian Bond's RSSify tool at *http://www. voidstar.com/rssify.php*.

Most blogs that offer RSS feeds have links to those feeds on their sites. A new technique that's gaining popularity is to embed in your web page a pointer to the RSS for that page. This makes it much easier to write tools that automatically discover RSS feeds.

RSS Aggregators

An RSS aggregator is a tool that regularly fetches RSS feeds and stores their contents in a database. A personal aggregator (such as Plucky, available at *http:// geoffreygrosenbach.com/plucky.html*, or AmphetaDesk, available at *http://www. amphetadesk.com*) is used as a kind of software agent, a tool that searches any RSS feed you specify for stories, filters them according to your preferences, and displays the results.

Some blogging tools, such as Radio UserLand, include aggregators. You can fetch and filter RSS feeds from all over the Internet, from blogs to major news-organs such as the *New York Times*, which has a special arrangement with UserLand Spftware to provide Radio UserLand users with exclusive news-feeds. Radio UserLand's aggregator makes it trivial to turn stories that you discover via RSS into blog entries, by ticking a box and adding some commentary.

Internet aggregators such as Meerkat fetch thousands of feeds and make them available to people and to software agents.

Syndic8 (*http://www.syndic8.com*) and NewsIsFree (*http://www.newsisfree.com*) maintain giant master-lists of thousands of feeds that can be downloaded and imported into personal aggregators. Both sites allow you to submit your own RSS feed for inclusion on the master-list.

Blogging Tools

While it's possible to generate and maintain a blog by writing and updating each page by hand, you'd have to be a masochist to do so. The remainder of this book is devoted to several tools that automate the administrivia of blogging: Blogger, Radio UserLand, Movable Type, and Blosxom.

This isn't the full spectrum of blogging tools—products such as Greymatter, Manila, LiveJournal, and others all have strong user bases. The tools we've chosen to cover in-depth, though, represent various niches in the blogging spectrum—some are for gurs, some are for novices; some require you to install software on your PC, some can be run completely from afar; some work with your own domain, others host your blog for you; and so on.

This section discusses the features of several blog management systems, not just the ones we describe in detail in the book. Table 1-1 lists the systems covered in this section and their URLs.

After reading this section, you can make an informed decision about which tool is right for you.

Table 1-1. Blog management systems

System	Home page
Blogger	*http://www.blogger.com/*
Blogger Pro	*http://pro.blogger.com/*
Blosxom	*http://www.raelity.org/lang/perl/blosxom/*
Greymatter	*http://www.noahgrey.com/greysoft/*
LiveJournal	*http://www.livejournal.com/*
Manila	*http://manila.userland.com/*
Movable Type	*http://www.movabletype.org/*
Radio UserLand	*http://radio.userland.com/*
Slash	*http://www.slashcode.org/*
Zope	*http://www.zope.org/*

Hosting

A blog takes up disk space and must be served from a web server. If you already own (or pay for space on) a web server, you probably want to host your blog there. For example, Neil Gaiman's web site contains a biography, a bibliography, FAQs, a message board, and much more, so it's the logical place to keep his blog.

Some tools (for example, Greymatter, Movable Type, Blosxom, Slash, Zope, and Manila) can be installed on your server. Others (for example, Blogger and Radio UserLand) can publish your blog to your site by uploading files via FTP. FTPing your blog files can become very time consuming, though, for blogs with many entries.

Installing software on your web server requires some know-how (logging into Unix or adding software to a Windows or Macintosh server, where are the CGI programs kept, and so on) that may eliminate some choices for the less tech-savvy.

If you don't already have web hosting, or you're just getting started online, or even if you're an old hand but simply don't want to pay for the bandwidth used by your blog, you can choose to host it on someone else's server. Radio UserLand, Blogger, and LiveJournal come with free hosting.

There are caveats to blog hosting services, though. Blogger's free service, BlogSpot, puts banner advertisements on your blog (they do offer an ad-free service for $13/year). The LiveJournal service doesn't let you host your blog on anywhere but LiveJournal's web site. In all cases, when you use someone else's hosting service, you're at the mercy of their quality of service—both Blogger and UserLand have had occasional outages. And although it hasn't happened yet, if your blog hosting service goes broke, your blog could be a victim.

Table 1-2 summarizes the installation and hosting requirements, and choices for the blog systems.

Table 1-2. Hosting and installation

Tool	Publish blog on own server?	Publish blog on free service?	Must be installed on the server?	Free hosting?
Blogger	Y	Y	N	Y
Blogger Pro	Y	Y	N	Y
Blosxom	Y	N	Y	N
Greymatter	Y	N	Y	N
LiveJournal	N	Y	N	Y
Manila	Y	Y	Y	N
Movable Type	Y	N	Y	N
Radio UserLand	Y	Y	N	Y
Slash	Y	N	Y	N
Zope	Y	N	Y	N

Price

LiveJournal, Blosxom, and Blogger are completely free. Blogger has an upgrade path, however: for advanced features such as RSS and Weblogs.com notification, you have to pay for Blogger Pro (now $35 per year, will be $50 per year, once all the planned features are available). LiveJournal sells a subscription ($5 for 2 months, $15 for 6 months, $25 for 12 months) that provides you with benefits such as a *livejournal.com* email address, text messaging, advanced customization, and faster servers.

Radio UserLand has a free 30-day trial and costs $39.95 per year. This gets you free software updates and blog hosting. You can continue to use the software after your subscription expires, but you won't receive updates and you must make separate arrangements to host your blog.

Greymatter is completely free. The author accepts donations through PayPal, however. This may seem odd at first, but it enables those who can afford to pay for their software to name their own price. If you can't afford to pay, you can still use the software and not be a criminal.

Movable Type is free for personal and non-profit use. Commercial users need a $150 commercial license. Personal and non-profit users can donate in a PBS-like model— $20 gets you a key to be listed on "Recently Updated Movable Type Blogs" and $45 gets you all that and support for instant messaging within certain hours.

Manila is part of the $899 commercial product called Frontier. Manila is the blog hosting and management part of the larger Frontier content-management system. You can get a free 60-day trial of Manila from *http://manila.userland.com*.

Slash and Zope are both open source software. You can download, install, and use them without paying. Slash is released under the GNU General Public License (GPL), while Zope is released under the Zope Public License (ZPL).

Table 1-3 summarizes price and optional services for each blog system.

Table 1-3. Price and optional services

Tool	Free?	If you pay	You get
Blogger	Y	$35-50/yr	Advanced features
Blosxom	Y	N/A	N/A
Greymatter	Y	Anything	A warm feeling inside
LiveJournal	Y	$2-$2.50/month	Advanced features
Manila	60-day trial	$899	Frontier
Movable Type	Y	$20 or $45	Listed on the home page and (for $45) support
Radio UserLand	30-day trial	$39.95/yr	Hosting space and updates
Slash	Y	N/A	N/A
Zope	Y	N/A	N/A

Syndication

As we saw earlier in this chapter, there are two aspects to syndication: producing an RSS feed for your blog and consuming the RSS feeds from other sites.

LiveJournal automatically creates RSS feeds for you and autoaggregates the feeds from your buddies in the LiveJournal community. There is no way to aggregate RSS feeds of non-LiveJournal blogs.

Blogger does not create or consume RSS by itself, although you can use the RSSify script mentioned earlier in the "Syndication" section to produce an RSS feed of a Blogger blog. If you upgrade to Blogger Pro, you can create an RSS feed of your blog. Blogger has no way to consume an RSS feed, though the Fyuze aggregator has a way to automatically incorporate its feeds into Blogger blogs (*http://www.fyuze.com/blog/*).

Radio UserLand is built for and around RSS. It automatically creates an RSS feed of your blog and can incorporate the RSS feeds from other blogs into your blog, Radio UserLand functions as an RSS reader, letting you subscribe to feeds and read the latest articles, and this makes it trivial to turn a syndicated story into a blog entry.

Radio UserLand is the only product with a built-in RSS reader—Manila creates and incorporates RSS but does not include an RSS reader.

Also built around RSS, but in a different way, is Blosxom. Blosxom automatically offers RSS feeds, and the optional Blagg aggregator can incorporate feeds into your blog.

Greymatter neither produces nor consumes RSS out of the box; however, a third-party modification from *http://www.foshdawg.net/gm/mods/* makes Greymatter produce RSS.

Movable Type automatically publishes an RSS feed of your blog. While it doesn't come with the ability to aggregate RSS, you can use Blosxom's Blagg to insert stories from an RSS feed into your blog.

Slash produces RSS feeds and can incorporate other RSS feeds into pages. Zope does not come with the ability to offer an RSS feed, but it's simple to write an RSS generator.

Table 1-4 summarizes the RSS capabilities of each blog system.

Table 1-4. RSS capabilities

Tool	Produce	Consume	Read
Blogger	Requires third-party add-on	Requires third-party add-on	N
Blogger Pro	Y	Requires third-party add-on	N
Blosxom	Y	Y (with Blagg)	N
Greymatter	Requires third-party add-on	N	N
LiveJournal	Y	Y (but only other LiveJournal feeds)	N
Manila	Y	Y	Y
Movable Type	Y	Requires third-party add-on	N
Radio UserLand	Y	Y	Y
Slash	Y	Y	N
Zope	Y	N	N

Local versus remote

Almost all the blog management systems we've talked about offer web interfaces. That is, regardless of whether you're using Radio UserLand, Blogger, or Movable Type, you can use your web browser to post and administer your blog. Some server-based systems such as Blogger and Movable Type also offer an XML-RPC interface (called the Blogger API, although it's not specific to Blogger) that lets you edit posts and templates remotely.

If your chosen blog management system offers the Blogger API, you can choose one of several *desktop clients* (programs you install on your desktop PC) to administer your blog. Chapter 2 discusses some of these desktop clients in detail.

Blogger is a web application that resides on the *blogger.com* server. You can interact with Blogger from any web browser. There is no desktop component to Blogger, however, you can use a desktop client to post to your blog. Blogger can also be used to post to any blog that supports the Blogger API.

LiveJournal is a web application that runs entirely on the LiveJournal servers. While it does offer an API so that desktop clients can post to a LiveJournal blog, it's not the Blogger API. Thus, the desktop clients discussed in Chapter 2 do not work with Live-Journal. You can't post to another blogging system's blog from LiveJournal.

Radio UserLand is a desktop application, meaning you download and install a program that runs on your desktop PC. This program contains a web server, and a typical Radio UserLand user maintains their blog through a web browser. Power users can go into the desktop application, however, for more advanced content-management features.

Manila users interact with their blogs through a web browser. There is no client component like Radio UserLand, although you can use Radio UserLand to maintain a Manila blog. A Manila blog can be posted to via the Blogger API. You can also use Manila to post to another blog via the Blogger API.

Movable Type has no desktop component—once you've installed it on your server, you are ready to blog. It offers an XML-RPC interface, so you can post to it from a desktop client, including any Blogger API client. You can't, however, post to another blog from Movable Type.

Greymatter is also web-based, with no desktop component. It doesn't understand the Blogger API, so you can't post to a Greymatter blog from a desktop client nor use Greymatter to post to another blog.

Slash and Zope are also purely web-based server-side systems. Each offers a web interface for administration. Neither Slash nor Zope speak the Blogger API, but Slash does have its own SOAP interface for posting to journals.

Blosxom offers neither a web interface nor a desktop interface. To post to Blosxom or change your blog's appearance, you must create files on your server. A plug-in for Blosxom lets you upload posts to another blogging system via the Blogger API, but you can't post to a Blosxom blog from a desktop client.

Table 1-5 summarizes the interfaces for each blogging system.

Table 1-5. Desktop versus web

Tool	Web interface	Installs on your PC	Post to blog via Blogger API	Post to other blog via Blogger API	Own interface?
Blogger	Y	N	Y	Y	N
Blogger Pro	Y	N	Y	Y	N
Blosxom	N	N	With Third-Party Addon	N	N

Table 1-5. Desktop versus web (continued)

Tool	Web interface	Installs on your PC	Post to blog via Blogger API	Post to other blog via Blogger API	Own interface?
Greymatter	Y	N	N	N	N
LiveJournal	Y	N	N	N	Y
Manila	Y	N	Y	Y	Y
Movable Type	Y	N	Y	N	N
Radio UserLand	Y	Y	Y	Y	Y
Slash	Y	N	N	N	Y
Zope	Y	N	N	N	N

Summary

Blogger and LiveJournal are low-impact, easy-to-get-started services. However, they have their limitations: you must pay to use advanced features, and LiveJournal doesn't support the Blogger API, which would let you use a desktop client. LiveJournal users tend to be part of the LiveJournal community, whereas Blogger users tend to form their own communities.

Also good for entry-level bloggers is Radio UserLand. More so than Blogger and LiveJournal, Radio UserLand offers something for people who like to program and experiment. Radio's not only a user-friendly blogging system, it's also a fully-fledged content-management system. You must pay for it after the free trial period, however.

To host your blog on a Unix server, you probably want Movable Type or Greymatter. Of the two, Movable Type is more actively maintained and has more features (e.g., it supports the Blogger API). Manila is a good choice if you want to host many blogs on a Windows or Macintosh server, although Movable Type does run on Windows.

If you're a programmer and a tinkerer looking to learn and experiment about the insides of blogging, take a look at Blosxom. The Blosxom code is short and easily extended in Perl. Radio UserLand is also extensible and programmable using its own scripting language, Frontier.

To build a full portal site, try Slash or Zope. If both support the features you're looking for, the choice between the two probably comes down to language preference. Slash is written in Perl, and Zope is written in Python. While Zope does support extensions in Perl, you'll soon run into Python if you hack Zope for any length of time. We don't cover Slash or Zope in this book, but you can learn about them from books such as *Running Weblogs with Slash* (O'Reilly) and web sites such as *http://www.zope.org*.

CHAPTER 2
Desktop Clients

As we saw in Chapter 1, most blog systems provide web-based interfaces. Browser text fields, though, are primitive, constrictive, and awkward to use. It's very easy to accidentally delete a post you're working on, and there are no autosave or "Are you sure you want to lose this message?" prompts.

Desktop clients are a more convenient way to blog. A desktop client is an application that runs on your desktop PC and communicates with a blogging system using a protocol called the Blogger API. Many blog systems understand the Blogger API, including Blogger, Radio UserLand, and Movable Type.

The typical desktop client features a text editing window with buttons to add images, mark sections as bold or italic, create headings, etc. Most support two commands: Post, which sends the post to your blogging system but doesn't make it appear on your blog; and Publish, which sends the post and makes it visible on your blog.

This chapter provides a quick survey of six popular blogging applications that make use of the Blogger API. While they do vary in completeness, compliance, and usability, they're all simple to install, configure, and use; you should make use of the same handful of settings and sport a range of features designed to take your blogging experience beyond that cramped browser window and into an environment better suited to writing.

The Settings

While each sports its own particular preferences, all the Blogger API-based applications hold certain API-specific settings in common, usually:

Username

The username with which you identify yourself to your blogging system.

Password

The password associated with your username.

XML-RPC URL

The URL of your blog system's Blogger API interface (the default is often Blogger's *http://plant.blogger.com/api/RPC2/*). Sometimes this is broken up into Server and Path settings (e.g., Server *http://plant.blogger.com*, Path */api/RPC2/*).

Weblog ID

Many blog systems support multiple weblogs—for example, with only one installation of Movable Type, you can publish as many different weblogs as you like. Some desktop clients understand the concept of multiple weblogs and will let you select the blog to which a particular post is to go. Others require you to hardcode the ID of a particular blog. A Blogger ID is a string, such as myblog, while Movable Type uses numerical IDs.

Figure 2-1 shows a fairly representative configuration panel. Beyond these standard options are features such as Ping Weblogs.com, which notifies *http://www.weblogs. com* each time you post a new story. Check the desktop client's documentation for details of such features.

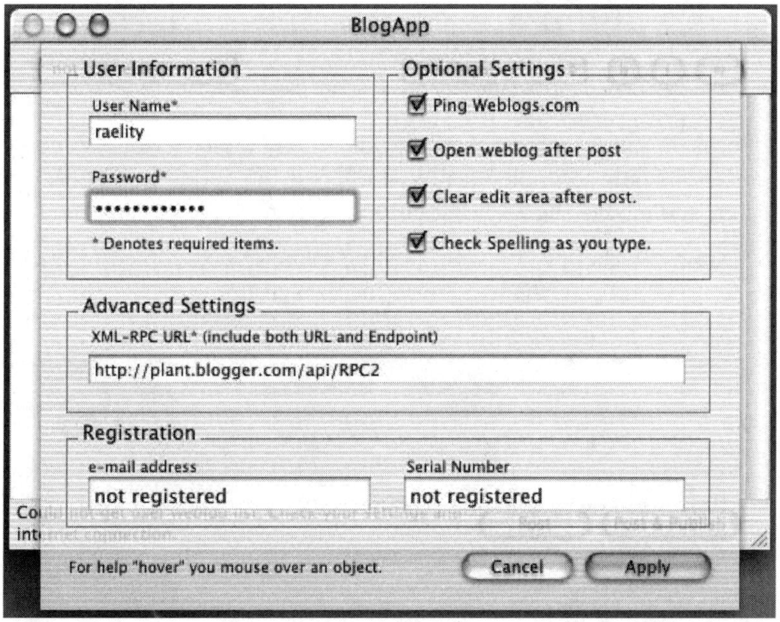

Figure 2-1. BlogApp's fairly representative configuration panel

BlogScript

BlogScript by WebEntourage (*http://www.webentourage.com*) is a free AppleScript script for Mac OS X that simply posts the contents of the clipboard to a weblog via a single menu selection. The obvious advantage is the ability to write in any environment you choose, by copying the text you wish to blog and activating BlogScript when you're ready to post (see Figure 2-2).

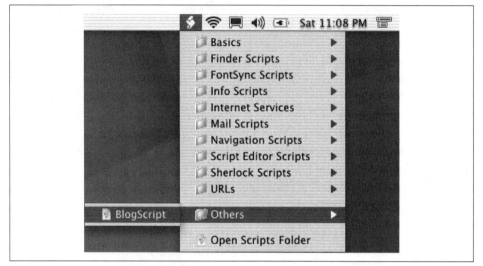

Figure 2-2. Running BlogScript from the Mac OS X Script menu

Given its focus on simply being a copy-to-blog function, BlogScript is understandably rather sparse. The only additional feature it offers is the option to ping weblogs.com. You can copy and modify the AppleScript to manage multiple accounts and weblogs.

Figure 2-3 shows BlogScript in action, posting a line of text copied to the clipboard from Mac OS X's TextEdit (the window in the background).

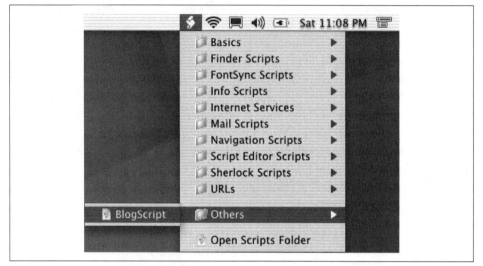

Figure 2-3. Running BlogScript from the Mac OS X Script menu

Installation is a snap; simply drop the script into your Scripts folder, and it'll be available from your toolbar Script menu. The only prerequisite is Script menu for OS X 10.1, available for free download at *http://www.apple.com/applescript/macosx/ script_menu/*.

BlogApp

Also from WebEntourage is BlogApp, a $6 shareware Mac OS X application that offers a rudimentary drag-and-drop text editor with bold, italic, and hyperlink buttons (see Figure 2-4), as-you-type spell-checking, the ability to maintain multiple weblogs and weblog entries, and template maintenance functions: Store Post, Edit Last Post, Edit or Delete Recent Post, Edit Main Template, and Edit Archive Template.

Figure 2-4. BlogApp and resulting Blogger weblog entry (browser window in the background)

BlogApp requires Mac OS X, Version 10.1.2 or higher. Downloadable as a compressed disk image, installation is just a matter of decompressing and mounting the image and copying the application to your Applications folder.

blogBuddy

blogBuddy (*http://blogbuddy.sourceforge.net*) is the Windows (95/NT/ME/2000/XP) equivalent of BlogApp, providing a basic text editor with bold, italic, underline, and hyperlink buttons (see Figure 2-5), web service–based spell checking (meaning you don't need to install a big dictionary), support for multiple weblogs (but not multiple accounts), and the ability to edit previous posts and main and archive templates.

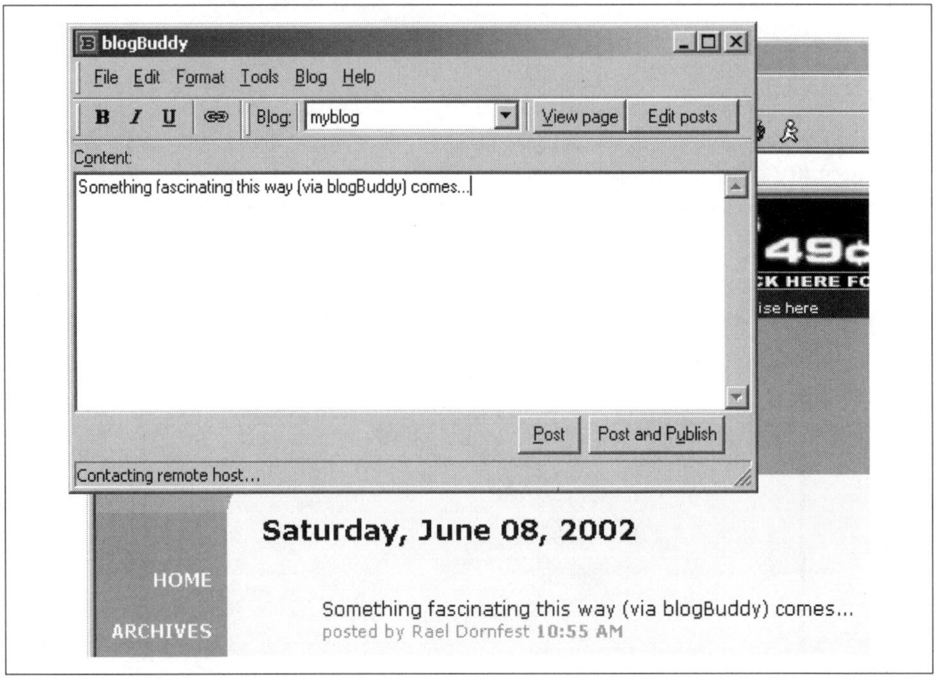

Figure 2-5. blogBuddy and resulting Blogger weblog entry (browser window in the background)

blogBuddy is open source software, distributed under the GNU Public License, downloadable as both a self-installing executable and a ZIP archive.

w.bloggar

The most featureful desktop client is w.bloggar (*http://www.wbloggar.com/*) for Windows. It sports a colorized HTML editor (including tables and images) with text formatting (bold, italic, font, color, size, alignment, and so forth), an integrated preview window, and everything else one would expect to find under the File and Edit menus. Toolbar drop-down lists provide instant access to previous posts and main and archive templates. Figure 2-6 shows w.bloggar in action.

Figure 2-6. w.bloggar showing off its HTML editor with the resulting nicely formatted weblog entry in the background

w.bloggar supports not only multiple weblogs associated with a particular account, but multiple accounts across weblog systems and services; simply choose Select Account and you're posting elsewhere. And w.blogger allows you to post a particular weblog entry to multiple weblogs simultaneously—associated with a single account, mind you.

w.blogger is freeware, downloadable as a self-extracting installer. It requires Microsoft Windows and Microsoft Internet Explorer 5.0 or newer.

Slug

Slug (*http://www.3e.org/slug/*) is designed to work specifically with Movable Type via the Blogger API, UserLand's proposed MetaWeblogAPI (a more generalized and extensible API based on Blogger's), and some API calls specific to Movable Type. Other than the addition of Movable Type's categories, Slug is rather rudimentary and reminiscent of BlogApp for Mac OS X and blogBuddy for Windows. Figure 2-7 shows Slug.

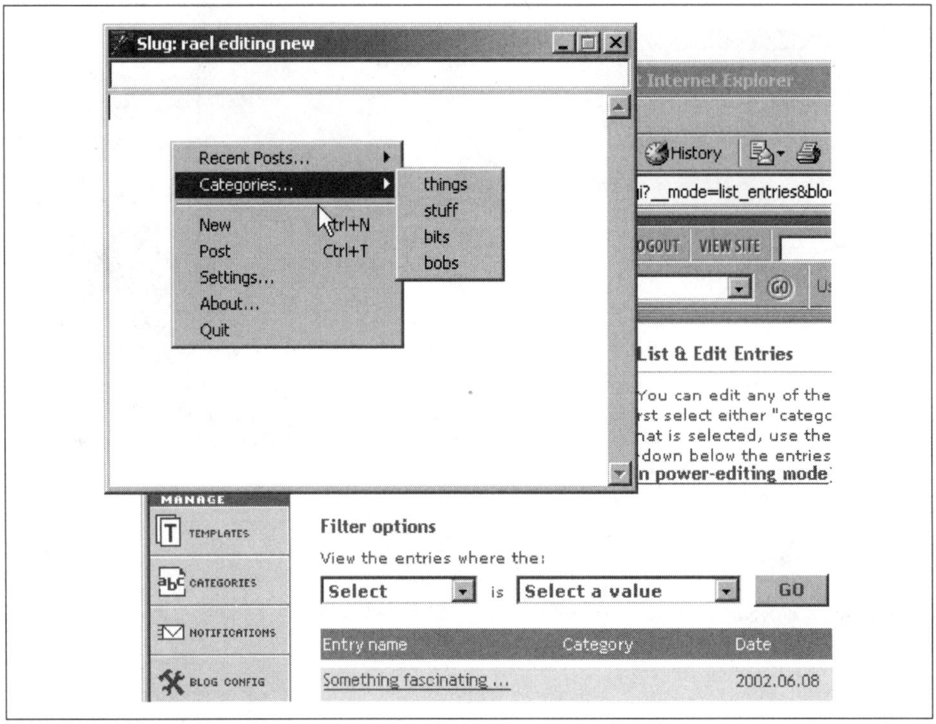

Figure 2-7. Slug's support for Movable Type categories; the resulting entry appears underneath in Movable Type's usual browser-based interface

Slug comes as a self-installing Windows *.msi* application with included source code. It does require the installation of the Microsoft .NET Framework, a separate 19-megabyte download.

Radio UserLand

Radio UserLand can be used to post to another blog system (e.g., Movable Type or Blogger). The experimental Manila-Blogger Bridge Tool lets you mirror Radio UserLand blog posts via the Blogger API. Detailed instructions are available from *http://radio.userland.com/manilaBloggerBridgeTool/*.

Figure 2-8 shows the configuration screen for the Manila-Blogger Bridge. As you can see, it takes the same parameters as the other tools.

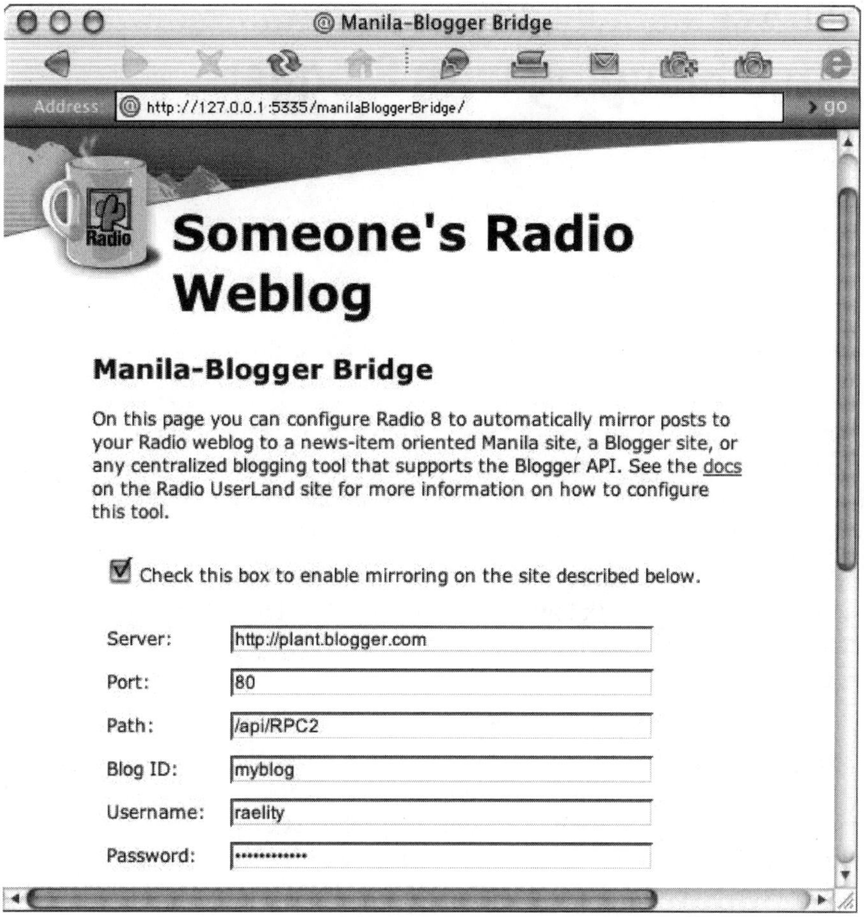

Figure 2-8. Manila-Blogger Bridge configuration

CHAPTER 3

Hosted Blogging with Blogger

The most commonly used blogging tool is Blogger. It requires the least amount of commitment in time or resources, allowing you to go from wanting a blog to having one in about five minutes and at no cost. This simplicity, ease of access, and no-risk aspect of Blogger is the reason many people have started blogging.

The Blogger software is the property of Pyra Labs (*http://www.pyra.com*), a company headed by Evan Williams (known as "Ev" within the blogging community). Blogger is often credited as the reason for the explosion of blogging that's occurred in the last couple of years.

While it is incredibly easy to use, Blogger's popularity can lead to unexpected results at times, such as postings that are lost during the publication process, archives that go missing, and server errors when accessing Blogger or your blog on BlogSpot. Throughout this chapter, we'll point out the problems that exist at the time of this printing and suggest ways to lessen or resolve these problems. Pyra is aware of all these problems and is working on fixing them.

Regardless of the occasionally unreliable nature of Blogger, it's a great tool to use to get your blogging feet wet. This chapter provides an overview of Blogger, from signing up for an account to creating your first blog. It also looks at the features built into the standard version of Blogger. The enhancements available in the subscription Blogger Pro service are discussed in Chapter 6.

How Blogger Works

Blogger is a web-based tool, requiring no installation of software on your personal computer or on your server if you happen to already have a web site. You access the tool through the Blogger web site (located at *http://blogger.com*), and the blog pages are posted to your web site or to Pyra's BlogSpot (*http://blogspot.com*) community blog server.

Architecturally, your template, archival information, and blog content are stored in databases at Pyra. It's only the generated main blog page, associated supporting files such as images, and archive files that get stored on the blog server. Figure 3-1 shows this.

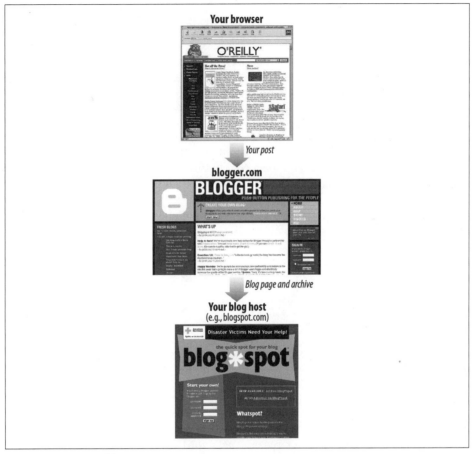

Figure 3-1. Posting a blog

While most people interact with Blogger through the web interface, it's not the only way. You can also use a desktop client from Chapter 2 to maintain your blog. In Chapter 6, you'll learn about Blogger Pro's blog-by-email service.

Requirements

To use Blogger, all you need is a browser that Blogger supports. The standard version of Blogger works with most major browsers including Internet Explorer, Netscape, and Mozilla. Until recently, browser support for Blogger Pro was limited to Internet Explorer, which meant Blogger wasn't accessible from a Linux or other Unix-based box. However, Blogger support has been added to Mozilla Release Candidate 1.0 and up, which means you can now manage your Blogger account from Linux and other non-Windows environments.

You can work around the browser completely by using the Blogger API. Once you've created the initial account and blog, post and maintain it via XML-RPC, using one of the client-side tools describe in Chapter 2.

You don't need to have a web site or a preregistered domain name to create a Blogger blog. You can use Pyra's community blog server, BlogSpot, to host your blog pages. However, if you want to host your own pages, you'll need a web site that allows FTP posting of content. It doesn't matter whether it's a Unix or Windows server, but it must have FTP access.

Other than these two very minimal requirements, there are no technical restrictions to running a Blogger blog. If you meet the minimum requirements, you're ready to create your first Blogger blog.

Your Blog, Quick Start

The best demonstration of the simplicity and ease of use of Blogger is to create a Blogger account, then create your first blog—a process that takes five minutes from start to finish.

Creating Your Blogger Account

To set up a Blogger account, access the main Blogger web site at *http://blogger.com*. In the page that opens, there's a box in the center titled "Create your own Blog" and a button labeled Start Now!. Click the button to go to the signup page, shown in Figure 3-2.

Enter your preferred username and password, your name and email address, and your organization, if any. Don't reuse a password from another system you have access too—the web traffic between you and Blogger is not encrypted, and your password may be emailed to you in plain text. By picking a unique password, you ensure that a malicious packet sniffer can gain access only to your Blogger account and not your email, ISP account, etc.

If you don't see the Start Now! button on the Blogger main page, look for a form with the words "If you don't have a blogger account, sign up!". In the form, type in your Blogger username and password. When you submit the form, you are taken to a second page to type in the rest of the account information.

You only have to create a Blogger account once; you can use the one account to create many different blogs.

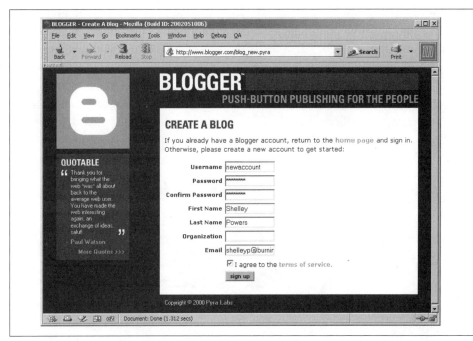

Figure 3-2. Blogger account sign-up page

Creating Your First Blog

Once you have your Blogger account, you can log into your account and begin using the blogging tool by going to the Blogger main page and entering your username and password. At this point, you can also check the option box labeled "Remember me?" to have the web site remember your login information and log you in automatically every time you access Blogger.

Once logged in, click on the link labeled Create a New Blog, listed on the front page. In the page that opens, provide a title and description. As you'll see later in this chapter, this information can be printed on your blog page if you so choose. For the demonstration blog, we'll use "O'Reilly's Weblogging" as the title, and the following for the description:

> All you ever wanted to know about starting and maintaining a Blogger weblog

You can also choose to publicize the blog through the Blogger Directory (*http://www. blogger.com/directory/*) by checking the Public Blog option. Because you're just starting the blog and trying out the tool, you won't want people coming around and peeking over your shoulder, so choose No for now—you can change this later.

The next page asks if you want to host the blog on your own server or host it at BlogSpot. This option is covered in more detail in the later section titled "Self-Hosting." For now, accept the default of hosting the page on BlogSpot, an option that can be changed later.

The third page that opens asks you to provide a physical name for the blog. It, combined with the *blogspot.com* domain, forms the URL by which your blog is accessed by your reading public. For example, choosing "hemp" here would give your blog the URL *http://hemp.blogspot.com*. Use a name you won't mind being publicly known by and one that is easily remembered.

In the example shown in Figure 3-3, I used "oreilly" as the name. I also checked the box agreeing with the Blogger Terms of Service required to use Blogger, which you'll want to take time to read—carefully—before proceeding with posting your first publicly accessible blog posting.

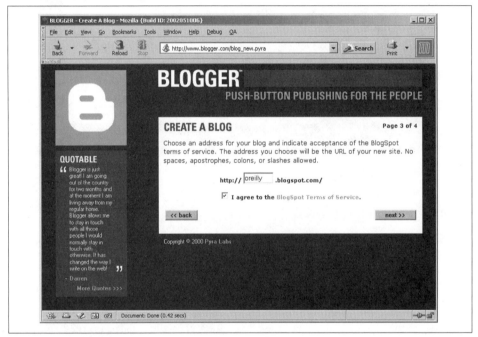

Figure 3-3. Providing a blog URL and agreeing to the Blogger TOS

After creating the URL, a template page opens, displaying a set of predefined blogging templates. Templates form the basis for how the content is displayed and organized within your blog. Pick one from the list in order to proceed; don't worry if you don't like the selection—later in the chapter, we show you how to easily change the template.

Only a random sampling of the Blogger templates are shown on this page. For the demonstration blog, I've picked one of the most commonly used templates within Blogger, the Chroma template. For your own blog, if this template doesn't show, pick any of the others that are displayed. Click the Finish! button at the bottom of the page to finish the process of creating your default blog. You're now ready to starting posting.

Posting

Once Blogger is finished creating the default blog, the Edit view page opens. The top part of the page is an open text box where you enter your content. This is headed by a toolbar containing content-formatting buttons, as well as buttons to Post or Post & Publish the content. The bottom part of the framed application page will usually contain previous postings but first contains posting instructions. To the right of this is a calendar with which to access specific day's postings and a search option with which to search among previous postings.

To add a post, type something into the text box at the top of the page. You don't have to use HTML—the Blogger tool will generate enclosing HTML tags for your text. Type in the ubiquitous "Hello, World!" as shown in Figure 3-4.

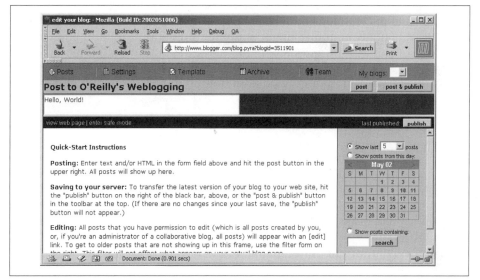

Figure 3-4. Typing in your first posting

Once you've typed your test message, post and publish it to the blog by clicking the Post & Publish button. This not only stores the content you just typed into the Blogger-maintained databases, it also generates your first blog page.

Once you publish the content, you can view the blog page by typing the URL into your browser or clicking on the link labeled View Web Page, located in the bottom frame of the tool.

In the generated page, an ad is placed across the top. This is due because your blog is hosted on BlogSpot. The ad can be removed if you pay a set fee of $12 a year per blog. If you're content with the default implementation of the blog, as shown in Figure 3-5, you can continue adding new content to the existing blog, or you can customize your blog using techniques discussed later in the chapter.

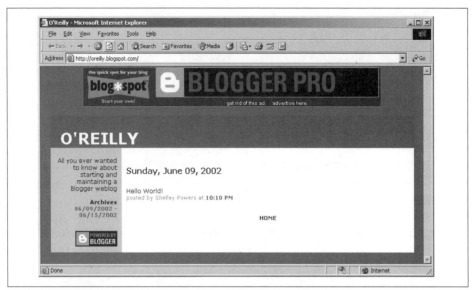

Figure 3-5. Blog displaying your first posting

Basic Blogger Settings

In the previous section, you created a blog and made your first posting, accepting the default behavior of Blogger. However, over time you'll most likely want to customize the blog to provide a look and feel uniquely your own. The first step in customizing your blog is understanding the components of a Blogger blog and how to adjust the settings related to each of them.

Title and Description

Figure 3-5 shows the blog description at the top of the lefthand column and the title in large type across the top of the page.

To change the title, return to the Blogger Edit view page and select the Settings option from the toolbar at the top of the web page. This opens a page that allows you to change various settings of your blog, as shown in Figure 3-6.

You can change the title in the first field, as we did for the example. You can also edit or remove the description in this Settings page. For the example, we'll leave the description as is.

Change the URL field to specify your blog's subdomain on *blogspot.com*. For example, Figure 3-6 shows a URL of "oreilly," so the blog is visible at *http://oreilly. blogspot.com*. Blogspot will give you an error if you try to set the URL field to something that's reserved or already taken(e.g., "www").

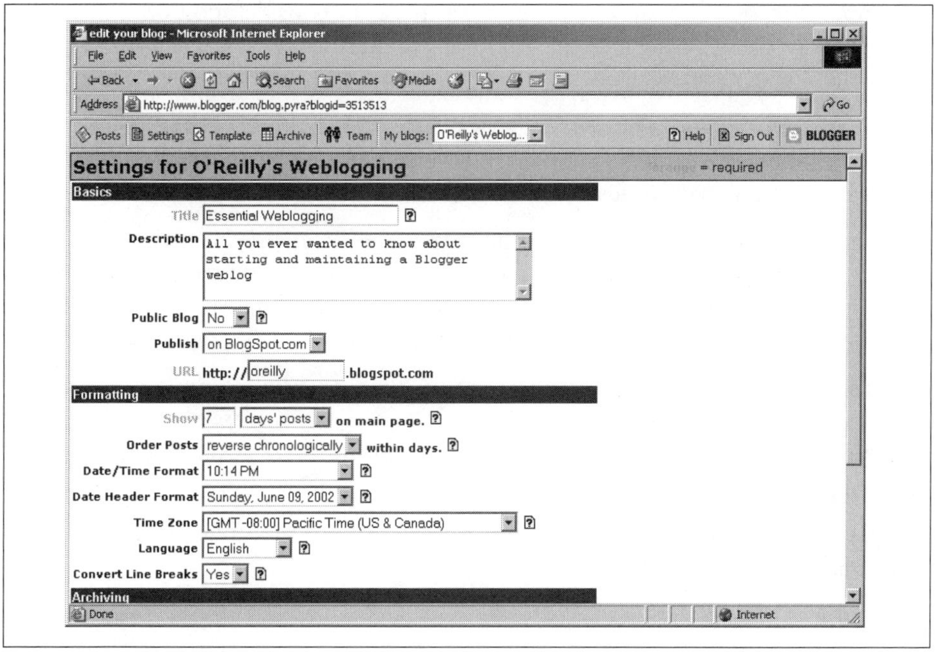

Figure 3-6. Changing the blog title in Blogger Settings

Once you've made the changes, save them by clicking the Save Changes button at the bottom of the page. Be careful with this button—right next to it is one that will delete the blog!

After saving the changes, you're returned to the Edit view page. To promote the changes you made to your displayed blog, click the Publish button that shows above the calendar in the bottom half of the page. View the blog again to see the new title on the page.

Formatting Basics

As described in Chapter 1, blog postings are commonly date- and timestamped and displayed in reverse chronological order (latest at the top of the page).

In the Blogger Settings, shown previously in Figure 3-6, you can see that the date formatting and posting display sequence can be adjusted for your blog. For instance, the number of postings displayed on the main page can be adjusted from the default of seven days' postings. Instead of displaying a set number of day's postings, you can choose to display a certain number of postings at a time. This approach is popular if you post frequently throughout the day.

The greater the number of postings, the larger the main blog page and the more time it takes to download. If you have large postings or post frequently, consider adjusting the number of postings shown on the main page, in consideration of your readers who might be using a slow modem and have slow access times.

Another thing you can change is the ordering of the posts, choosing to display postings in strict chronological order. However, before doing this, consider the fact that probably about 99% of bloggers post in reverse chronological order, and changing this default setting may confuse your blog readers.

If you prefer to post in a language other than English, the default, you can choose from among other language such as French and German. If you subscribe to Blogger Pro, you have access to even more language choices, including Arabic, Croatian, and several variations of English, German, Spanish, and so on.

Other formatting settings you can alter are the date- and timestamp associated with your postings. By default, each posting is date- and timestamped, and a date field heads each day's postings. In addition, the date itself is controlled with the Time Zone field. Use whatever matches your time zone.

For your blog, change the posting number to show 15 of the latest postings. In addition, change the Date/Time Format to:

```
M/D/YYYY HH:SS:MM AM/PM
```

And the Date Header Format to:

```
Day of week, Month Date
```

Alter the Time Zone and Language settings to reflect your own preferences. The settings at this point should be similar to those shown in Figure 3-7.

Once saved, republish your blog to reflect the changes.

Blogger Archives

By default when you create your new Blogger blog, archives are stored by week, which means there is a separate archive file for each week. These archives are accessible through hypertext links within the blog, as shown earlier in the blogging snapshot in Figure 3-5.

Archives by week are particularly useful because your blog page readers can reference an archived entry though a smaller weekly file rather than a larger monthly one. However, after a time, you can have so many archive files that the listing within your blog page is cluttered and hard to view. For this reason, a lot of bloggers prefer to store their archive files monthly.

You can adjust your archive frequency in the Settings. For your blog, change this to monthly. Once you save these changes and republish your blog, you'll see that the archive link changes to reflect the new date period.

Now that you've made some basic adjustments to your blog settings, it's time to focus on the blog content itself—your writing.

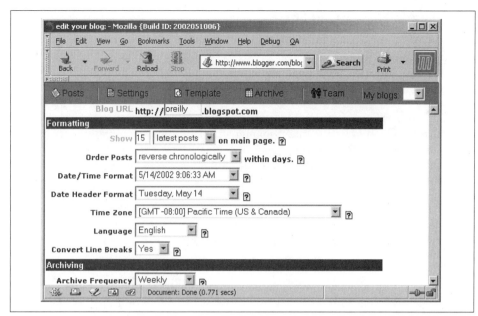

Figure 3-7. Blog Settings after modifications in formatting

Managing Your Posts

Your first blog posting was small and without a lot of embellishment. For the most part, though, your postings can be larger, and may feature hypertext links to other web pages or embedded graphics and other media. In addition, you can use HTML formatting to make certain aspects of your content stand out, such as with bolding or italicizing, or indenting text you've pulled as a quote.

Once you've created a post, you might need to modify it, adding new information or perhaps correcting existing information (or to correct typos, an all too frequent occurrence in blogs). In addition, you might regret a posting and choose to delete the whole thing.

All these blog posting management tasks—adding, modifying, and deleting—are performed through the Blogger Edit view page.

If you're creating an extensive or long post, or making significant modifications, we strongly recommend that you do this work in an offline text tool, such as Notepad, and then copy and paste the text into the Blogger edit window. If problems arise during posting, you won't lose your work and can resubmit your post safely a second time. Alternatively, use one of these desktop clients mentioned from Chapter 2.

Adding and Formatting Entries

Line breaks in the posting are reflected in the generated HTML by default. As an example, two break tag entries (<BR>) are added when you hit the Enter key twice in your content. Unless you want to add these tags manually, leave the line break conversion setting as is.

Though line breaks are managed for you, any other use of specialized HTML formatting must be added to your content manually. Thankfully, there are Blogger buttons that handle some of this for you. The formatting buttons do not display when you use Mozilla. They display only within Internet Explorer at the time of this writing.

For example, you might want to italicize text in your posting for emphasis. You can do this in Blogger by embedding italic (<i> <i/>) or emphasis (<em> </em>) tags directly in the page. Clicking the Blogger toolbar button labeled "I" generates italic tags and embeds these at the cursor location directly for you.

You can bold text by surrounding it with embedded tags (<strong> </strong> or <b> </b>), typed in directly or generated by using the "B" button in the Blogger toolbar.

If you prefer to add more complex styles, use CSS styling and enclose the text in either span tags (with no associated line breaks surrounding the text) or within div blocks.

If you're adding a link to another web page, use the button labeled with the small globe and link. When you click on it, a new window, as shown in Figure 3-8, opens providing you a place to type in the URL of the link. Once you're finished typing, clicking the OK button will close the window and generated hypertext link HTML with the URL embedded in the page at the cursor location.

Figure 3-8. Adding a hypertext link to a posting using the Blogger toolbar URL generator

To add HTML formatting yourself, create a new entry in your blog by clicking your mouse in the top window and placing the cursor at the start of the text edit block. Type in the paragraph, as shown in Example 3-1, using the Blogger buttons to add the HTML tags shown in the text or by typing the tags directly.

Example 3-1. Posting containing HTML formatting

```
<b>Blogger</b> is a weblogging tool that's accessed online. It can be found at the <a
href="http://blogger.com">Blogger web site</a>, and takes <i>very little effort</i> to
create either an account, or your first weblog. Once you've seen how easy weblogging can
be, you'll wonder why you didn't try weblogging sooner.
```

Don't worry about the line breaks; type in the content until the line automatically wraps. Once you're finished, save the content without publishing it by clicking the "Post" button. This stores your posting in the Blogger database but doesn't add it to your blog. This allows you to check the posting for typos and to review the HTML formatting in the bottom window before publishing.

Once you're satisfied with the text and formatting, click the Publish button to publish the content.

Modifying Entries and Adding Images

Up until this point, you've only added new blog entries. In the Edit view window, click the link labeled Edit, located directly beneath the item, to change an existing entry. This loads the item text into the editing window where you can make as many modifications as you want.

For instance, you can modify the new posting you made in the last section by embedding an image in the posting. To add a graphic to the new post, load it for editing, then add an img tag pointing to the URL of the graphic, wherever it's located. In the example, we "borrow" O'Reilly Network's Web DevCenter image to use. (In practice, you shouldn't point to images without the owner's permission, as explained in Chapter 1.)

Once the posting is loaded into the Edit window, add the following HTML tag just before the content:

```
<img src="http://www.oreillynet.com/images/javascript/javascript_logo.jpg"
align="right" vspace="10px" hspace="10px">
```

This embeds the image into the page, aligned to the right of the posting text, with a 10-pixel vertical and horizontal space. To see the results of adding the image, click the Post & Publish button to both save the content to the Blogger data store, as well as publish the modified posting to your blog. Figure 3-9 shows the blog with the image added.

This example also demonstrates the downside of hosting your blog within a constrained environment such as BlogSpot—you can't upload images or other media to the server. If you plan on making use of these types of files, move your blog off BlogSpot to a server of your own.

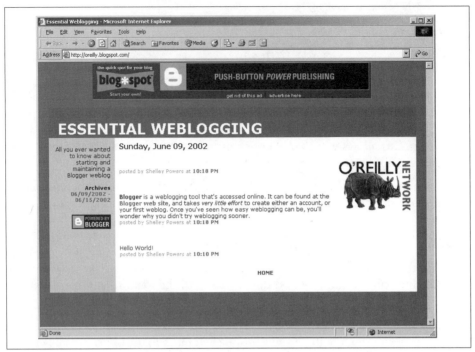

Figure 3-9. Blog page showing new posting, including image

Embedding other media content is just as easy as embedding images—you simply specify the appropriate HTML for the content's media type and publish your blog page.

Cleaning Up

Occasionally, you regret making a post. You may decide it's too personal, too angry, not appropriate, not politically correct, or whatever, and you want to eliminate the post.

Deleting a posting within Blogger is easy. Load the posting to be zapped into the Edit window, then click the Delete button on the Blogger toolbar. When you do so, a message box opens asking you to confirm this choice. Clicking on the OK button removes the posting from Blogger's data storage. To remove the posting from the blog page, click Publish and you're finished.

Try this by removing your first Hello, World! posting. After publication, view the page to see that the first post has been deleted.

Archiving in Detail

When you added, modified, or deleted a posting in the last section, the modifications were applied to the associated archive file, as well as the main blog page. Not all changes are reflected this way—if you customize the template or choose a new default template, you have to republish the archive pages to pick up this change.

Generating New Archives

To generate new archive files due to a change in the template, click on the Archive button on the Blogger toolbar. The Blogger Archive view page opens, listing each archive file with icons next to it to republish or delete the specific archive file. Because you've just started your blog, only one archive file is present, as shown in Figure 3-10.

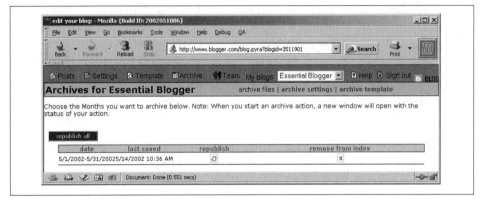

Figure 3-10. Blogger Archive view

To republish one specific archive, just click the small recycle button next to the archive filename. When you do, a page opens providing the status of the republication process. When finished, this window closes and the new date and time the archive was republished is shown in the Last Saved column.

Note that occasionally, a blog error page appears instead of a status page. This usually means the Blogger system is under a great load at the time. Wait about an hour and then republishing the archive file again—this time you should be able to see the status page.

If you have more than one archive file, you can click the Republish All button. This forces a republication of all archive files, disseminating any template change throughout all the archives.

Over time, you might decide not to keep a reference to an older archive. To remove this reference, click the delete icon next to it. You still need to physically remove the file if you host your own blog.

 The Archive view page is changing. At the time of this writing, archive handling was being modified, and individual archives are no longer accessible.

Troubleshooting

As stated in the beginning of the chapter, Blogger is a heavily used system and this causes problems at times. Probably the most infamous of the Blogger problems is the missing archive problem. You'll see this—and you're almost guaranteed to see this at least once—when you add a posting and publish your blog and the archive links don't show in the blog page (or in the archive page if you're using a separate page). The actual archive files aren't missing—just the reference to them. However, people won't be able to access these archives without the links, so you're going to want to fix the problem.

There are a couple of approaches to take to restore the links. We've found that if we go into Archive view and click the Republish All button, the links will usually re-appear. If this fails, though, another approach is to turn archiving completely off (set Archiving to No Archives in the Settings), reset archiving to your desired frequency (weekly or monthly), and then click the Republish All archives button again.

Finally, if the first two approaches don't work, try publishing a new posting. You can always delete this immediately, if you wish, if this solves the missing archive links.

 At the time this was being written, Ev was testing a new publishing engine, which should eliminate the missing archive problem.

Changing Your Account Profile

Over time you might need to change your email address or want to change your user-name. In addition, for security reasons, you should consider changing your pass-word every three months or so. All this information is kept in your account profile.

To modify your basic account profile information, click on the Team button in the Blogger toolbar, and in the page that opens, click on your name. Another page opens listing Organization, URL, Time Zone, and other information. In the right side of the toolbar is a link labeled Edit My Profile; follow this link.

The user account profile page is shown in Figure 3-11. This page is where you can modify your username, email, personal URL, and so on. In particular, this is where you can change your password. Once you've made your modifications, click the Save Profile button to commit the changes.

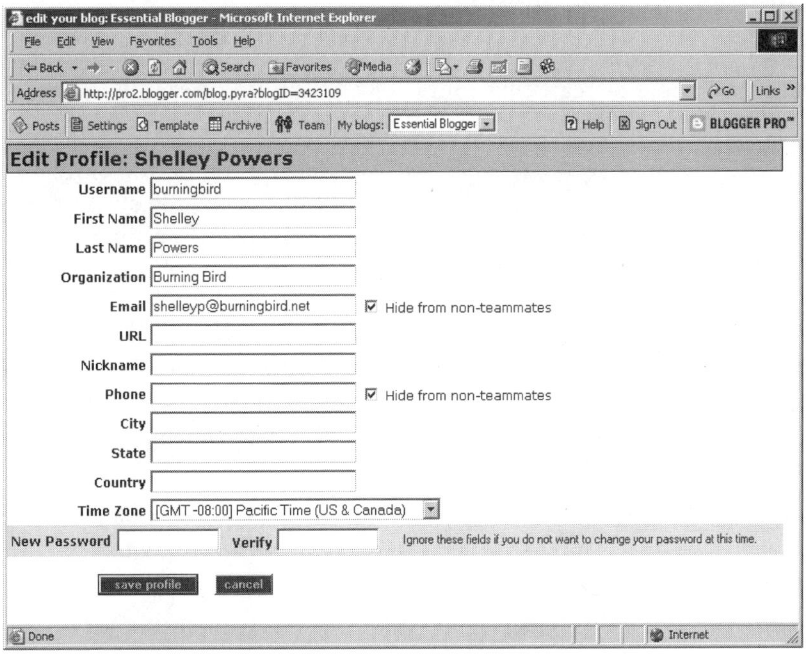

Figure 3-11. Changing your account profile

Change your password frequently, and use a combination of characters—alphabetical, numerical, and other. In addition, you'll want to use a username that's not that easy to guess. For instance, don't use the name of your blog or other publicly known information.

In the Profile page, you can also set what information is hidden from people who aren't part of your blogging team. (See "Group Blogs" later in this chapter for more on this.)

Basic Use of Templates

The most important aspect of your blog is the writing. However, the overall appearance of the blog can affect how people perceive the writing. If the blog has a bright, cheerful, and silly appearance, but the writing is somber and very serious, the mixed messages can jar your readers.

Additionally, blog formatting can adversely impact people's ability to read the writing. If the font is small and light-colored against a white background, your readers might have a hard time making out the words.

The current style on the Essentials blog, Chroma, is one of the most popularly used, primarily because the words are very legible and its neutral format fits most writing and content styles. However, it's fun and interesting to try new looks.

Changing the Blogger Template

When you created your blog, you picked a default template. You might be happy with it, or you might be regretting your choice about now. Regardless, changing the default template is easy within Blogger.

To change the existing template, click the Template button on the Blogger toolbar. When the Template view page opens, a large text box at the top shows the existing template HTML, including the embedded Blogger tags (to be discussed in more detail in Chapter 6). When you pick a new Blogger template, you lose everything in this block—including any additions and modifications you may have added. If you've customized the template, make a backup of the existing template first. Then you can work on incorporating your modifications into the new template. (Backing up your template is as easy as selecting all the text in the textbox, clicking the Copy button in the Browser Edit menu, and then pasting the contents into your favorite text editing tool, such as Notepad.)

To change the existing template, click the link labeled Choose a New Template. In the page that opens, you'll see several different template formats from which to choose, including the one you currently have.

Before selecting a new template, think about the layout you prefer for your blog. Background colors, images, and font styles are easy to change, but page layout can be complex, particularly when you have to work around the necessary Blogger template tags. As a general rule, pick a blog that has the layout that you want and fine-tune the selection with color and style.

For instance, you might prefer centered content, in a fairly traditional three-column style. Or you might prefer a left-justified blog, two-column style blog. If you're not concerned about displaying archive hypertext links and a blogroll next to your blog content, you can also pick a single-column layout.

Play around with the template styles. As an example of changing templates, in your test blog click the Use This button next to the Sports Cut template. You get a warning message about losing your template customization if you proceed. Clicking OK accepts the change and takes you to a page where you can either proceed to the Edit view page to publish the content with the new template or the Template HTML view page to modify it. For now, go to Edit view and publish the blog with the new template. Figure 3-12 shows the demonstration blog formatted with the new Blogger template.

Notice in the template that instead of a list of archive file links, it has a link to a separate archive file that has a listing of the links. As stated previously, not all templates have the same layout—and this can include changes to how the Blogger template tags are managed. Again, this isn't as much of an issue if you haven't customized your template, but you could be in for considerable rework otherwise.

Figure 3-12. Blog with the Sports Cut template

Once you decide on a new template, republish all of your archives to pick up the new style.

Blogger isn't the only location of templates that you can access. The next section talks about downloading and incorporating a template from another web site, blogskins.com.

Incorporating a Non-Blogger Template

Blogger templates are nice, but sometimes it seems as if every blog you view has one of five or six Blogger templates; you'd like something different but without having to manage the layout and style yourself. Because Blogger templates are nothing more than text, it's not surprising to find that people have published templates that you can download and use for free.

In particular, the BlogSkins web site (*http://blogskins.com*) offers several Blogger "skins," or templates. All the templates we've seen at the site are free for the downloading, and most even have comments attached that can provide useful feedback about why people do like or dislike the template.

To try out a template, once you've access the web site, follow the Browse Skins link on the left. The templates are listed by name but aren't displayed. Read the description associated with the template, then click whatever link that provides a view of the template. If none is provided, clicking the link associated with the template page takes you to another more detailed page that has a Preview link.

For the Essentials blog, let's try a skin called "Sim-Gray." To access it, set up a BlogSkins account (no charge). Click on the name for the skin, and within the skin detail page, click the Apply button. BlogSkins uses the Blogger API to get the names of blogs from your account, then overwrites the existing template with the selected one. After returning to Blogger and republishing the blog, the newly skinned blog is displayed, as shown in Figure 3-13.

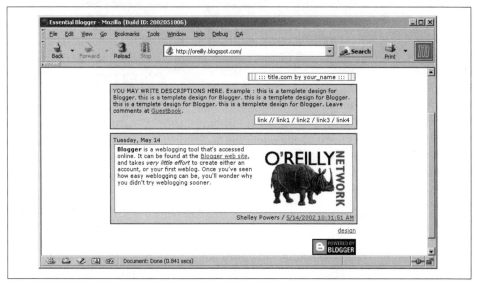

Figure 3-13. Newly skinned blog

The new skin requires editing to provide links, a description, and so on—but the basic formatting and layout has been added and is ready for customization. Many of the skins also have archive templates for separate archive index pages. These also get uploaded during this process. Republishing all of the templates propagates the template change to all archive files.

After playing around with different templates, return to the Chroma style. In the Template view, select Choose a New Template Link.

The Sim-Gray template didn't require any graphics, but many templates do. In addition, you might want to use other graphics within your blog or add photos. This isn't a problem if you have your own web server, but it is if you're using BlogSpot.

Self-Hosting

Where you locate your blog can impact what you can do with it. If you host your blog on something such as BlogSpot, you can only host your web pages on this site, not additional files, such as graphics or other media files. However, hosting your own web site for your blogs isn't always a trivial exercise.

Why Self-Host?

BlogSpot (*www.blogspot.com*) is a handy place to park your blog when first starting out. The cost is very cheap—$12/year to eliminate the ad if it bothers you (it will!). No maintenance, no hassles with working things out with an ISP, and so on. However, there are two primary disadvantages to hosting your blog on BlogSpot.

The first is, as stated earlier, you can't load other files on to the server or run other technologies such as PHP or ASP. You can work around this limitation, somewhat, by hosting your graphics at a free web server, such as *freeservers.com*. In addition, other bloggers are usually willing to give up some space for graphics, though, you may have to work through them to get the graphics uploaded. Unfortunately, this won't help if you want to use server-side technologies such as PHP. For this, you'll have to self-host.

The second reason not to use BlogSpot is that it is, at times, an extremely overworked server, leading to slow page loads and occasional server failures. The subscription-based Blogger Pro gets you access to faster and more reliable servers, however.

You will almost definitely need a subscription ISP service to run your own blog. Many free web sites, such as GeoCities, won't allow you to FTP pages from Blogger.

Configuration

To self-host your Blogger-generated pages, you need a web account with an ISP that provides FTP access. We're not aware of any ISP that doesn't provide this, so you shouldn't have any trouble finding one. The only decisions that exist, then, are what environment you want (Windows or Unix), web server (such as IIS or Apache), and the cost. Because you don't have any requirements for specialized technology—you only need the ability to host HTML pages—you don't have to sign up for an account that provides specialized application support.

Once you have your account, the next step is to FTP your files to their new home.

After logging into Blogger, access the Settings view. In the drop-down menu labeled Publish, change from "on BlogSpot.com" to "via FTP...". The form changes and new text boxes display for entering your FTP information.

Here are the fields you'll need to add values for are below:

Blog URL
> The URL of your new blog (e.g., *http://essentials.burningbird.net*).

FTP server
> The hostname of the FTP server to which your blog will be uploaded (e.g., *essentials.burningbird.net*).

FTP path
> The filesystem location and path where blog pages will be placed (e.g., */vhosts/ essentials/docs*). Check with your ISP if you're unsure of what your published page path is.

Blog filename
> You probably want to keep this as *index.html*.

FTP username and password
> Leave blank for security purposes (explained later).

FTP Archive path
> The relative location of archive files. Leave blank to put the archives into same directory as the main blog pages, specified in FTP path.

Figure 3-14 shows the Blogger settings after the information is added. Notice that we left the FTP username and password blank. This is for security purposes—if Blogger is ever compromised, your web site could also be compromised if the crackers obtain your username and password. You're better off providing this information once per session than storing it in the Blogger database.

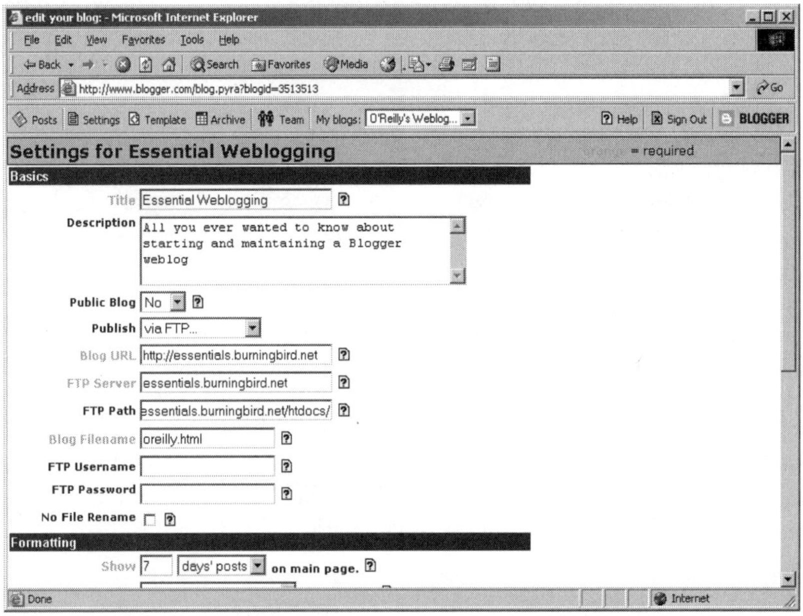

Figure 3-14. Changing settings to publish blog on your personal web server

Unfortunately, your username and password are transmitted over the network as plain text. This is a security risk as this information can be "sniffed" by specialized packet-sniffing software, giving someone access to your username and password.

Once you've made the changes, save them and return to the Edit view page. To publish the pages at the new site, click the Publish button. Because you didn't supply an FTP username and password, you are prompted for the username and password, as shown in Figure 3-15.

Figure 3-15. Prompt for web server username and password

You must republish all your archive files to restore the archive links and to move these files to your server. First, make sure the archive files are going to the correction location by accessing the Archive view and then clicking on Archive Settings. In the page that opens, check and see that the FTP Archive path is specified. You can also check this value within the Settings. When finished, republish all the archives by clicking the Republish All button.

Once you've moved your blog to your own server, you'll be free to post pages in ASP or PHP format or to incorporate other technologies.

Troubleshooting

If you submit a posting for publication, but the blog page, archive page, or posting aren't showing up, chances are the publication process is still working—this can take a few minutes when the system is under load. You should also make sure that your browser cache has been refreshed.

However, if the page doesn't show after a considerable time—at least a couple of minutes—something has happened during the publication process. This can range anywhere from not providing the correct FTP path or username and password (when publishing the first time) to not being able to get a connection for one reason or another (problems with your server or Blogger).

To start the troubleshooting process, click on the Status link that appears above the calendar in the Edit view page after you publish your blog. Information about the most recent publication process appears in the titlebar, such as "Transaction successful" if the blog was successfully published. If the publication wasn't successful, additional information is provided, including a link to an FTP file. For instance, if you get the following error:

```
Transfer Error: 550 /usr/local/somepath/index.html No such file or directory
```

chances are the location you specified doesn't exist or you don't have permissions to FTP to this location. Get more information by clicking the View FTP Log link, opening the transcript of the FTP attempt, as shown in Figure 3-16.

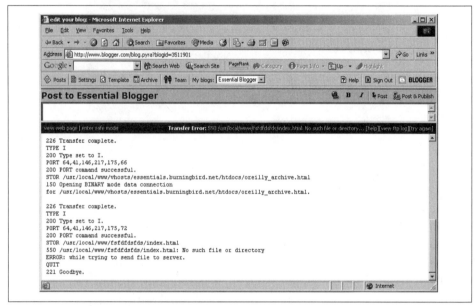

Figure 3-16. Viewing FTP transcript when FTP error occurs

This file usually gives you enough information to correct your settings, such as providing the correct username or password, or providing the correct FTP path.

Failure to publish can occur due to other causes. If your web site is hosted on an ISP that also provides your connectivity (through DSL, modem, or other means), you might get a failure because the actual FTP is originating at Blogger's IP address rather than through the IP provided by the ISP. If your ISP prohibits this as a security measure, you'll need to check with them about how to work around the issue of hosting your Blogger pages.

AOL members that host Blogger pages on their AOL Hometown space can't use the AOL Hometown system but can FTP the pages directly. Contact AOL for more information about hosting generated blog pages.

Finally, Blogger itself can fail, easily determined by the message displayed. If this occurs, your best bet is to sign off, wait an hour, sign back in, and try publishing your page again. Check *http://status.blogger.com* for information about planned or unplanned outages.

Browser Shortcuts

Blogger has a shortcut that allows you to easily select text from another web page and post the selected text as an attributed and linked post to your blog. The feature is called BlogThis!.

BlogThis! gives you the ability to go to any web site—not just another blog—select some text and then click a link that'll open a Blogger window that includes the high-lighted text *and* a hypertext reference to the page. You can edit the text as much as you want. When you're finished, click a button and the material is then posted to your blog with no other required effort. This is particularly handy if you quote and reference material in other blogs. No more having to select, copy, paste, and create a link when you want to quote another blogger.

To enable BlogThis!, access the Settings view and scroll down to the bottom of the page. There are two links in the page, each corresponding to a different way to get BlogThis! functionality. One link points to a registry file that can be downloaded and then run against your registry. The second link adds BlogThis!, manually, as a link to your Favorites menu.

To update the registry, right-click on the registry file link and select the Install BlogThis! option. A window opens providing some feedback. Click OK to open another window to download the file or run it from the current location—choose the option to save the registry file to your drive. Once the file is downloaded, open the file. When prompted to update the registry, specify Yes to update the Registry.

In theory, you can now select text and right-click on it to get a menu that lets you create a new blog entry from the selected text. Unfortunately at the time of this writing, the registry version of BlogThis! is problematical with IE 6.0, even with published workarounds. Hopefully BlogThis! will be fixed by the time you read this. In the meantime, you can use the second approach, which is to add a link to the BlogThis! functionality in your toolbar.

To manually add BlogThis! to your browser toolbar, go to Blogger help at *http://publicmind.blogger.com/enduser/group.jsp?node=171*. This page contains instructions for adding BlogThis!, organized by operating system and browser. Click on the appropriate link and drag it to the toolbar to install BlogThis! on your browser. The currently supported operating systems are Windows and Mac OS, and the currently supported browsers are IE and Mozilla.

To use BlogThis!, select text from a web page and then click the link in Favorites. A page opens that asks for your Blogger login. Once you provide this, a second page opens that contains the quote and a link to the quote. The hypertext link generated surrounds the name of the blog name, as pulled from the page title.

If you're using Blogger Pro, there's an updated version of BlogThis! accessible from the Blogger Pro main web page (*http://pro.blogger.com*). Drag the specified link to IE's Links toolbar to install.

Once installed, the Blogger Pro version works in a manner similar to the standard Blogger version; select the text to quote and click the BlogThis! button on the tool-bar. A window opens containing the quoted material, with title, and the ability to post it to your blog. At this point, you can add or edit material in the window, as shown in Figure 3-17.

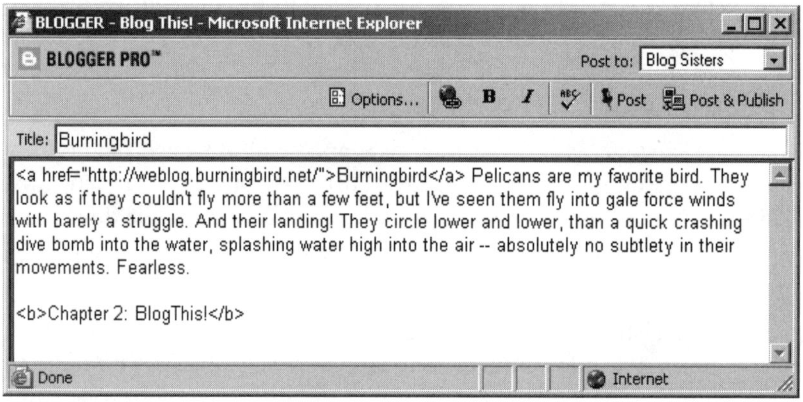

Figure 3-17. Blogger Pro BlogThis! window

The Blogger Pro version of BlogThis! allows you to use the Edit view features from Blogger Pro. See Chapter 6 for more on Blogger Pro.

If you keep several blogs, use caution with the Blogger Pro BlogThis! functionality. It's easy to forget to change the blog you're posting to and end up posting to the wrong blog.

Blogger Buzz

Up until now, you haven't been promoting your blog to the public as you've been trying out new features. When you're to the point where you want to attract visitors to your blog, you'll introduce your blog to the world, inviting people to stop by and read what you have to say. In the blogging community, this is known as generating buzz.

The first step to promoting your blog is to change the settings from being a non-public blog to a public one. This is accomplished through the Blogger Settings view, by changing the drop-down menu value of No for the field labeled Public Blog to Yes. Once you've done this, this adds your blog to the blog verification process—Pyra reviews the entry to ensure that it doesn't violate the TOS. Once verified, your blog is then added to the Blogger Directory. It also shows up on the Blogger web site when you make blog updates (though only briefly, and only if your update is within the time frame of the current view on Blogger).

The second step is Ping Weblogs.com whenever you make a change to your blog. You can do this through various automated approaches, outside of the scope of this book. Or you can do this manually, through the Weblogs.com update notification form at *http://newhome.weblogs.com/pingSiteForm*. In this form, type in the name of your blog (keep it short) and your blog URL. For the demonstration blog we've built so far, the values would be:

```
Essential Blogger
essentials.burningbird.net
```

This adds the update to the Weblogs.com queue, and your blog will show—within a minute or two—on the Weblogs.com page. By adding your update notifications to Weblogs.com, you're also "adding" it indirectly to several other resources that use Weblogs.com as feeds to their own notification systems.

If you're a Blogger Pro user, there's a checkbox in the Settings view, in Publishing, that you can check. This makes edits to your blog automatically update Weblogs.com.

The third step to promoting your blog is to add it to Blogdex and Daypop. They are services that scan blogs to see what people are pointing to. See *http://blogdex.media.mit.edu* and *http://www.daypop.com*.

Group Blogs

In addition to maintaining a Blogger blog for your own personal use, you can also create a group blog and then invite people to participate.

As you are the owner of the blog, you'll be the designated administrator and the only person who can add or remove other blog team members. To add a new member, click the Team button on the Blogger toolbar. In the window that opens, you should be the only person listed as a team member at this time, with a check underneath the column heading labeled Admin.

To add a new member, click the Add New Member(s) button on the toolbar. In the window that opens, there are a couple of boxes, including one with a list of Available Users, one for team members being added, and form fields to add a member who isn't in the list of Available Users. The Available Users list is made up of people who are team members of other group blogs to which you belong.

Figure 3-18 shows an invitation. The message that goes with the emailed invitation explains what's going on. Click the New >> button to add the invitee to the list.

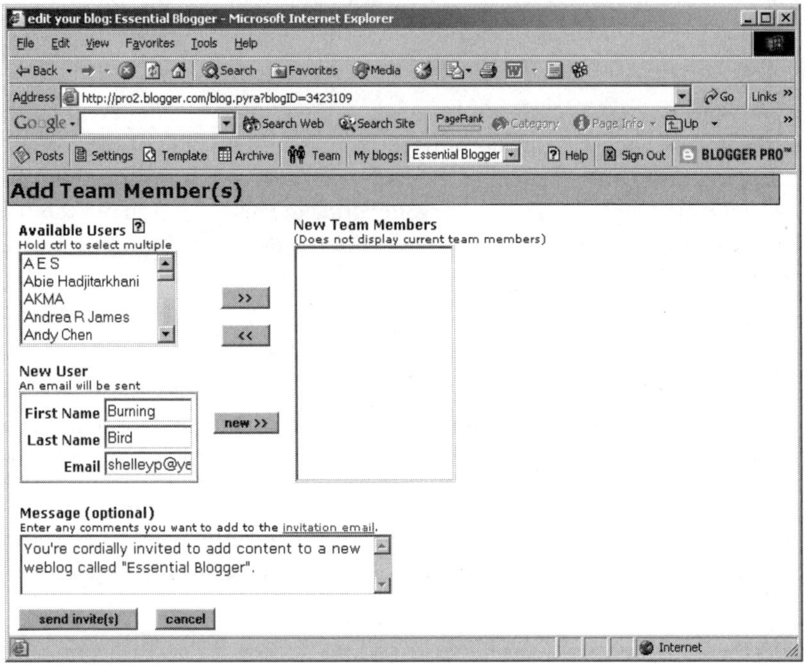

Figure 3-18. Inviting new team members to a group blog

Repeating this process adds yet more invitees to the list. When finished, click the Send Invite(s) button to send the invitation. This returns you to the Team view, where you'll find that the invitee has been added to the page, with a status of pending until they either accept or decline the invitation.

The invitee receives an email with a subject line of "Blogger blog invitation from *your name*". The invitation includes a link to accept or decline the invitation, and instructions how to process the invitation whether they're a current Blogger user or not. Clicking the link then takes the invitee to a page where they can accept or decline the invitation.

Invited team members do not have all the options on the Blogger toolbar that the blog administrator has. For instance, a team member will not see the Settings, Template, and Archive buttons as they won't be able to adjust any of global settings of the blog; they can only add, modify, and delete their own postings.

When the new team member posts to the blog, their name will be attached to the posting rather than yours. This will be the name the person uses to set up the account, not the one you used for the invitation.

To remove a Team member, click the Remove checkbox associated with their name within the Team View window. In addition, if you want to give another team member administration capabilities, check the box labeled Admin. Note, though, that the team member will now be able to modify any team member's post, nor can she add or remove members or modify the blog. Use caution before giving this privilege to others.

Removing a Blogger Blog

The procedure to remove a Blogger blog differs based on whether the blog is hosted on BlogSpot or your own server. If hosted on your own server, you can manually delete the blogging pages and then delete the Blogger blog.

Until recently, if your blog was hosted on BlogSpot, you had to manipulate the Blogger template to remove the files. However, with recent changes, deleting the Blogger blog also deletes the pages on BlogSpot.

To delete a Blogger blog, access the Settings view, scroll down to the bottom and click the Delete this Blog button. You are then asked to confirm your decision. Once you do, the blog is removed from Blogger's data stores, and blog pages are removed from BlogSpot. If you hosted the blog on your server, you must manually remove the pages.

Support

Throughout this chapter, we've talked about some of the quirks of Blogger, and what to do to minimize problems associated with them. There are a few other things that you can do and places to turn to when you run into problems.

There's a help system at *http://publicmind.blogger.com/enduser/category.jsp*, and FAQs at *http://archives.blogspot.com* and *http://profaq.blogspot.com*. These latter two publications were created by Phil Ringnalda, who has provided help to Blogger users for a considerable length of time.

The blogging community is always willing to lend a helping hand to other bloggers. Once you have a few readers, you're likely to get an answer if you post a question to your blog.

CHAPTER 4

Desktop Blogging with Radio UserLand

Radio UserLand, by UserLand Software, is a desktop blogging tool. You build your blog using the Radio UserLand software (henceforth referred to simply as Radio) that runs on your computer, and then Radio publishes it to a web server for the world to read. Because Radio is a desktop blogging tool, a writer can take it with him and blog wherever he is—the beach, a coffee shop, a plane, anywhere. For many writers, this alone is a compelling reason for using Radio over other blogging tools.

Radio can be downloaded for free, and from download to your first blog post takes only a few clicks. Your blog source text is stored on your computer, but blog pages are served from an *upstream server*—a server out on the Internet to which your copy of Radio can send files (upstream them). UserLand Software provides hosting space on its upstream servers for every Radio UserLand customer as part of the license. You can start to use this immediately. Alternatively, you can use any web hosting account with FTP support to serve your Radio UserLand blog. Radio provides many options for connecting to other servers, including acting as an upstream server itself; thus, Radio "power users" can control every stage of blog publishing from their own desktop.

Radio provides an integrated News Aggregator (see Chapter 1). This is a powerful tool for monitoring web sites of interest to you. Radio can automatically capture news from subscribed-to sites as it is published, add it to your blog with one mouse click, and publish your own RSS feed to which other bloggers can subscribe. Overall, Radio provides exceptionally powerful RSS capabilities both for reading blogs and publishing your own blog.

Given Radio's powerful RSS capabilities, people tend to use Radio in two different ways for blogging. You can create original content in your blog—this is referred to as a "writer" blog. Or you can comment on existing content in your blog—this is referred to as a "router" blog, because it usually ends up sending or *routing* people to other places on the Web.

Because Radio can be used both online and offline, it is an ideal tool for writers—they can work wherever they are. And for people who are commenting on content, the News Aggregator is a tremendous convenience.

Although you download and run your own copy of the Radio application, you don't have to reinstall this when Radio is enhanced (or when bugs have been fixed); you can enable a UserLand automatic software-update mechanism, which can upgrade your Radio installation while you sleep.

In this chapter, we're going to discuss how to download, install, and configure Radio, then walk through publishing your blog and using the News Aggregator.

Some powerful features of Radio—themes, macros, and content management—will be introduced in this chapter and then described fully in Chapter 7.

Installing Radio UserLand

Installing Radio is your first step toward using it as your blogging environment. Radio can be easily downloaded and installed in about 10 minutes, using a cable modem. Your time may vary if you have a dialup connection or a slow Internet link. Directions for installing, on both Windows and Macintosh, platforms are covered in the following sections.

Downloading

Radio, like many Internet applications, is not sold in stores. It is available for download directly from UserLand Software. You can download it via the download link at *http://radio.userland.com*.

Choose the right version for your computer and click the download link to begin. For convenience, you probably want to save it to your desktop. Once you download Radio, you can use it for 30 days under the evaluation license. After 30 days, your copy of Radio will stop working, and you can then either uninstall it or purchase it for full use. At the time of this writing, the cost for a copy of Radio is $39.95 per year. This covers the Radio software and hosting your blog at *http://radio.weblogs. com/YourUserNum/*. The *YourUserNum* is a unique user number that is issued to every Radio download and distinguishes your blog from that of another user. For example, a UserNum of 0103087 gives the blog a location of:

> *http://radio.weblogs.com/0103807/*

If you download Radio and start using it but decide not to purchase it, UserLand maintains the data on your blog for 30 days following the 30 day evaluation period to give you the opportunity to change your mind. After this it is deleted.

Installation

These download instructions are for Radio 8.07. There might be a slightly more advanced version available by the time that you read this. The same basic steps, however, should apply.

Windows

From your desktop, double click the Radio installer (it should be named something like *RadioUserLand807Setup.exe*). Your screen should look like Figure 4-1.

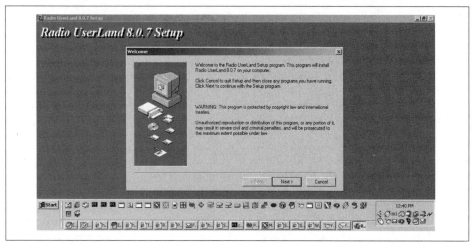

Figure 4-1. Radio UserLand setup screen

Click the Next button to advance to the Install program to view the license agreement. If you agree with the license agreement, click the Next button.

Choose where you want to Install Radio. Using the default *C:\Program Files\Radio UserLand* is generally best. Click the Next button two more times to start actually copying the Radio files to your computer.

When the files are done copying, click the Close button to end the installer. Radio will start for you.

Macintosh

Radio for the Macintosh comes as a self extracting Stuffit file. Double click the Stuffit file and follow the prompts to install Radio.

If you need to uninstall Radio, first backup your data (very specific instructions are later in Chapter 7) and then drag the Radio UserLand folder to the Trash.

To install under Mac OS X, extract the downloaded archive. Double-click the extracted disk image to mount it on your desktop then copy the Radio UserLand folder into the Applications folder. Make sure your web browser is running, and then double-click the Radio UserLand application icon. The browser will open the Radio UserLand Setup page.

To install under Mac OS 9, unstuff the archive if it hasn't been unstuffed automatically. Launch Radio UserLand 8.0.7 Installer and follow the straightforward instructions. At the end of the installation process, the installer will offer to launch the program for you. Accept this offer. Your web browser will open the Radio UserLand Setup page.

Registering

When Radio starts up, it displays the form shown in Figure 4-2.

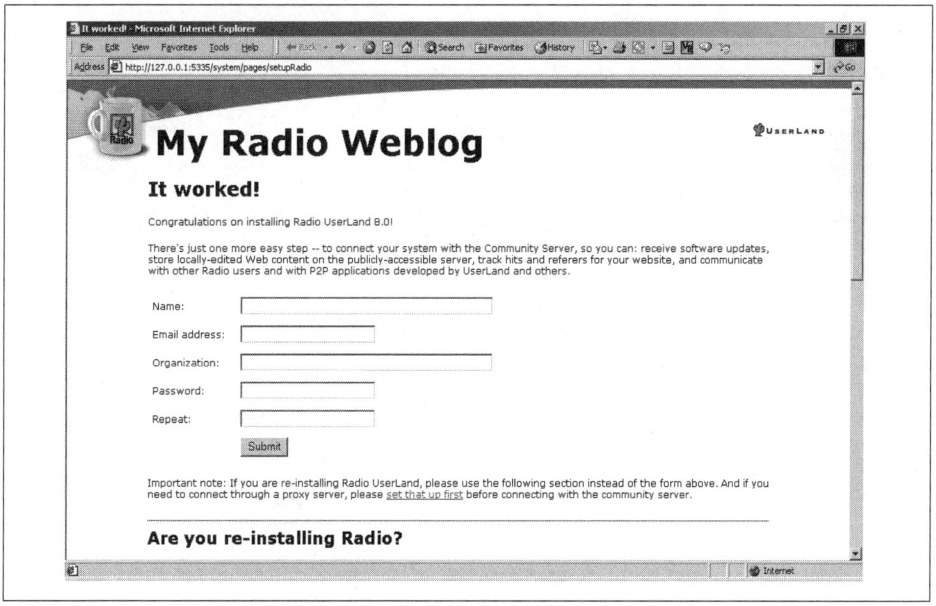

Figure 4-2. Successful installation of Radio UserLand

Before you can begin using Radio, you need to fill out this web form to finish configuring Radio. This creates an account on the UserLand server for you. Obviously, you want to make note of your password (and remember which email address you specified if you have more than one). Once you click the Submit button, you should see the page shown in Figure 4-3.

Click the Continue button to begin using Radio and you should see the page shown in Figure 4-4.

Congratulations! You have now installed Radio and are ready to begin blogging.

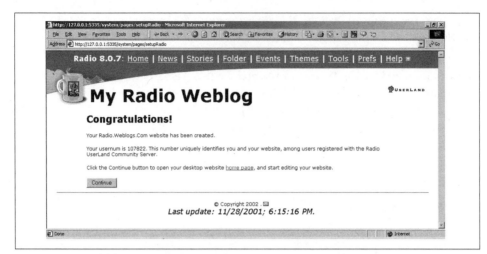

Figure 4-3. Successful creation of a UserLand account

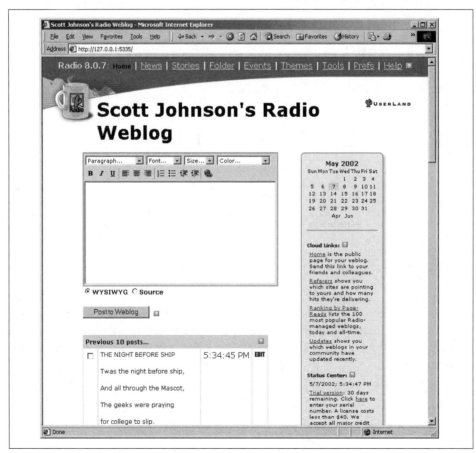

Figure 4-4. Installed and ready to blog

Welcome to Radio

Radio is an application that runs (usually) in the background on your machine. It acts as a web server, so most of your interaction with Radio takes place through your web browser. The terms we'll use are Radio Application for the program that runs mostly behind the scenes, Desktop Website for the administrative pages served by the Radio application to your web browser, and Your Weblog for the final publicl visible product of all this: your blog.

Figure 4-5 shows the interaction between your browser, the Radio Application, and your blog on the upstream server.

Figure 4-5. Radio UserLand components

Starting the Radio Application

The Radio installer launches Radio for you automatically. To start it manually on Windows, go to the UserLand group in your Programs menu and run Radio. If you are on Mac OS X, Option-click on the Radio icon in the Dock and choose Home Page.

The Desktop Website

Figure 4-6 shows the Desktop Website with the various components labeled.

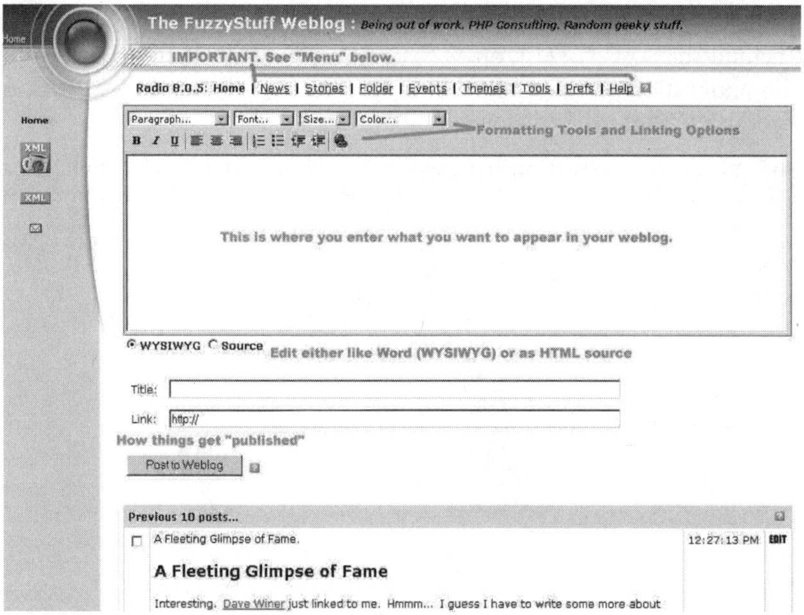

Figure 4-6. Desktop Website in Internet Explorer

The important parts of the Desktop Website are:

Radio command bar
> Links to the different commands in Radio (Home, News, Stories, etc.)

Formatting tools and linking options
> Tools for formatting and linking your content (font, size, color, etc.)

Editing window
> Where you type your blog post

Editing options
> Under Windows, you can edit text graphically (WYSIWYG or what you see is what you get) complete with fonts and pictures, or you can use straight HTML

Post to weblog
> Publish your blog entry to the Internet

Previous 10 posts
> List of your previous posts

A Visual Tour of Using Radio

In this section, we walk through Radio, illustrating all the common steps that a new user takes. This starts with making your first post, checking that it gets to the Internet correctly, changing your preferences, switching your theme, and using the News feature to post to your blog. View this section as an introduction only—these features are covered in more detail later in this chapter and in Chapter 7.

To make your first post, type anything you want into the editing box you see on the Desktop Website home page (shown in Figure 4-7).

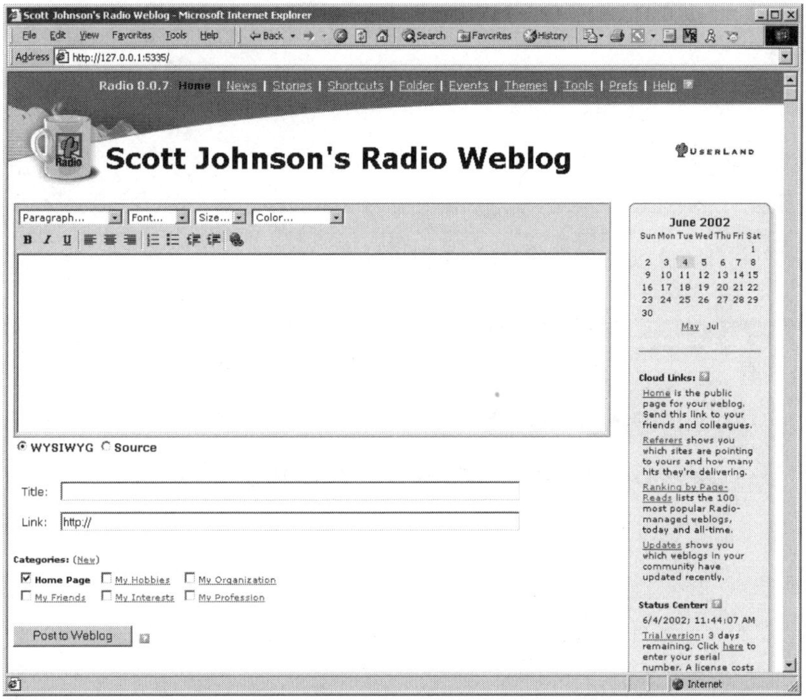

Figure 4-7. Desktop Website home page

"Hello World" is a fine first blog entry. Once you're done, click the Post to Weblog button to your blog entry only. Radio immediately posts your entry to the Internet. You can view it by clicking the Home link shown in the Cloud section of the gray sidebar. While your URL and title will be different, you should see something pretty much like Figure 4-8.

Now that you know how to make a basic post, the next step is to customize the title and description for your blog. These are preference settings, or Prefs. Click the Prefs link at the top righthand side of your Radio window (first return to the Desktop Website with the Back button in your browser). Figure 4-9 shows the Prefs page.

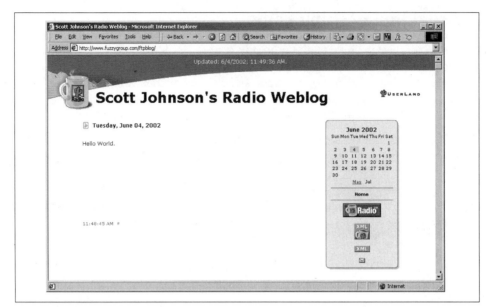

Figure 4-8. Blog with a successfully posted entry

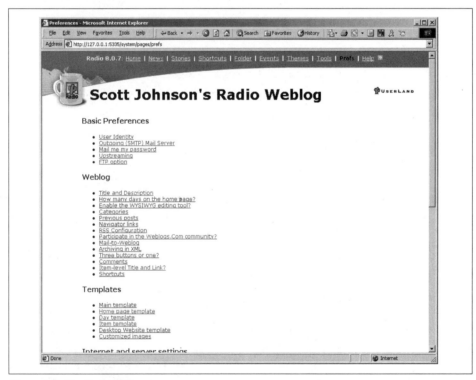

Figure 4-9. The Prefs page

The Prefs page shows the different preferences you can set. Click on Title and Description in the second grouping. Figure 4-10 shows the Title and Description preferences.

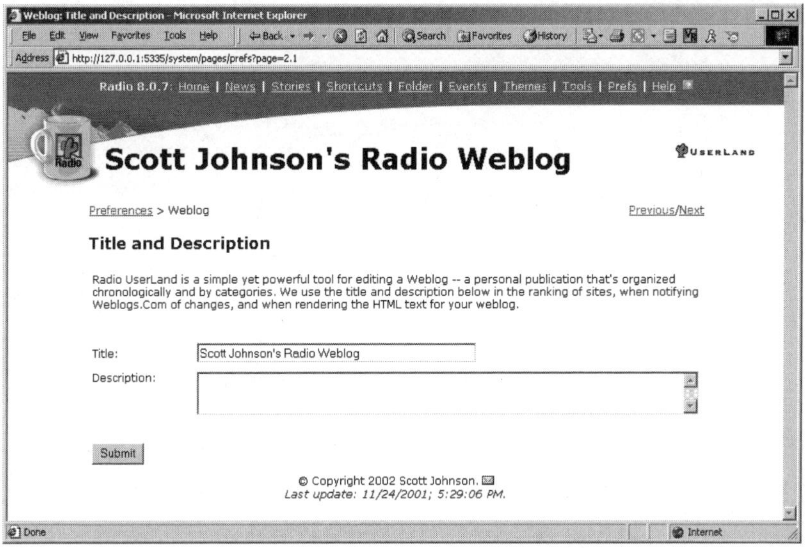

Figure 4-10. Title and Description preferences

Change the Title and Description as you need to and then click the Submit button. Radio will make these changes and then return you to the Prefs page so you can make additional changes if needed.

The next change you probably want to make will be to upgrade the look and feel of your blog—its theme. Click on the Themes link at the top of the screen. The Themes page looks like Figure 4-11.

Select a theme that sounds appealing to you and click its radio button. Scroll down the page and select the Submit button. The resulting page is shown in Figure 4-12.

Before you change your template, Radio warns you that you could lose any customizations that you might have made. Click Apply Theme to continue.

Radio applies the theme and returns you to the main Themes page in case you want to try another theme. Click the Home link to return to the main Radio page to see the theme in action. You may need to click Refresh or Reload in your browser to see the new theme as in Figure 4-13.

As you can see, the new theme, Woodlands, is now used for your blog. Click Home in Cloud links to see it applied to your blog, as in Figure 4-14.

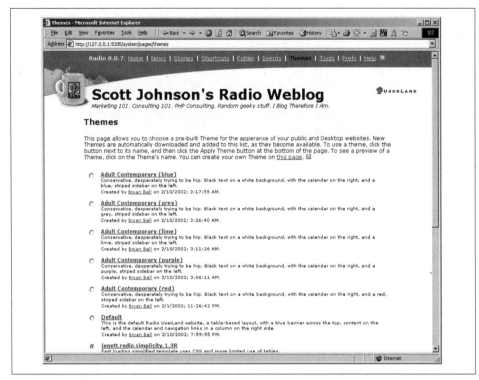

Figure 4-11. The Themes page

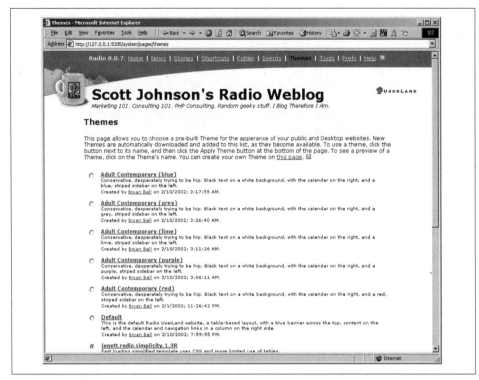

Figure 4-12. Theme change confirmation page

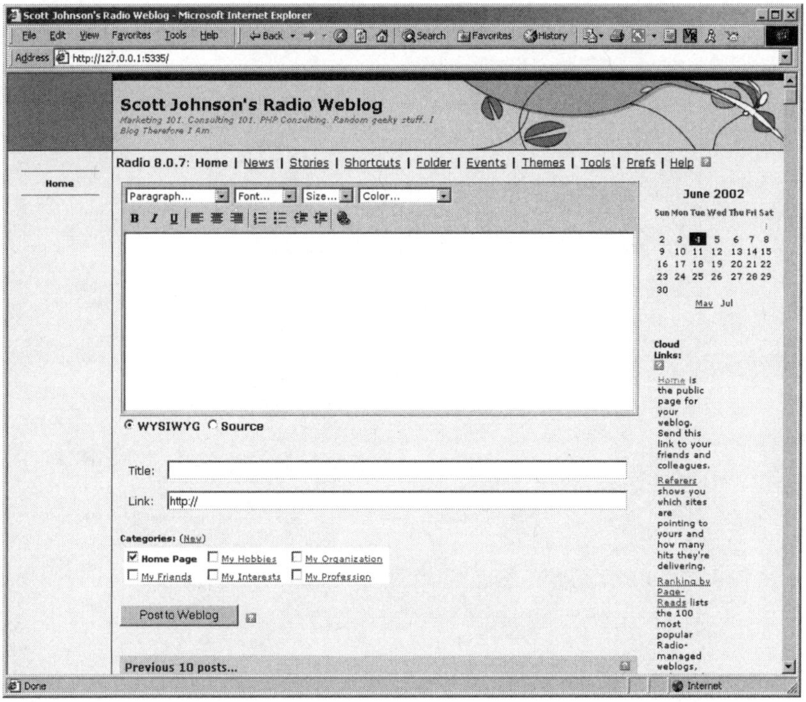

Figure 4-13. A new theme, Woodlands

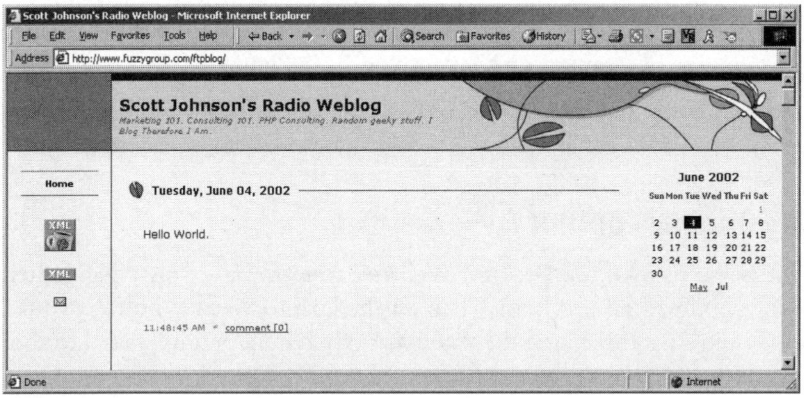

Figure 4-14. Woodslands-themed blog

The final step in your tour is to use Radio's news feature, the News Aggregator, to post content to your blog from another source. Return to the Desktop Website and click the News link. The News Aggregator page is shown in Figure 4-15.

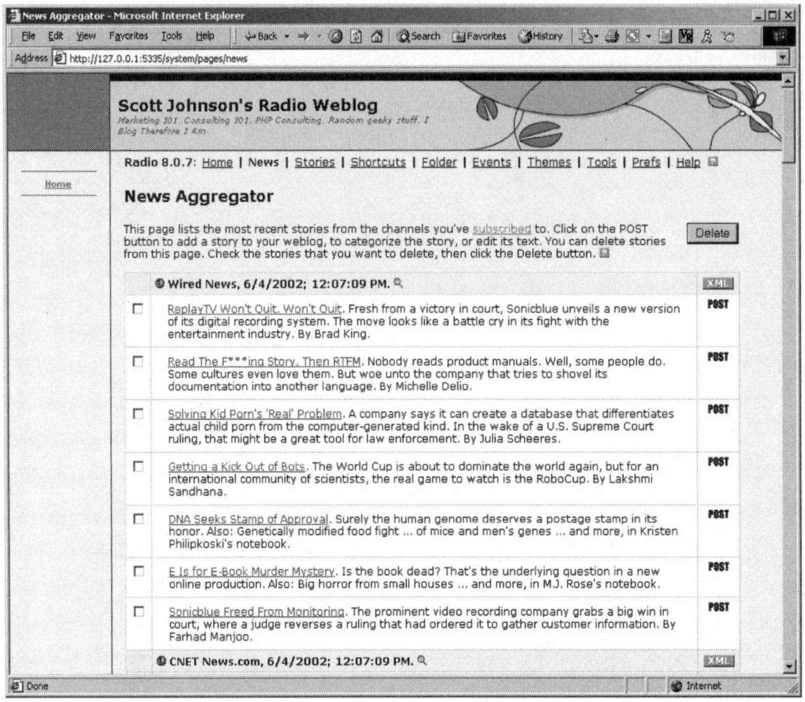

Figure 4-15. News Aggregator

What you see above is a set of news items from different feeds to which you subscribe. Click the Post button next to any news item, and Radio will add it to your editing window so you can post it to your blog, as in Figure 4-16.

Click the Post button and Radio will publish this entry out to the Internet complete with all links and any changes you made. See Figure 4-17 for an example.

Writing Original Content

From the home page of the Desktop Website, type or paste your blog content into the editing window (the text box). Then hit the Post to Weblog button. Your post is stored in Radio's database, and the web pages are rebuilt and uploaded to the server where you can view them.

This is where most Radio users make their first wrong turn. Radio is a browser-based application. This means that the browser does not save your information unless you hit Post to Weblog. If you have text typed in the Editing window and you move away from it by using the Back button or any other link, that text just goes away. Given that everything that controls Radio is a hyperlink, its surprisingly easy to lose content.

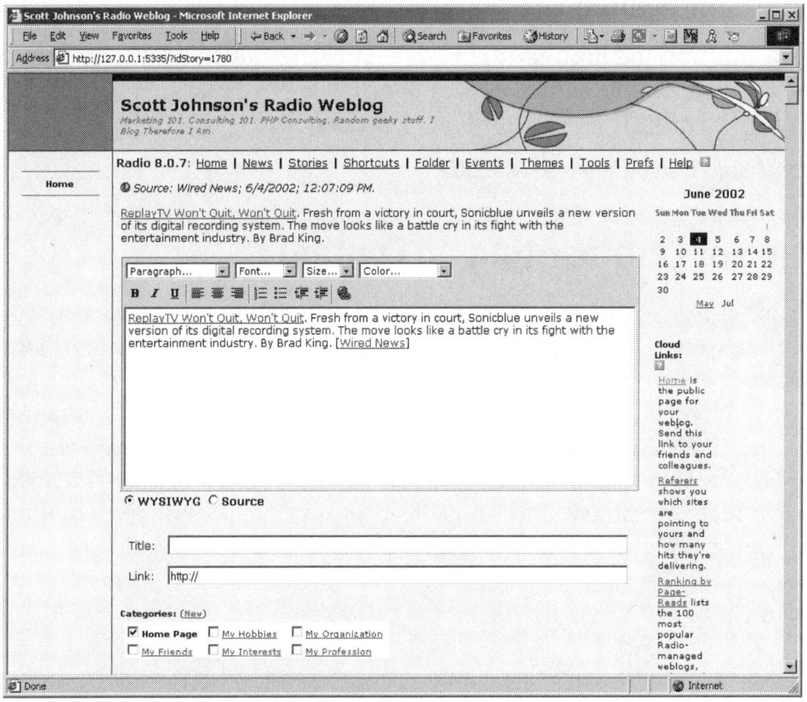

Figure 4-16. Item from News Aggregator in post editing window

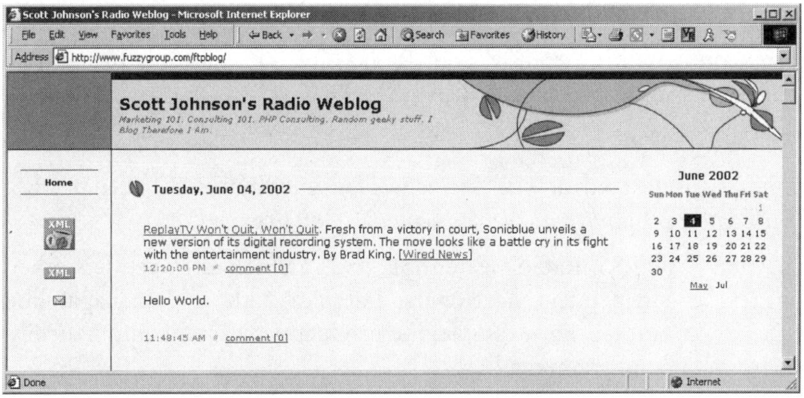

Figure 4-17. Blog post from News Aggregator

Reading Your Weblog

If you use the provided hosting at *http://radio.weblogs.com*, the URL for your blog is *http://radio.weblogs.com/usernum/* where *usernum* is your user number padded with leading zeros to make it seven digits long. For example:

http://radio.weblogs.com/0107822/

Routing or Commenting on Content

Radio's News Aggregator is a feature in Radio that regularly receives news updates based on RSS news feeds to which you subscribe. These can be other blogs, web sites such as News.com or Slashdot.com, or even "real media" such as the New York Times or CNN. Once you've subscribed to a news feed, Radio automatically receives those feeds and then lets you add them to a blog posting with just one mouse click. A very useful feature of the News Aggregator that Radio newcomers overlook is that you can use it to simply read your personal news from multiple web sites, all condensed into one easy-to-view web page.

RSS in Radio

It's important to understand that Radio has very powerful RSS features beyond the News Aggregator. In addition to accepting RSS input, Radio automatically creates an RSS feed for your blog. This lets anyone in the world subscribe to your blog and read it through a News Aggregator. And, because Radio feeds are always in the same relative place in every blog, it's easy to susbscribe to any Radio blog.

Unless you configure it differently, your Radio blog automatically has an RSS feed, containing your current posts located at:

BLOGURL/rss.xml

If your blog was located at *http://radio.weblogs.com/0103807/*, then its RSS feed would be located at *http://radio.weblogs.com/0103807/rss.xml*.

Going beyond basic RSS, Radio's extensible tools architecture even lets other products, written by independent developers, interface with its RSS capabilities and extend them even further. For example, the product news2mail, automatically delivers news from Radio to your email.

This has a number of advantages for regular news readers. News is changed from a push to a pull model where the news automatically comes to your inbox as opposed to your having regularly visit Radio's News page. Because most people check email regularly, this is very convenient. Additionally, this allows you to receive the benefits of the News Aggregator even when you are traveling and away from your desktop computer. Finally, news2mail even allows posting to your blog right from the email it sends you. For more on news2mail, see:

http://www.rds.com/doug/weblogs/news2mail/

For more information on Radio's Tools feature, see Chapter 7.

Another powerful news-related feature is the Radio Express bookmarklet, which gives Radio users the equivalent of the Blogger feature Blog This! (described in Chapter 3). More details are available at:

http://www.newsisfree.com/blog/stories/2002/01/20/radioexpress.html

Subscribing to a Feed

To subscribe to a news feed, first click on the News link in the Radio command bar. The News Aggregator is displayed. Click on the Subscribed link to get the subscriptions page, as in Figure 4-18.

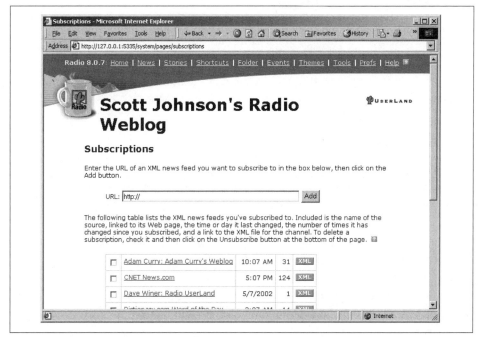

Figure 4-18. The news subscriptions page

Enter the URL of a news feed and click the Add button. You can also subscribe to news feeds on any Radio blog by clicking the orange XML coffee mug button, as shown in Figure 4-19.

Beyond the XML coffee cup, there is also the XML button icon shown in Figure 4-20.

Figure 4-19. XML coffee mug icon

Figure 4-20. XML button

This indicates that a site has an RSS news feed but that you need to manually cut and paste the URL into your News Aggregator.

Click on the News link in the Radio command bar to return to the News Aggregator. Refresh your browser, and Radio should start collecting news from your subscribed feeds.

Commenting on a Feed Item

To add a news feed item to a blog post and comment on it, first click on the News link in the Radio command bar. This brings up the News Aggregator, shown earlier in Figure 4-15.

Click on the Post button to the right of the news item. Radio moves the news item to your entry form, where you can edit it, add comments, or just post it.

The Radio Menu

Almost everything you do in Radio is controlled from the Radio command bar, the row of links across the top of your screen. Here's a quick rundown of what each menu item does. This is called either the Radio menu or the Radio command bar.

Home
> Jumps you back to the main editing window. You may have to refresh your browser window to see any changes you made.

News
> Radio's RSS News Aggregator, which lets you subscribe to syndicated RSS feeds and easily base your blog posts on stories from those feeds.

Stories
> Essentially longer essays but written in the Radio environment.

Folder
> Browse the Radio server layout so you can see how the data is stored. This lets you find URLs to your blog posts so you can link to them. It also enables uploading content such as pictures and other files to your blog.

Events
> Traces what Radio does behind the scenes.

Themes
> Change the look and feel of your blog with two clicks.

Tools
> Utilities within the Radio environment.

Prefs
> Configures Radio and makes it function. For example, getting Radio to FTP to your own web server is something you'd set up here.

Help
> Documentation.

Setting Your Radio Preferences

Radio is a very configurable product that lets you set many different preferences. Radio's Prefs screen mixes together two very different types of preferences: how your blog operates (blog properties), and how your copy of Radio operates (Radio preferences).

In this section, we'll cover the Radio Prefs screen and point out the options that really matter for your blog and for your system.

To get to the Radio Prefs screen, click on the Prefs link in your Radio command bar. The Prefs screen is shown in Figure 4-21.

The Radio Prefs options are broken down into different categories:

Basic Preferences
> System-level configuration

Weblog
> How your blog operates for readers and for yourself, the author

Templates
> The presentation of your weblog

Internet and server settings
> How connectivity functions in Radio

News Aggregator
> Settings to control the News Aggregator

Advanced
> Changing passwords, backup, and URLs

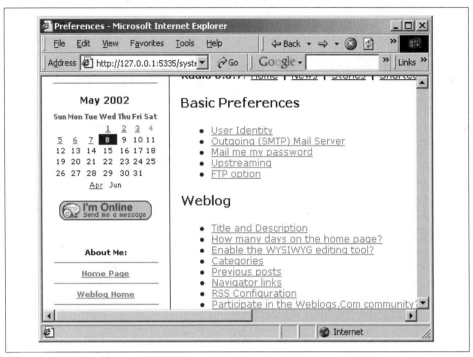

Figure 4-21. FTP Preferences

In total, there are approximately 50 different preference screens, each with one or more options. To make configuring Radio easier, we are going to make the following assumptions about how you blog with Radio:

- You are both a "writer" and a "router." That is, you both write new content for your blog and comment on news items. Radio's news preferences, as set to the defaults, are usually correct for most users, and don't need to be changed.

- Your blog is hosted at *http://radio.weblogs.com/usernum/*.

- You want one or more categories for your blog. Categories, which are covered fully in Chapter 7, let you group related blog posts together. This is useful for readers because they can see like items in one place.

Even though the Radio Prefs screen includes the look and feel of your blog, this is complex enough that we cover it separately in Chapter 7 and not in this section.

Blog Title and Description

To set or change the title and description of your blog, select Title and Description from the Weblog group of preferences. Enter the title of your entire blog (e.g., "The Sherlock Holmes Casebook"). This is shown at the top of your blog.

Then enter a description of what's in your blog (e.g., "Gossip from 221B Baker Street"). Click the Submit button to save your changes. The description appears under the title.

Blogdex or Navigator Links

To create or edit your list of links, select Prefs from the Radio command bar. Select Navigator links. This brings up a form with a text box where you enter URLs and titles for the links as XML.

Your block of links should start with <navigator> and end with </navigator>. In between is a set of <item /> tags. The two attributes of an item tag are name and pagename. The name will be shown to the user as a link, the destination of the link is the pagename. For example:

```
<item name="O'Reilly" pagename="http://www.oreilly.com/" />
<item name="Home" pagename="/" />
```

The URLs given as pagenames can be either absolute (as in the case of the O'Reilly link) or relative to your blog's home page (as in the second link).

Save your Navigator links by clicking the Submit button. Reload your blog to see the effect of the navigation bar.

Adding Titles to Your Posts

By default, Radio posts are untitled and simply appear in a series under the date on which they were blogged. To give each post its own title, select the Prefs option from the Radio command bar. Click on Item Level Title and Link. Turn on both checkboxes and then click the Submit button. This adds two extra fields to the Desktop Website page for adding a new blog entry: Title and Link.

The Title field is used in your RSS feed to provide a title for your blog post when it is viewed in a reader's News Aggregator; it is not displayed in your blog post. The Link field stores a hyperlink to an alternate representation of your post. For example, you might have a post that talks about a new music CD. The link field could go to the CD's page on Amazon. In general though, you tend to leave the Link field blank and Radio then inserts a PermaLink to your post.

Click the Submit button to save your change. Select Home from the Radio command bar to see the blog entry page with its two new fields.

Not Using Internet Explorer?

When you start Radio, it launches a web browser to view the Desktop Website. The WYSIWYG editor builds on the editor built into Internet Explorer on the PC and doesn't exist in other browsers and other platforms.

One way to get roughly equivalent functionality in another browser is to enable the JavaScript-based editor via Radio's preferences. To do this, click on the Prefs link located on Radio's command bar.

Then click on the Enable the WYSIWYG editing tool option. Turn off the checkbox and click on the Submit button. Radio then saves your changes and redisplays the preferences screen so you can see that your changes were saved.

Click on the Home link, located on Radio's command bar. The editor now has a slightly different interface. If your browser supports JavaScript to the appropriate level, there's a toolbar. The JavaScript interface, which doesn't offer the same WYSI-WYG formatting, does provide the same features, such as applying tags, inserting formatting elements, and creating links. Use this interface by selecting text in the writing area with the mouse and then choosing a command from the toolbar.

If your browser doesn't have sufficiently advanced JavaScript, there's simply a rectangular text box and no toolbar. In this case, you must create your blog posts using HTML. See *Learning Web Design* (O'Reilly) if you are in this situation and don't know HTML.

Saving Without Publishing

The Post to Weblog button below the editing panel saves your content and publishes it. This forces you to go live with things that might not be ready. To save an entry without publishing, set your Radio preferences to have both Post and Publish buttons off.

Choose the Prefs link on the Desktop Website's command bar. Under the Weblog grouping, click on the Three Buttons or One option. A checked box corresponds to three buttons, an unchecked box to one. Check it to enable separate Post and Publish buttons.

Click the Submit button, then select the Home link at the top left of the command bar to continue adding new entries. If you don't see three buttons where the previous Post button was, Refresh the browser. You should now see something like Figure 4-22.

The Post button saves the material to your local database. The Publish button makes it public and the Post & Publish button does both.

Publishing Your Blog

By default, Radio upstreams to *radio.weblogs.com*. This is a service run by UserLand and is paid for by your annual subscription. However, you can also instruct Radio to upload the blog it builds to any machine that runs an FTP server. This lets you publish your blog, for example, to your ISP's server, where you have an account with your own custom domain name.

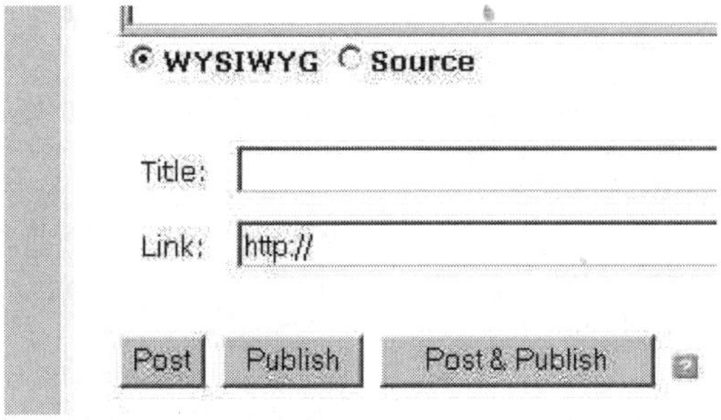

Figure 4-22. Separate Post and Publish buttons

Publishing to radio.weblogs.com

By default, Radio is configured to publish to *radio.weblogs.com* so all you really need to do to publish to this destination is to create a blog entry and click the Publish or Post and Publish buttons (depending on how your Prefs are set up). Radio will automatically send your blog entry to the *radio.weblogs.com* site. Table 4-1 shows the pros and cons of hosting your blog at *radio.weblogs.com*.

Table 4-1. Advantages and disadvantages of radio.weblogs.com hosting

Advantages	Disadvatages
Extremely easy as Radio is configured for this out of the box.	No security on content (you can't limit access with passwords).
Publishing is faster than using FTP.	No control over the server farm—if UserLand has problems, your blog goes down temporarily.
Your blog is part of a growing, expanding community of blogs and blog readers. Many people treat *radio.weblogs.com* as a destination and have an affinity for its content.	No ability to publish AVI files.
Server farm is managed, maintained, and backed up.	No ability to customize your blog with a language such as PHP or Perl.
Google regularly crawls *radio.weblogs.com* for new pages and adds them to the index.	The domain name is long and difficult unless you use a third-party, blog-aware service to create a domain name.
No bandwidth charges regardless of how popular your blog is.	Limited to 20 megabytes of disk space with no clear way to purchase more.

A list of third-party, blog-aware domain name services is available at *http://www.fuzzygroup.com/go/?blognameservices*.

Publishing to Your Own Site via FTP

The pros and cons of publishing to your own web site via FTP are given in Table 4-2.

Table 4-2. Advantages and disadvantages to publishing your blog via FTP

Advantages	Disadvantages
You can use standard web server security tools to protect your content.	You have to handle the server maintenance and backup.
You can integrate your blog into your home page.	Radio has some interesting issues with FTP covered in the later section "Limitations on Upstreaming Files."
Your own domain name is easier for people to remember than the long *radio.weblogs.com* domain name.	You pay the costs for Radio's hosting without taking advantage of it.
	You cannot publish to an FTP directory that is actually a symbolic link—in this case, Radio will appear to work, moving a single file up the destination and then fail completely.

To publish to your own server, first configure Radio's FTP settings. Here is the information that you need to know before publishing:

User name and password
> Your login and password for the FTP server.

Server name
> The hostname of the FTP server. This is often something like *ftp. yourservername.com.*

Path
> Where the published blog files are stored on the FTP server. The trailing slash is important to Radio. The exact value of this depends on where your web server HTML files go.

URL to your published blog
> You need this for permalinks. Often it's something like *http://www.yourname. com/blog/*, although this will obviously depend on where you choose to publish your blog on your site.

Whether or not your FTP server supports passive mode (PASV)
> If you're running Radio behind a firewall, you may need to enable this.

Your systems administrator or webmaster should be able to help you with these settings.

To publish to your own server via FTP, first click on Prefs in the Radio command bar. Select the FTP option from the group of Basic Preferences, which brings up the form seen in Figure 4-23.

Fill in the values you collected earlier, and hit the Submit button. If you have any unpublished blog posts or stories, Radio will begin publishing them at once. If not, the best way to force Radio to publish is to add a new post or edit an existing post.

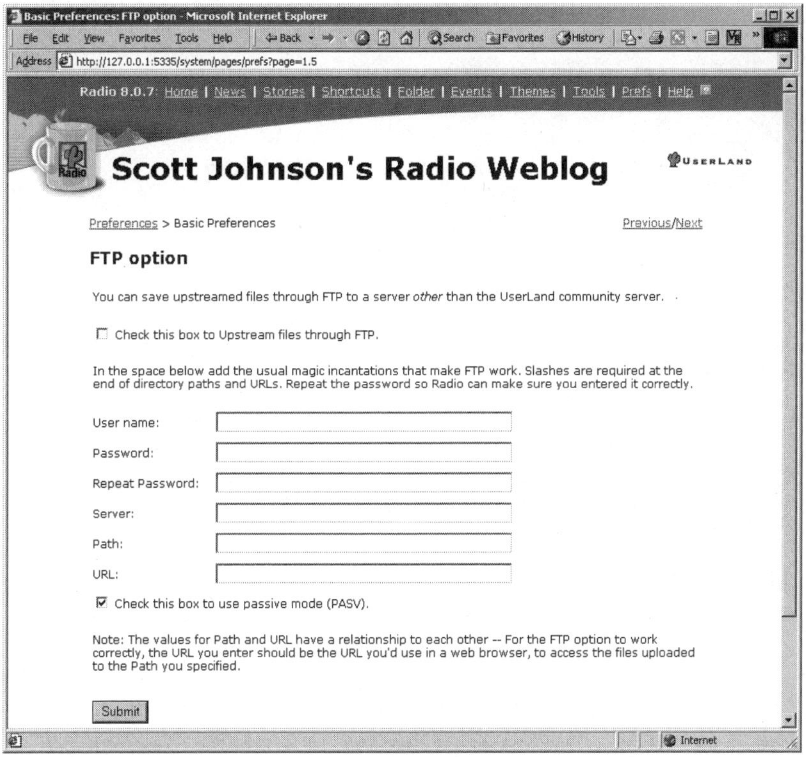

Figure 4-23. FTP Preferences

Checking Publishing Status with Events

Whenever a computer needs to communicate with the outside world, there is always the chance for problems. Radio handles this by logging all its actions as "events." This activity record is called the Events Log. These events are very helpful in analyzing problems with upstreaming, particularly with FTP problems. For example, if you mistype the FTP password, the Events Log tells you there was a password error.

Access the Events Log by clicking on the Events link in the Radio command bar. Figure 4-24 shows a typical Events Log.

The Events Log lists the 50 most recent events. If you don't see the results of your last publishing action listed, other events may have pushed it off the list. In that case, just republish your post by editing it and clicking the Publish or Post and Publish button.

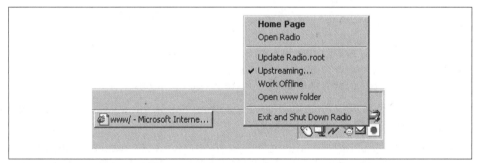

Figure 4-24. Events Log

Republishing Your Entire Blog

All your entries and preferences are stored in a database. *Republishing* consists of regenerating your blog from that database. Publishing pages in Radio is also referred to as *rendering* them.

To republish your entire blog, you have to interact with the Radio Application. Right-click the Radio icon located in the Windows System Tray and select Open Radio from the pop-up menu. This is shown in Figure 4-25.

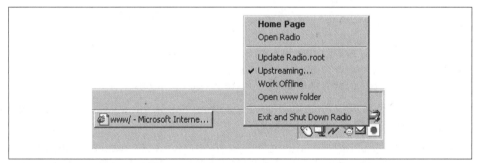

Figure 4-25. Launching the Radio Application from the system tray

The Radio Application is displayed in Figure 4-26.

Select these menu options: Radio → Publish → Entire Website. Answer Yes to the Republish Entire Website question and Radio republishes the entire web site.

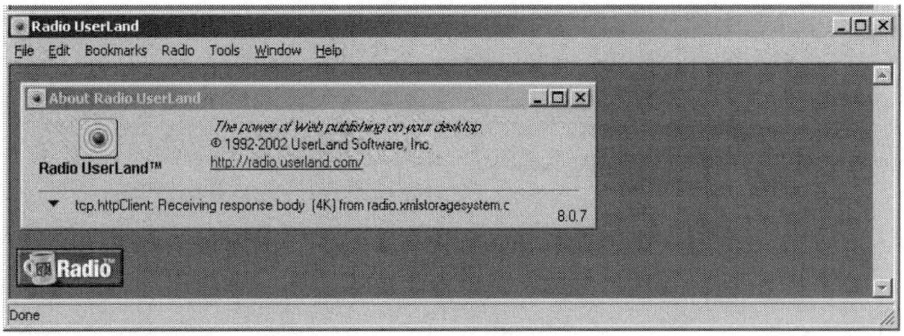

Figure 4-26. The Radio Application

Depending on the size of your blog, Radio may take a bit of time to upstream all the files involved. Radio upstreams files until your entire blog has been updated and published across the Internet.

Stories Instead of Posts

Blog posts are typically short entries between one and four paragraphs in overall length. While this isn't a hard and fast rule, it is the norm. When working in Radio, you often find the need to create longer documents than posts. Radio handles this with the Stories feature. Stories in Radio are designed to be longer essays. They also feel more permanent in nature than posts because their URLs include the date and title of the story. Here's a sample story URL:

> *http://radio.weblogs.com/0103807/stories/2002/05/06/*
> *marketing101ItsAllAboutTrust.html*

Creating Stories

To create a story, click on the Stories link on the Radio command bar. Scroll down to the bottom of the list. Click the Create New Story option to add to this list. This brings up an editing window like Figure 4-27.

The story is displayed in an editing window similar to the editing window where a post is created. A key difference is the presence of the Title field, which must be filled in to save the story. Enter your story as if it were a normal Radio post.

Click the Create New Story button to save your story when you are ready to save it and make it available.

If you write a series of stories, such as articles on marketing, it can be useful to title each story with a common keyword or prefix. For example, in a series of articles on marketing for high tech companies, you might use the prefix "Marketing 101: ".

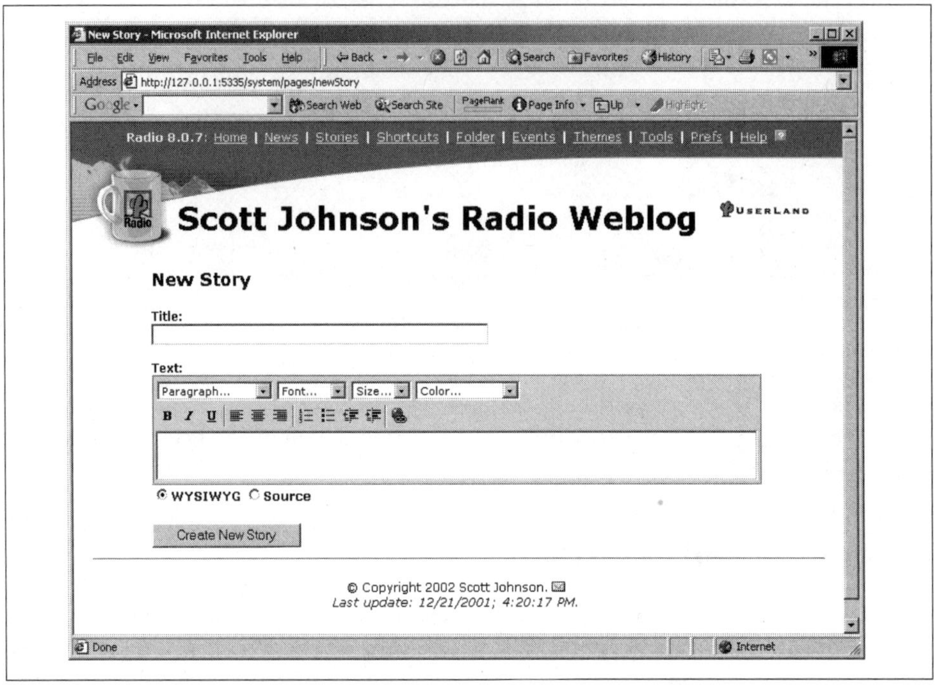

Figure 4-27. Creating a new story

Editing Stories

To edit a story, click on the Stories link on the Radio command bar. From the list of all stories that is displayed, click the story you want to edit. The story is displayed as a user sees it. Click on the Edit This Page button at the bottom of the screen.

The story is displayed in an editing window similar to the editing window where a post is created (the difference is that the size of the editing window is the length of the story, not a fixed height). Make your changes and click the Post Changes button.

Besides editing stories, you can also delete them. To delete a story, click on the Folder link in the Radio command bar. This displays the Folder view, which shows you all the content that makes up your blog, in every folder. Click on the Stories link. Click on the year, the month, and the day of the story. Radio then displays a list of all stories published on that day. To delete a story, click the Edit This Page button. A folder from your desktop environment will be displayed. You can now just click on the story and delete it, as shown in Figure 4-28.

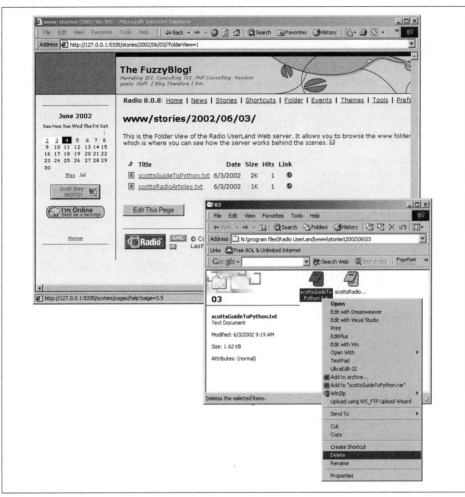

Figure 4-28. Deleting a story

Limitations

While stories are very useful, they do have several limitations such as the following:

- Stories cannot be placed in categories.
- Stories are not automatically referenced on your home page—you have to create a separate blog posting a link to the story. By not posting them automatically, Radio allows you to promote a story as you see fit.

- Titles of stories cannot be changed once they have been saved.

- The built-in index of stories in Radio is just a flat list organized by date. If you have many stories, it can be difficult to locate the story for which you are looking. Suggestion: when you are editing your stories, use the Find feature in your browser, generally Ctrl-F or Command-F.

- When editing a story using the WYSIWYG editor in Internet Explorer for Windows, the Page Up and Page Down keys do not work. You can use Ctrl-Home and Ctrl-End to jump to the beginning or end of the story.

You shouldn't be put off, though—stories are a great feature in Radio and definitely worth using and exploring.

Adding Pictures to Your Posts

Radio offers several different ways to add pictures to your posts ranging from shortcuts and global shortcuts to pasting from Internet Explorer and image uploading, using Radio's upstreaming model.

Pasting from Internet Explorer

If you use Internet Explorer for Windows, the easiest way to add pictures to your blog is to copy them from another source on the Web. Let's say, for example, that you have an existing web site where your pictures are stored. The Copy command in Internet Explorer lets you copy images from other URLs and paste them into Radio.

To paste an image from Internet Explorer, find a picture on your web site and view in your web browser. Right-click the mouse button with the mouse pointer over the picture you want to copy. Choose the Copy command from the pop-up menu. Go to a story or post in Radio's WYSIWYG editor, set the cursor where you want the image, and press Ctrl-V, or choose Paste from the right click pop-up menu. The picture is then pasted into your editor. Make it available to your readers by publishing the post or story.

Adding Pictures by Uploading Files

The problem with adding pictures using the WYSIWYG editor, is that the picture file must already be somewhere on the Internet, accessible as a URL. If you have local picture files on your computer, you can use Radio's upstreaming feature to upload your pictures to the server where your blog is located.

Upstreaming occurs every 10 seconds when Radio is running. This time interval can be set using Prefs if you need to change it. Upstreaming can also be turned off by right-clicking the Radio icon located in the Windows System Tray.

Upstreaming works when your blog is located at *radio.weblogs.com/usernum/,* as well as when you use FTP to publish your blog to your own site.

To upstream a picture or pictures to your blog, open the *www folder* contained in the folder where Radio is installed. On Windows, this is usually *C:\program files\Radio UserLand\.* Find a picture or pictures on your filesystem and drag them into the *myPictures* folder that was created for you when Radio was installed.

Provided that you have an Internet connection, Radio will automatically upstream any pictures you moved into the directory and save them into your *myPictures* folder on your server.

Once the picture has been upstreamed to your blog, you can insert it into a blog posting or link to it, using the Folder command. Selecting the Folder command from the Radio command bar displays all the files and directories located on your server in the *www* directory, as in Figure 4-29.

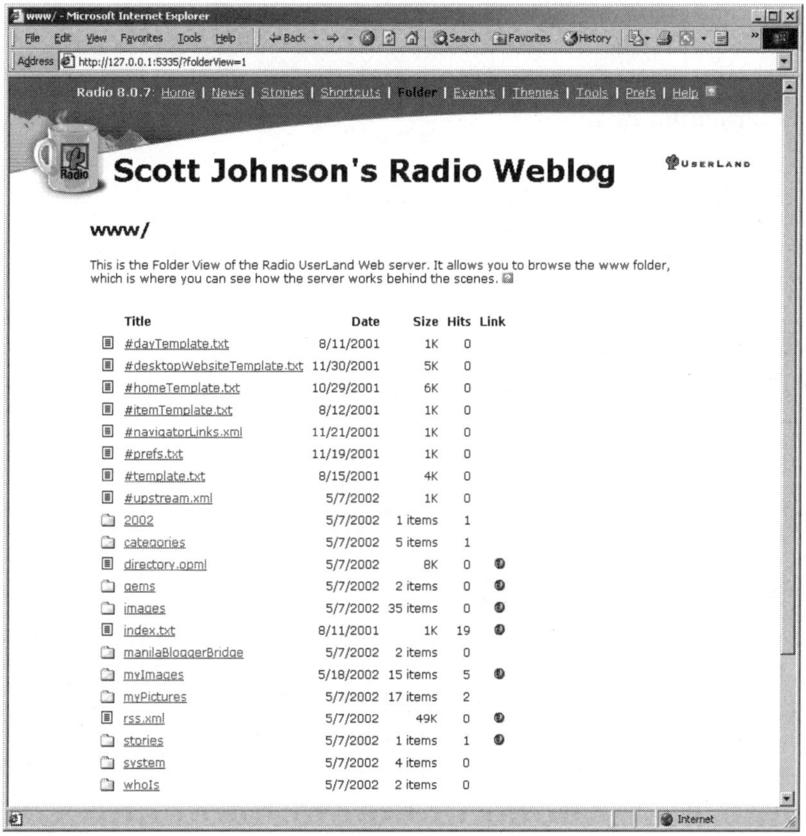

Figure 4-29. The Folder view

Click on the link to the *myPictures* folder. This displays all the files in that folder. If you click on the globe icon next to the picture to which you want to link, the picture will be displayed.

If you are using Internet Explorer for Windows, you can insert the picture into your blog by right-clicking it, selecting Copy, and going to your blog and pasting it into a post or story. This is the same process described in the preceding section.

To get an uploaded picture into a blog post or story if you aren't using Internet Explorer for Windows, you need to copy the URL of the picture, not the picture itself. Once the URL is copied, go to the blog story or post where you want the picture.

If you want to create a link to the picture, you need to enter the HTML code for a hyperlink. This is entered in this format:

```
<A HREF="PASTE_PICTURE_URL_HERE">Link Anchor</A>
```

If you want to insert the picture itself into the blog post or story, enter the HTML for an image. This is entered in this format:

```
<IMG SRC="PASTE_PICTURE_URL_HERE">
```

Of course, any standard HTML code for formatting pictures can also be specified (borders, alignment, etc.).

Notes on Upstreaming Files

This approach of dragging a picture file into a folder within the *www* folder can be used to upload any type of file to your blog (except for *.avi* files). Radio uploads all files, not just picture files. You can also create any folders you need beneath the *www* directory to organize your uploaded files, and those folders with their contents will be uploaded to the server. You can use the same linking method discussed above to create links to any uploaded files.

For a very powerful picture gallery for Radio, see:

http://www.fuzzygroup.com/go/?radioGallery

Limitations on Upstreaming Files

Radio operates differently when upstreaming files to a web site via FTP than it does when upstreaming files to *radio.weblogs.com/usernum/*. When your files go to a blog located at *radio.weblogs.com*, they always remain in the *myPictures* directory. When you use FTP, these files are moved up to the server and deleted from the *myPictures* directory. An additional limitation is that Radio's linking mechanism via the Folder command does not show the correct URL for FTP'd files. You will have to correct the URLs that Radio creates.

Using the MyPictures Tool

In the preceding sections, we discussed manually uploading individual image files. This is fine when you have only a few images, but what about when you have many images? The MyPictures tool monitors a specific folder on your computer and automatically uploads any images placed to a folder where your blog resides.

The MyPictures tool is not enabled by default. To turn it on, click on the Tools link in the Radio command bar. Tools are extensions to Radio that give it new features. This displays all installed tools. Click on the MyPictures link. Clicking the MyPictures link gives you the configuration options for MyPictures, as shown in Figure 4-30.

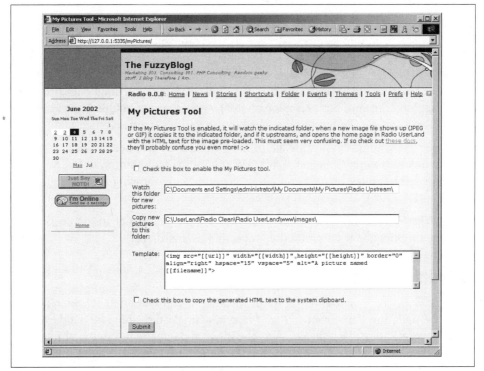

Figure 4-30. MyPictures Preferences

You probably don't want to use your main image directory such as "My Pictures" (in Windows). You should create a directory below this so that images you don't want put online can still be in this folder. The default folder name that Radio uses is Radio Upstream and, if you use this, all you have to do to start using MyPictures is create this folder, select the MyPictures checkbox, and click the Submit button. If you need to change the folder on your blog where images go when they are uploaded, just modify the option for *x:\www\images*. For example, if you were uploading photos, you might want them stored in a photos directory on your blog. In this case, set the folder to *C:\UserLand\Radio Clean\Radio UserLand\www\photos* to access them at *http://yourblog/photos/* or set it to *C:\UserLand\Radio Clean\Radio UserLand\www\images\photos* to access them at *http://yourblog/images/photos*.

If the MyPictures tool isn't installed with your copy of Radio, it can be downloaded and installed from:

> *http://radio.userland.com/myPicturesTool/*

This is also the place to go for more information on MyPictures.

Source Editing Your Radio Entry

If you are using Internet Explorer on Windows as your Radio interface, you probably enjoy its rich editing features. Being able to create your blog as though you were using a word processor with WYSIWYG formatting is tremendously convenient. However, in Radio, as in most graphical tools that product HTML, you sometimes need to change the HTML source directly. For example, you might find that list items that look fine in Internet Explorer actually are incorrect in Opera, due to missing <UL> or <LI> tags. To fix this, you need to use Radio's source editing.

To source edit your Radio posting, go to the post or story you need to edit. Click on the Edit link or button. Change the WYSIWYG/Source radio button to Source. This will change the display of your content to a source view showing HTML tags, as in Figure 4-31.

Change the HTML tags as needed. This may require making changes, posting the changes, checking the results, and then repeating several times.

Updating Radio.root

If you read any documentation on Radio UserLand, you will often see references to "Start by updating Radio.root." *Radio.root* is a single file, shipped standard with every copy of Radio. This file contains the internal database and much of its actual code. "Update Radio.root" really means "Update the Radio UserLand program but without exiting the product or running a Setup program."

Unlike most programs, Radio is able to update itself with new features and bug fixes over the Internet. While this happens automatically every night (if you leave Radio running), you sometimes need to do it manually to get the latest features. Additionally, if it has been more than 24 hours since you last ran Radio, it will automatically update itself when you launch it.

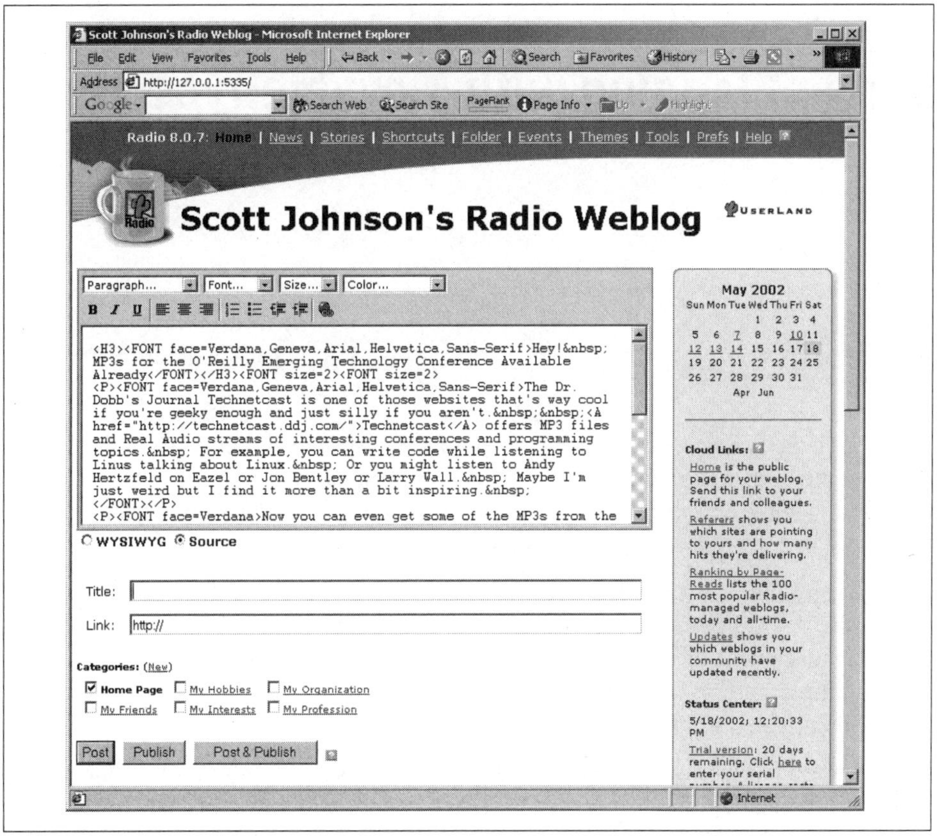

Figure 4-31. Source editing

To update *Radio.root*:

1. Make sure that Radio is running and you are connected to the Internet.

2. Point your browser at *http://127.0.0.1:5335/system/pages/updateRadioRoot*.

3. Click the Update Now button and Radio will update the *Radio.root* file.

CHAPTER 5

Server Blogging with Movable Type

Movable Type is a web-based personal publishing system designed to ease maintenance of regularly updated content. This content can consist of, but is not limited to, entries in a blog or online journal, photographs in an online photo gallery, news headlines on a newspaper site, or articles in an online magazine.

The system contains features common to many other blog applications: template-driven site design, allowing you to redesign your entire site by editing a set of templates; management of multiple blogs (or projects) with one instance of the application; multiple authors posting and editing, using a task-based permission system; and automatic RSS syndication of your content.

Beyond these fairly standard features, Movable Type offers much more. What started solely as a blogging tool has grown into a lightweight content management tool that can be used site-wide. Some of the system's features include:

Data import
> Imports your entries and comments from other content management systems (i.e., Blogger, GreyMatter, NewsPro), and manages those posts through Movable Type.

Entry categorization
> Groups your entries into categories for your own reference, for archiving purposes, and for display in your blog. You can assign multiple categories to a single entry (for example, if an entry about a book you read belongs in both "Reading List" and "Technology").

Built-in comment system
> Allows your blog visitors to post comments on your entries and engage in conversations.

Multiple archiving options
> Archives your content monthly, weekly, and daily; provides individual pages for each entry; archives by category. Archive filenames are fully customizable, and you can associate multiple archive templates with each archive type, allowing you to create multiple "views" of the same archived content.

Integration of file and image uploads

Uploads files and images onto your web server, then seamlessly integrates them into your new entries. Also, you can automatically create thumbnails from uploaded images.

XML-RPC API

Implements the Blogger and MetaWeblog APIs, allowing you to use existing client tools (w.bloggar, BlogApp, etc.) to manage your blog.

Flexible template editing

By linking a template to an external file, you can edit your template in an external editor such as DreamWeaver. The system will transparently synchronize the external file with the Movable Type database.

This flexibility allows Movable Type users to build sites that go beyond the standard blog format depicted in Figure 5-1. Some examples of non-standard blog content include photo logs (such as Figure 5-2), news headline sites (such as Figure 5-3), movie/music review sites, magazine sites (such as Figure 5-4), instructional sites (Figure 5-5), and project-oriented sites (such as Figure 5-6 and Figure 5-7).

Why Use a Server-Based Solution?

Currently, Movable Type is not an out-of-the-box solution. And, of all the software options profiled in this book, it would be the package voted "most likely to require a thorough read of the manuals." Still, a growing number of bloggers, diarists, and developers are choosing Movable Type as the solution for their blogging and site maintenance needs.

Independence and control are primary reasons for choosing this server-based solution. While you accept a more proactive role as maintainer of the system (installing and upgrading the software yourself), you reap the benefits of reliability, accessibility, and customization.

Independence from a Central Server

Because you install the software on your own server or on server space offered by a hosting provider, you are not reliant on a central server that may be subject to universal network outages due to system maintenance and upgrades. However, this is not to say that a server-based application is not susceptible to inaccessibility due to server outages. If you opt to install Movable Type on server space provided by a hosting provider, be aware that the quality of the provider greatly affects the overall performance of the application. If you install Movable Type and, subsequently, host your blog with a provider that is notorious for network outages and lackluster maintenance, the independence you gain from a server-based solution is a moot point.

Figure 5-1. Classic blog

To some users, total independence means running Movable Type and hosting your blog on a self-maintained server. If you fit into this group, you can expect an installation process fundamentally similar to the process of setting up Movable Type on a hosting provider's server. However, before you install the application, you may need to install some of the core prerequisites, which most hosting providers offer as a matter of course (for example, web server software and Perl).

A complete list of Movable Type's requirements is given later in this chapter.

Ability to Store Your Data Behind a Firewall

In addition to server performance, network security is another benefit of using a server-based application. While the average blogger actively seeks an audience for his content, there are some users who want to keep their blogs and data securely tucked behind a firewall. Blogs as portions of intranets and company sites are increasingly common, and developers need to seek solutions that require data security. In other words, hosting their content on a centralized or shared server is not an option.

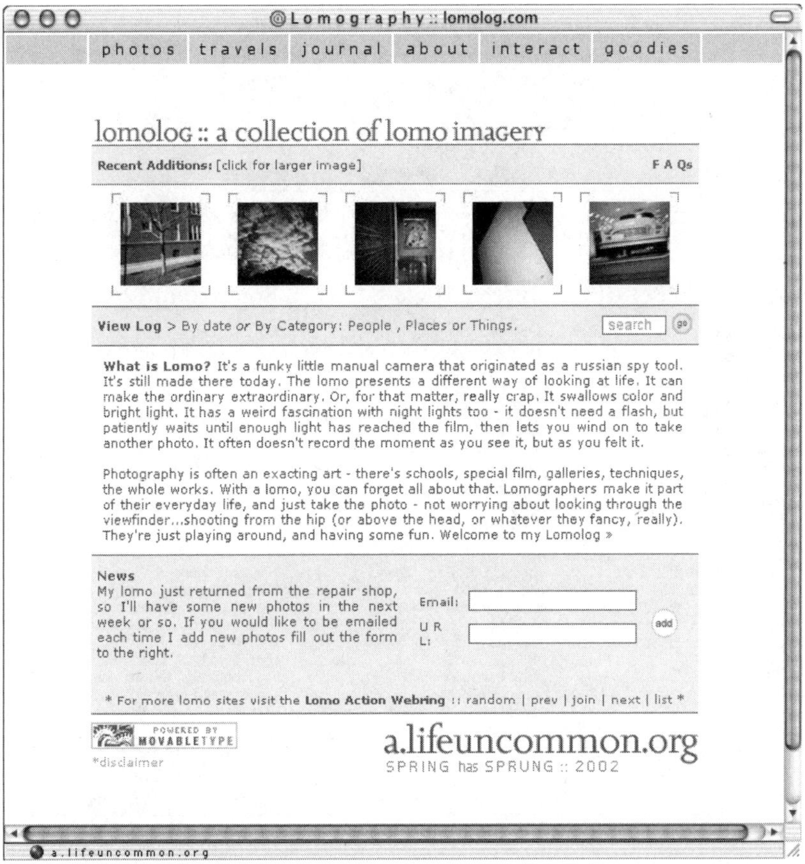

Figure 5-2. Photographic blog

Control over Your Data

As you begin publishing to your blog, backing up your data might not be a pressing concern. However, 2,000 posts down the road, the ability to back up your content is certainly a desirable option. In addition to the ability to manually back up all the datafiles, Movable Type ships with export functionality that allows you to export your data into a text file. Should you experience data loss on your server, you can import this text file back into the system to restore your data.

Installing Movable Type

Movable Type is free for personal use; if you're using the system for commercial purposes, a license fee of $150 is required. The software is donation-ware, meaning that a donation is appreciated. There are incentives for donating; for example, if you

Figure 5-3. News headline blog

donate $20, you will receive a key, allowing your site to appear on the Recently Updated List on *http://www.movabletype.org*.

As mentioned earlier in this chapter, the process of installing Movable Type can be time consuming, and the actual time spent installing the software will vary based on the amount of prior experience and familiarity you have installing server-based scripts. Users unfamiliar with the process of setting file permissions will no doubt have a different experience from those who are comfortable working in a command-line environment. However, as long as your server meets the requirements and you follow the instructions below, you should be able to get up and running without too much trouble. Let's get started.

Requirements

Does your web server meet the requirements for installing Movable Type? The system is a server-based application comprised of CGI scripts, Perl library modules, and

Figure 5-4. Magazine site

frontend display templates and images. Data is stored in Berkeley DB databases, which provide a solid data repository for all your important blog data.

To install and run Movable Type, you will need:

A web server
> The application itself is around 2 megabytes, but we suggest you have at least 25 megabytes of disk space available on your server to accommodate future files and posts.

FTP program or shell access (Perl 5.004_04 or greater)
> Most web hosts should have this version or greater installed. If they don't, ask them to upgrade. You can determine the version of Perl installed on your host's server from the command line:

```
% perl -v
This is perl, v5.6.1 built for i686-linux
Copyright 1987-2001, Larry Wall
Perl may be copied only under the terms of either the Artistic License or the
GNU General Public License, which may be found in the Perl 5 source kit.
Complete documentation for Perl, including FAQ lists, should be found on
this system using `man perl' or `perldoc perl'.  If you have access to the
Internet, point your browser at http://www.perl.com/, the Perl Home Page.
```

Figure 5-5. Instructional site

Berkeley DB and the DB_File Perl module

If your server does not have Berkeley DB or DB_File, you will need to have your hosting provider install it. Berkeley DB can be downloaded from *http://www.sleepycat.com*, and DB_File can be downloaded from the CPAN (*http://www.cpan.org*). If you are on a Windows server, you can install DB_File using the Perl Package Manager (PPM).

Downloading

The distribution can be downloaded from the Movable Type web site at *http://www.movabletype.org/download.shtml*. The file that you download is saved in *.tar.gz* format; this is a compressed bundle, containing all the files necessary to run the application on your web server. After downloading the archive to your computer's hard drive, unpack it.

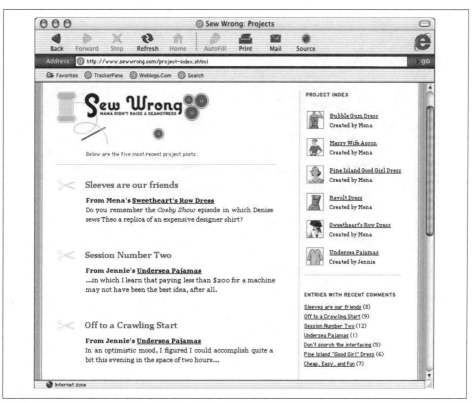

Figure 5-6. Project site

If you are in Unix, you can use *gunzip* and *tar* to unpack the archive:

```
$ gunzip file.tar.gz
$ tar -xvf file.tar
```

If you are on a Macintosh, Stuffit Expander can unpack the archive. If you are on Windows, PKZip or Winzip (in classic mode) can do the job.

If after unzipping the distribution archive you find a folder without a directory structure—that is, files dumped into one folder, rather than grouped into subfolders—you will have trouble installing Movable Type. This problem usually signifies you used Winzip's wizard mode to unzip the archives. If this is the case, delete the folder and try again with Winzip in Classic mode.

Locating Perl

The following files from the Movable Type distribution are Perl scripts: *mt.cgi*, *mt-comments.cgi*, *mt-add-notify.cgi*, *mt-load.cgi*, *mt-check.cgi*, *mt-xmlrpc.cgi*, and *mt-send-entry.cgi*.

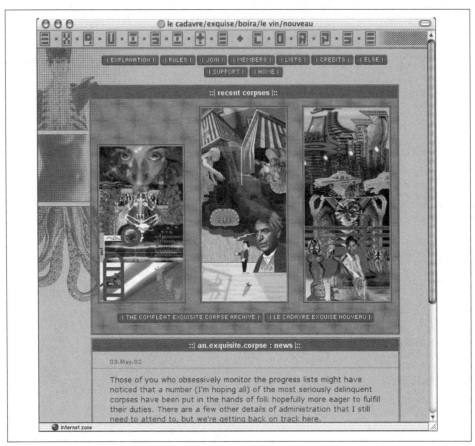

Figure 5-7. Project site

The first line of each file (called the *shebang line*) must contain the path to Perl on your web server; typically, this location is */usr/bin/perl*, so the first line of the file is #!/usr/bin/perl. You may need to change the first line of each file if Perl is in a different location on your web server.

To determine the location of Perl on your web server, take a look at the support pages for your hosting service. Alternatively, if you have a shell (command line) account and are comfortable using it, you can log in to that account then type:

```
$ whereis perl
```

This will give you the location(s) of Perl on your system.

If the location of Perl is not */usr/bin/perl* but instead */usr/local/bin/perl*, change the shebang line of each of the *.cgi* files to #!/usr/local/bin/perl. If you need to change the setting, take care not to remove the -w at the end of the first line in each file; this setting turns on warnings in Perl, and it is important that it be left on.

Installation Directories

There are three main components to Movable Type: the application, composed of CGI scripts, library files, and templates; the database directory, where your data is stored; and your blog itself, which is the public-accessible output of Movable Type (and is the reason that you're installing the system in the first place). The next step is to decide where to place these three components.

The location of the application

Choose where on your web server you would like to install the software. This is the location that you will use (from your web browser) when using the Movable Type system to publish to your web site. (It is not necessarily the same location as your blog, though it can be.)

If you are installing Movable Type into a *cgi-bin* directory, note that you will need to upload your *images*, *docs*, and *styles.css* files and directories into a directory outside of the *cgi-bin*. These are static files, and if they are left inside of the *cgi-bin*, the web server will try to execute them. This renders them unusable through a web interface.

A typical solution is to create a new directory in your web-accessible area called *mt-static*, then upload *images*, *docs*, and *styles.css* into that directory. Take note of the URL corresponding to the directory that you created, because you will need to use it later when configuring Movable Type. For example, if you created *mt-static* at the root of your web-accessible area, this value would be */mt-static/*.

The location of the Movable Type database

Choose where on your web server you would like to store your Movable Type database files. The database holds all the data stored by the system: your entries, comments, templates, configuration, authors, etc.

If you are installing into a *cgi-bin* directory, your database can be located in *cgi-bin*; otherwise, it is advisable from a security standpoint to create the database directory outside of your web-accessible directories. For example, many hosted accounts have a home directory that is not web-accessible, then a *public_html* directory that is the root of the web-accessible area. Placing the database outside of the web-accessible area prevents web browsers from seeing any of your database content; placing it in the *cgi-bin* directory has the same effect.

The location of your blog directories

Now you need to determine where to place the directories that will hold your blog files. These directories determine the URL that visitors will come to when they wish to view your blog. There are two directories: one for your main blog index files and one for the archives. The directories can be the same, if you'd like them to be. Note the path to the directories that you choose, because you will be creating them in "Installing Files," later in this chapter.

Configuring

The Movable Type system configuration is stored in the file called *mt.cfg*. This file contains system-wide settings, such as where your Movable Type databases are stored and the URL used to access the Movable Type system from a web browser.

On the computer where you unpacked the Movable Type archive, find the *mt.cfg* file and open it in a text editor.

1. Change the line starting with *CGIPath* to point to the URL where you chose to install the application in "Installation Directories." Make sure your URL contains a forward slash (/) at the end. For example, if you are installing Movable Type at *http://www.your-site.com/movabletype/*, you would change the *CGIPath* line to:

    ```
    CGIPath http://www.your-site.com/movabletype/
    ```

2. Change the line:

    ```
    DataSource ./db
    ```

    to instead read:

    ```
    DataSource /FULL/PATH/TO/DB
    ```

    where */FULL/PATH/TO/DB* is replaced by the full filesystem path to the Movable Type database directory (typically called *db*). For example, if you chose to locate your Movable Type database at */home/melody/db*, the above line would read:

    ```
    DataSource /home/melody/db
    ```

3. If you are not installing Movable Type into the *cgi-bin*, skip this step.

    In "Installation Directories," you chose a location for the *docs*, *images*, and *styles.css* in a directory outside of the *cgi-bin*, and you noted the URL corresponding to that directory. Find this line in *mt.cfg*:

    ```
    # StaticWebPath /mt-static/
    ```

    Uncomment it by removing the # character at the beginning of the line, then change the URL to the URL that you chose in "Installation Directories." For example, if the files are located in */mt-static/*, this line would become:

    ```
    StaticWebPath /mt-static/
    ```

4. If your server does not have *cgiwrap* or *suexec*, skip this step.

    cgiwrap and *suexec* are tools that allow for more secure Movable Type directories and files. When running your CGI scripts under either of these tools, your files and directories do not have to be world writable. This extra security is a very good idea in a shared hosting environment, where other users have access to the same server as you.

To take advantage of *cgiwrap* or *suexec*, uncomment the following lines in *mt.cfg*:

```
DBUmask 0022
HTMLUmask 0022
UploadUmask 0022
DirUmask 0022
```

5. Save *mt.cfg* and exit the text editor.

Installing Files

Now that you have decided where your files will be located and have configured the system accordingly, you are ready to install the application and create the necessary directories.

Connecting to your web server

Open your FTP program and open an FTP connection to your web server.

If the directory where you chose to install Movable Type in "Installation Directories" does not yet exist, create it. Then, open that directory.

Uploading the application

Upload all of the files in the *Movable Type* directory to your web server. Upload these files/folders in ASCII mode: *docs*, *lib*, *mt.cfg*, *styles.css*, *tmpl*, and all of the CGI scripts (*mt.cgi*, etc.) Upload these files/folders in Binary mode: *image*. Note: be careful when uploading your files, as certain files must be uploaded in ASCII mode, whereas others must be uploaded in binary mode. If you get it wrong, the system will not work.

If you are installing Movable Type into your *cgi-bin*, remember that you need to upload *docs*, *images*, and *styles.css* into the directory outside of the *cgi-bin* that you chose earlier in "Installation Directories."

Set the permissions on the following files to 755: *mt.cgi*, *mt-comments.cgi*, *mt-add-notify.cgi*, *mt-load.cgi*, *mt-check.cgi*, *mt-xmlrpc.cgi*, and *mt-send-entry.cgi*. If you are using your graphical FTP client to set the permissions, 755 permissions give read and execute access to all users (owner, group, and everyone else), and write access to just the owner. See Figure 5-8 for an example of 755 permissions.

If instead you are using the command line to set permissions, you should use the *chmod* command to set the permissions on each of the CGI files to 755 (Figure 5-9).

Creating your database directory

In your FTP program, open the directory you chose in "Installation Directories" for the location of your Movable Type database.

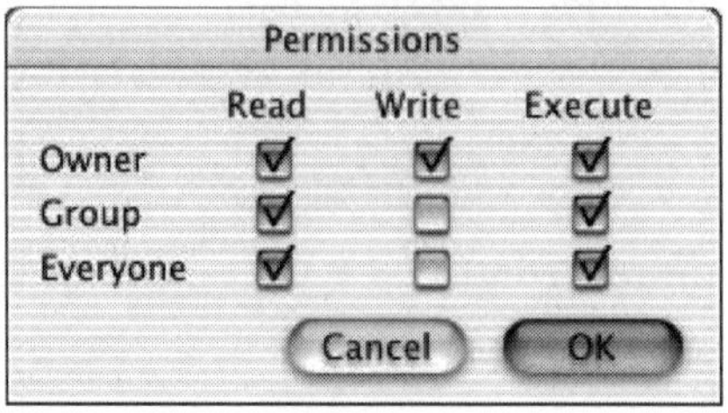
Permissions
Read Write Execute
Owner
Group
Everyone
Cancel
OK

Figure 5-8. Program permissions

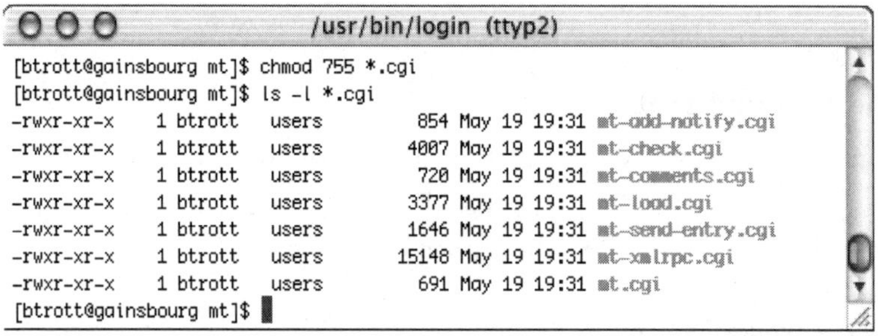
/usr/bin/login (ttyp2)
[btrott@gainsbourg mt]$ chmod 755 *.cgi
[btrott@gainsbourg mt]$ ls -l *.cgi
-rwxr-xr-x 1 btrott users 854 May 19 19:31 mt-add-notify.cgi
-rwxr-xr-x 1 btrott users 4007 May 19 19:31 mt-check.cgi
-rwxr-xr-x 1 btrott users 720 May 19 19:31 mt-comments.cgi
-rwxr-xr-x 1 btrott users 3377 May 19 19:31 mt-load.cgi
-rwxr-xr-x 1 btrott users 1646 May 19 19:31 mt-send-entry.cgi
-rwxr-xr-x 1 btrott users 15148 May 19 19:31 mt-xmlrpc.cgi
-rwxr-xr-x 1 btrott users 691 May 19 19:31 mt.cgi
[btrott@gainsbourg mt]$

Figure 5-9. Changing permissions with chmod

Create a new directory called *db*.

If you are not running Movable Type under *cgiwrap* or *suexec*, set the permissions of the directory *db* to 777 using the *chmod* command. If you are using your graphical FTP client to set the permissions, 777 permissions give read, write, and execute access to all users (owner, group, and everyone else). See Figure 5-10 for an example of 777 permissions.

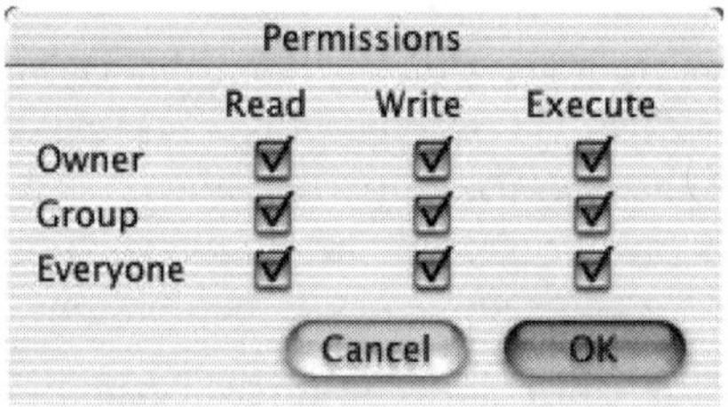
Permissions
Read Write Execute
Owner
Group
Everyone
Cancel
OK

Figure 5-10. db Directory permissions

Creating your blog directories

In your FTP program, create the directory where your blog files will be stored; this is the directory that you chose in "Installation Directories" for the location of your blog directories.

If you are using a separate directory for your archives, create the directory where your archive files will be stored.

Required and Optional Perl Modules

Open your web browser and point it at the URL for *mt-check.cgi* on your site. For example, if your site is *http://www.your-site.com* and you uploaded the Movable Type files into the */mt* directory, you'd type *http://www.your-site.com/mt/mt-check.cgi*.

mt-check.cgi is a Perl script that checks whether the required modules are installed on your server. If you get a 500 Internal Server Error when running this script, check that you set the permissions to 755 (mentioned earlier in "Installing Files") and that you uploaded the file in ASCII mode. If you continue to get errors, look in the server's error log for clues as to what is wrong.

If the script runs successfully, it displays a list of Perl modules, and for each module it tells you whether or not the module is installed on your web server. Modules under the Checking for Required Modules section are required by Movable Type; modules under Checking for Optional Modules are optional and are needed only for certain features. These features are disabled automatically if you do not have the optional modules installed, but the rest of the system is still useable.

In the current release of Movable Type (2.1), the following modules are required by the system: HTML::Template, Image::Size, File::Spec, DB_File, and CGI::Cookie. These modules are optional: LWP::UserAgent, File::Temp, SOAP::Lite, and Image::Magick.

Initializing

Open your web browser and point it at the URL for *mt-load.cgi* on your site. For example, if your site is *http://www.your-site.com* and you uploaded the files into the */mt* directory, you'd type *http://www.your-site.com/mt/mt-load.cgi*.

mt-load.cgi is a Perl script that loads initialization data into the Movable Type databases: an initial author, a blog, and some starter templates. If you get a 500 Internal Server Error when running this script, check that you set the permissions to 755 and that you uploaded the file in ASCII mode.

If successful, *mt-load.cgi* reports its success. If unsuccessful, it reports an error. The error that occurs most often when running *mt-load.cgi* is a Permission Denied error when trying to initialize the databases. If this happens, it means either the permissions on your *db* directory are incorrect or the path to the *db* directory is incorrect.

 After running *mt-load.cgi* successfully, you should remove *mt-load.cgi* from the directory where you installed Movable Type. Failure to remove *mt-load.cgi* could enable someone else to create a blog in your Movable Type installation and possibly gain access to your data. Failure to delete *mt-load.cgi* introduces a major security risk. Delete it now.

Troubleshooting

If you have problems installing Movable Type, head to the Movable Type support forums at *http://www.movabletype.org/support/*. The creators of the system, along with a dedicated set of expert volunteers, will help to answer your questions.

If after reading through the above steps you do not want to attempt to install Movable Type yourself, you can sign up for a paid installation at *http://www.movabletype.org/pay.shtml*. For $20, you can have Movable Type professionally installed and configured on your server.

Using Movable Type

Now that you have installed Movable Type, you are ready to start using the system. The first steps are to log in and change your username and password, because the system by default always uses the same username and password. The next step is to configure your first blog.

Logging In

Open your web browser and point it at the URL for *mt.cgi* on your site. *mt.cgi* is the main Movable Type application. For example, if your site is *http://www.your-site.com*, and you installed the application into the */mt* directory, type *http://www.your-site.com/mt/mt.cgi* to access Movable Type.

You should see the login prompt as shown in Figure 5-11. If you get an Internal Server error, check the permissions on *mt.cgi* and check that you uploaded the CGI scripts using ASCII mode. If you see a login prompt but the images do not appear, you may need to either move your *images*, *docs*, and *styles.css* out of your *cgi-bin*, or if you have already done that, adjust the Static Web Path setting in *mt.cfg*. See "Configuring" earlier in this chapter.

Log in with the author name "Melody" and the password "Nelson." Case is important. The author name "melody" does not work.

After a successful login, you see the screen in Figure 5-12. This is the Main Menu. On the left of the screen is a list of the blogs to which you have access; on the right is a list of system-wide options.

Currently the default username and password can still be used to log in to Movable Type. For the sake of security, the first thing you should is to change your author name and password. To do so, click Edit Your Profile. You will see the screen in Figure 5-13. Change the username and password, then click Save.

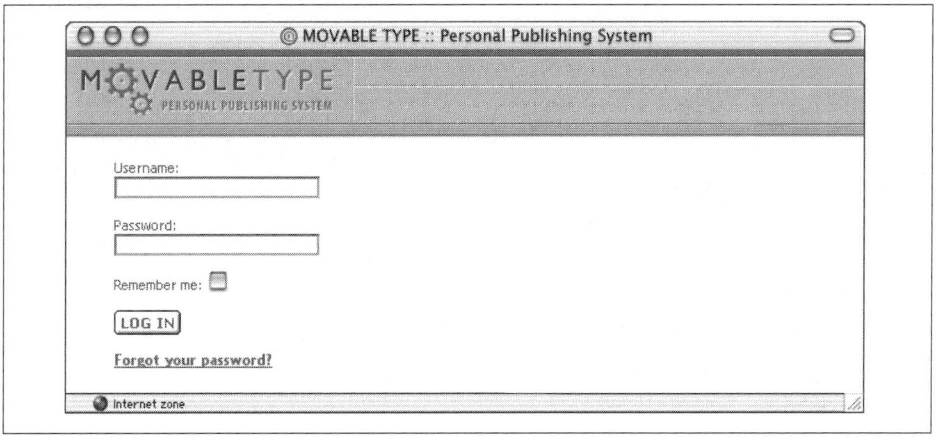

Figure 5-11. Login screen

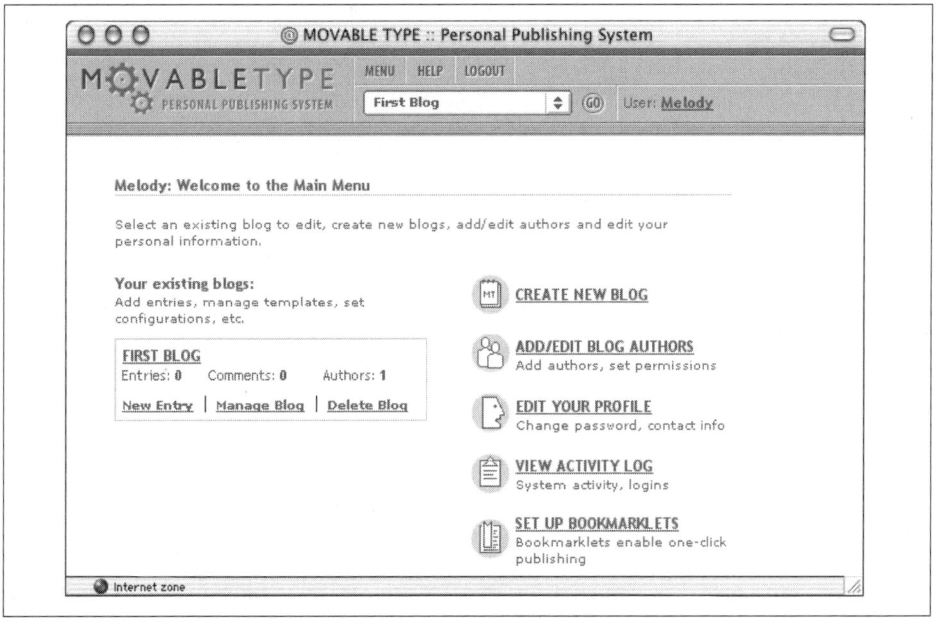

Figure 5-12. Main menu

Configuring Your Blog

The next thing to do is configure your first blog. A blog called First Blog already exists in the system. This blog gives you a head start in setting up your first blog in Movable Type. First Blog ships with default templates, which can be edited, customized, or deleted from the system. They provide a good starting point for blog customization and will give you a sense of familiarity with the Movable Type template tags and structure.

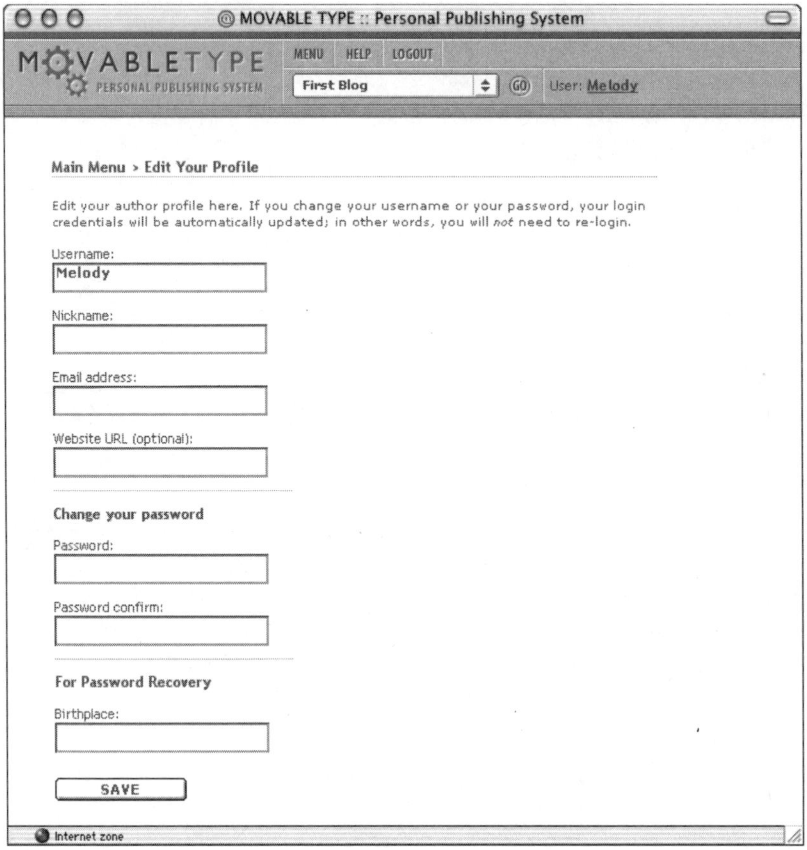

Figure 5-13. Edit Your Profile screen

To configure the blog for your own purposes, click on the link to First Blog under Your Existing Blogs. You now see the main Editing menu for First Blog (Figure 5-14).

To start configuring your blog, click on Blog Config from the left navigation bar.

In the blog configuration screen (Figure 5-15), name your blog in the Blog Name field. Then fill in the path and URL information (Local Site Path, Site URL, Local Archive Path, and Archive URL). Values for Local Site Path and Site URL are provided by default to give you a sense of what the paths should look like. All four of these fields must be filled in.

You should have already created the directories for your blog in "Installation Directories" earlier in this chapter. Fill in the local paths (site and archive) with the full paths to those directories, and enter the URLs corresponding to those directories.

Finally, select your timezone from the Timezone pulldown menu.

Click Save to save the configuration changes.

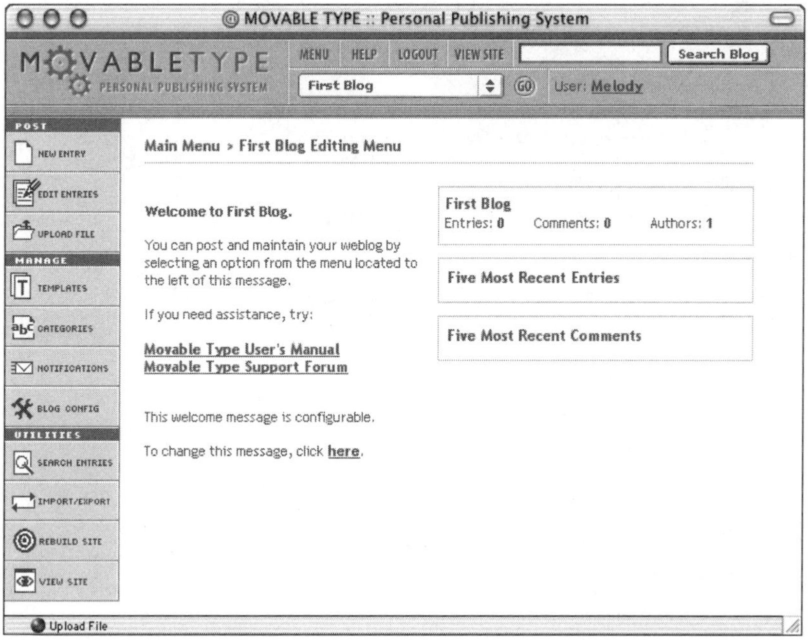

Figure 5-14. Editing menu

Note that there are many configuration options that can be set for each blog in the system. First Blog contains sensible defaults for all of these options. Chapter 8 contains more details on the preferences supported by the system.

Creating a New Entry

Now that your blog is configured, you are ready to post an entry. In the lefthand navigation bar, click New Entry. The New Entry screen (Figure 5-16) that pops up lets you create a new entry.

There are several fields on the screen:

Title
The title of your entry.

Main Entry Text
The main body text of your entry.

Additional Entry Text
An extended piece of your text.

Excerpt
A brief summary of your entry.

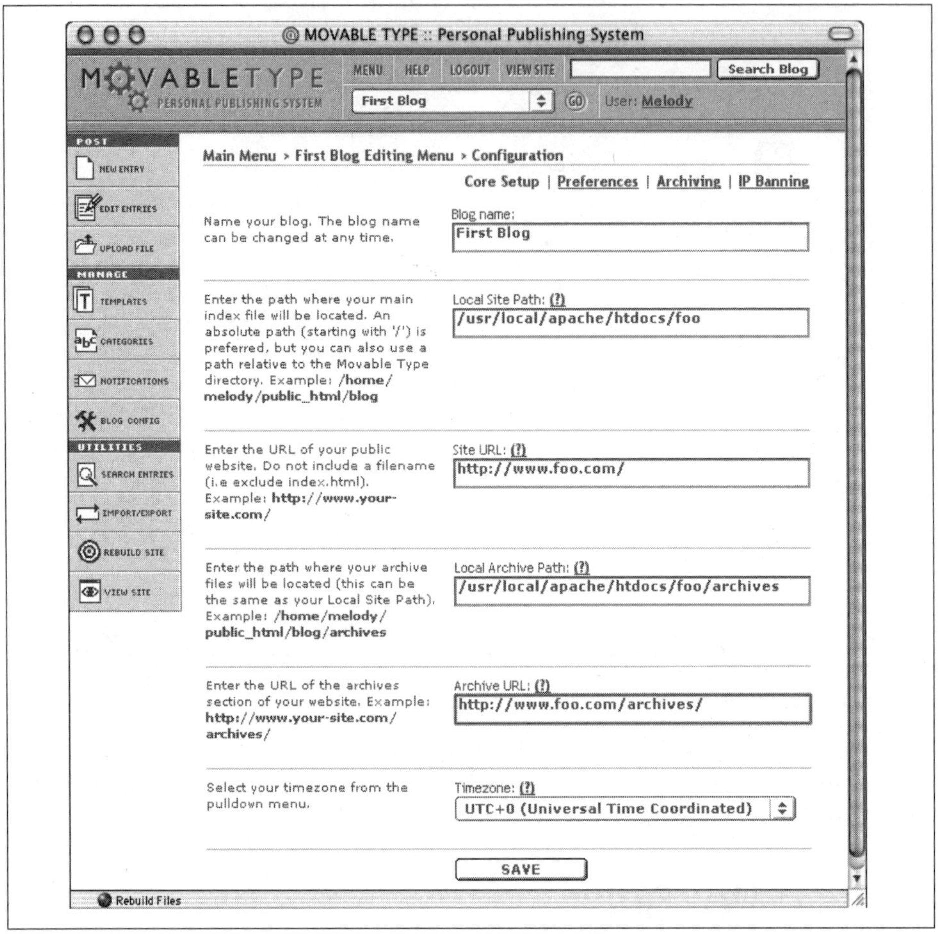

Figure 5-15. Configuration

Category

To assign categories to your entry.

Post Status

Determines whether or not this entry will be published to your public blog Entries marked "Publish" will be published, while entries marked "Draft" will be saved in the system, but not published to your blog.

Allow Comments

Determines whether you will allow readers of your site to post public comments.

Convert Line Breaks

Controls the appearance of the entry's text.

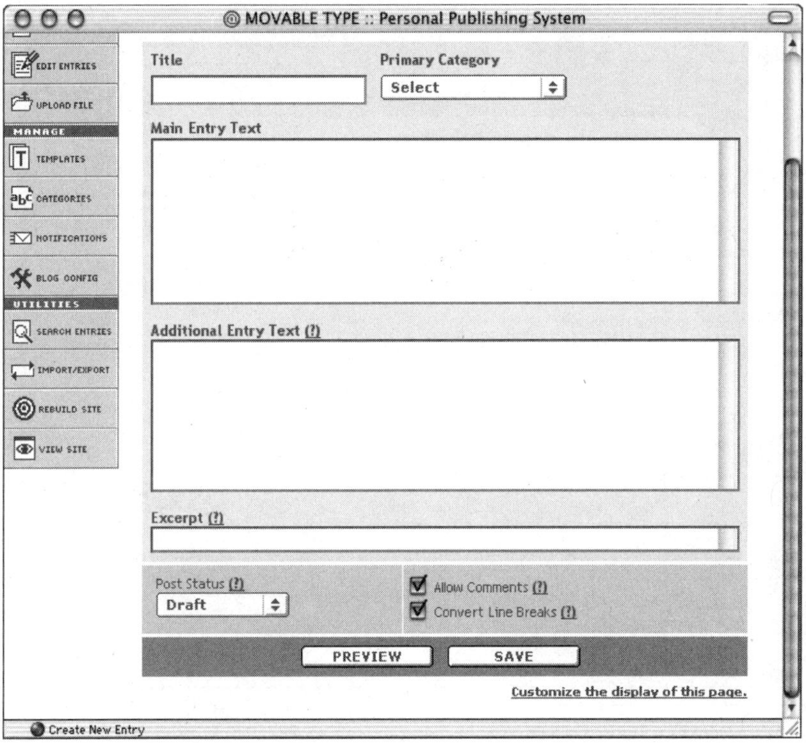

Figure 5-16. New entry page

You do not have to fill in the Additional Entry Text and Excerpt boxes. And in fact, if you do not want them to appear on this page, you can make them disappear. See Chapter 8 for more details.

Fill in the Main Entry Text with the body of the entry, type in an appropriate title into the Title box, and select Publish from the Post Status. Then click the Save button. The system should now tell you that your entry has been saved successfully (Figure 5-17).

If, instead, you see an error message, you should check the paths that you entered as your Local Site Path and Local Archive Path.

To view your new entry, click the View Site button. After doing so you, see the entry that you posted is styled using the default templates that come with the system (Figure 5-18). For information on modifying the default templates, see Chapter 8.

Now you have created your first entry. But suppose that you did not preview it first, and you made a spelling mistake, or you realized that one of your links was incorrect. To edit an existing entry, click the Edit Entries link in the lefthand navigation bar, find the entry you wish to edit in the list on the List & Edit Entries screen

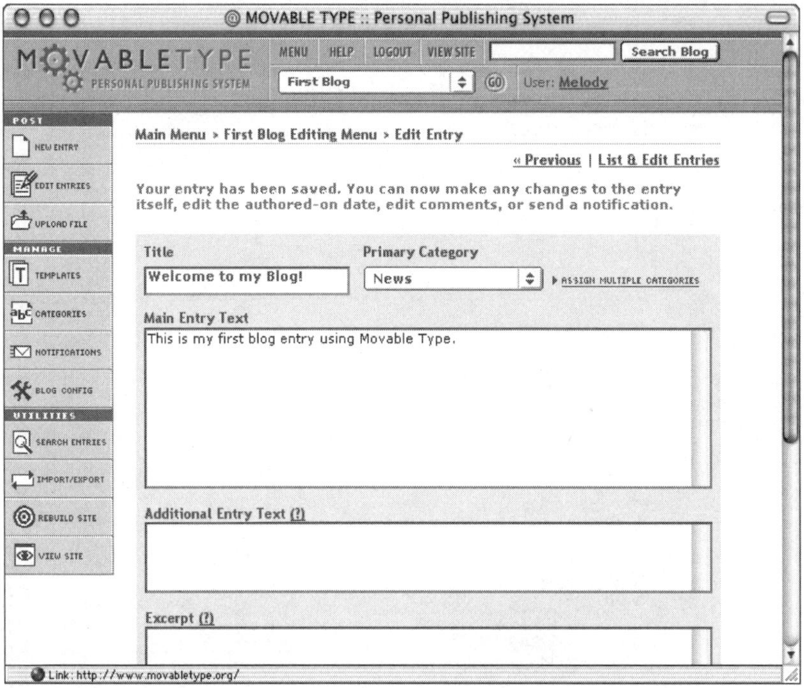

Figure 5-17. Successfully saved entry

Figure 5-18. Blog with new entry

(Figure 5-19), then click on the entry title to edit the entry. The entry-editing screen looks much like the new entry screen, but with some additional sections to edit comments and to send notifications regarding the entry. Once you have edited the entry to your satisfaction, press Save to save and rebuild the entry.

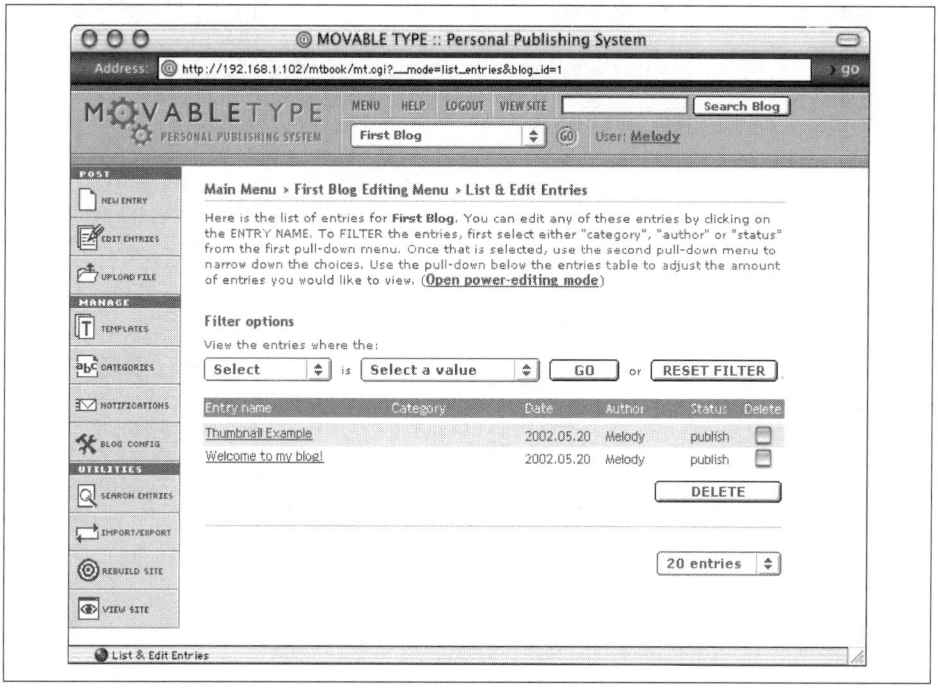

Figure 5-19. List & Edit entries screen

If you are so unhappy with an entry that you decide you would rather delete it, press the Delete Entry button to delete an entry. Or, if you would rather, you can delete an entry directly from the List & Edit Entries screen by clicking the checkbox next to it and pressing the Delete button at the bottom of the page.

Comments

Now that you've shared your thoughts with the world by creating a new entry, you have the option of allowing the world—visitors to your site—to respond. With Movable Type, those reading your blog can post comments on any entries where you have allowed comments. Remember the Allow Comments checkbox that was on the Advanced entry-editing screen? If that box is checked, visitors will be allowed to leave comments on your site.

To get a sense of what visitors to your site will see, click on the Comments link below the entry on your public page. In the window that pops up (Figure 5-20), visitors see a list of comments that have already been made, along with a form in which they can post their own comments.

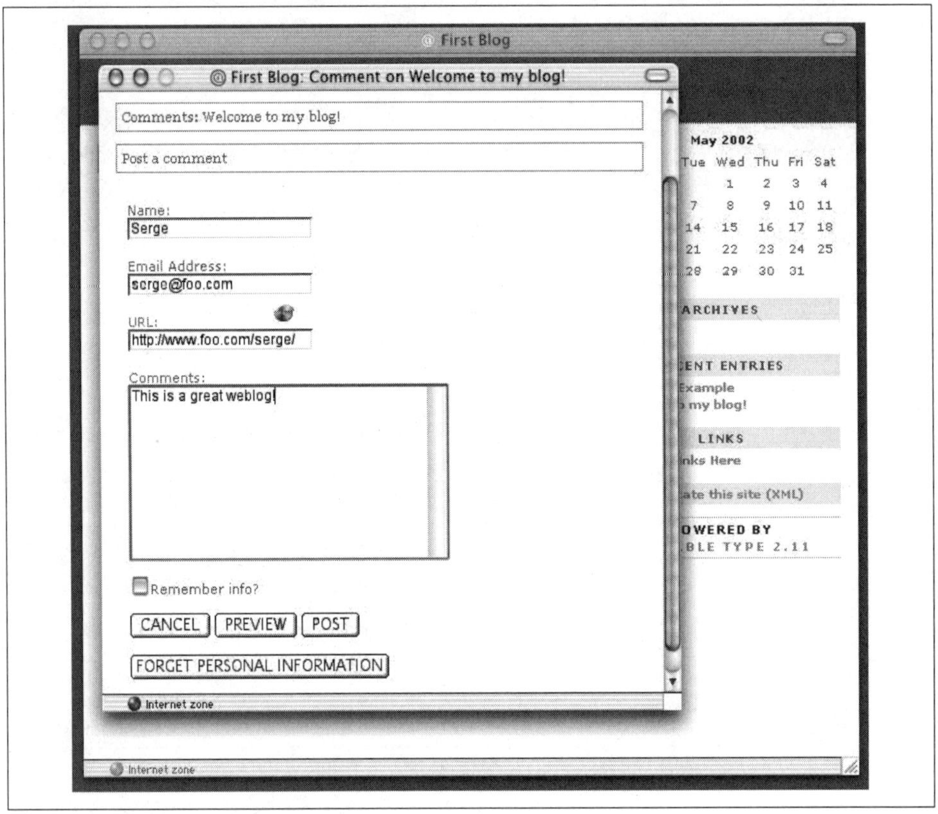

Figure 5-20. Submit a comment window

Create a comment by filling in your name and email address, then writing a comment. Then click Post to save the comment, and you see the new comment added (Figure 5-21).

If you would rather not allow visitors to your site to leave comments, you can set the default for the Allow Comments checkbox in your blog configuration. Or, if you generally allow comments but wish to disable comments for a particular entry, uncheck the Allow Comments box for that entry. When you disable comments on an entry, the Comments link will disappear from your public page (Figure 5-22).

If a visitor leaves an offensive comment on your site, you may want to edit or delete the comment. To do so, go to the entry-editing screen for the entry on which the comment was made and scroll down to the Edit Comments section (Figure 5-23)

To delete a comment, click the Delete checkbox, then click the Delete Checked button.

Figure 5-21. Submitted comment

Figure 5-22. Entries with and without Comments links

To edit a comment, click on the name of the author who left the comment. On the comment-editing screen (Figure 5-24), edit the appropriate fields, and then press Save.

Adding a New Author

Movable Type allows multiple authors to post to the same blog. This is often called a team blog, and it is very easy to set up in Movable Type.

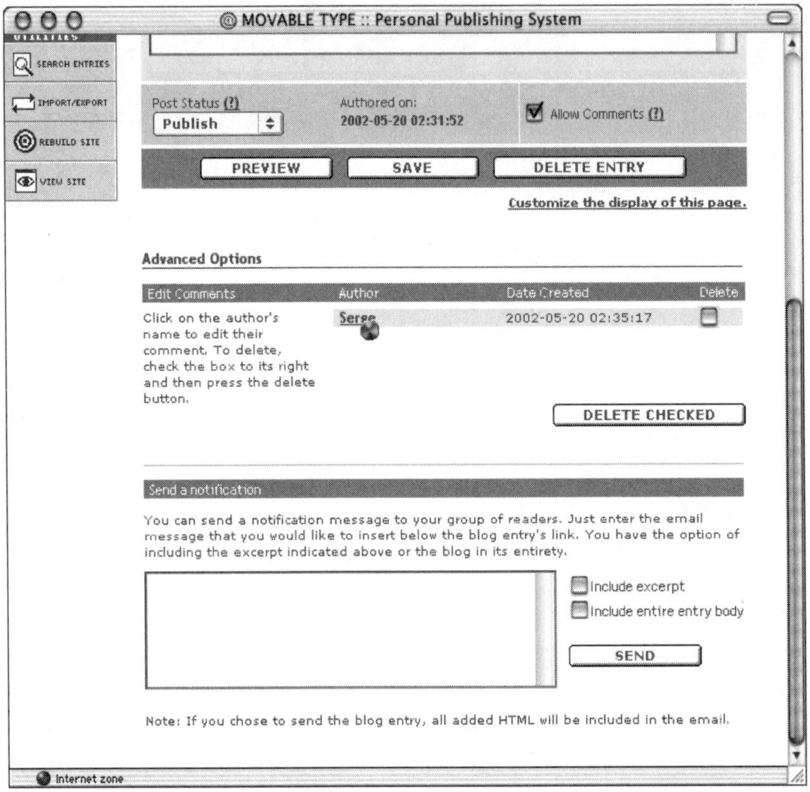

Figure 5-23. Edit comments list

First, go to the Main Menu by clicking on the Menu link in the top navigation. Click on Add/Edit Blog Authors. This screen (Figure 5-25) allows you to add new authors to your blog and to modify the permissions of existing authors. Movable Type uses a task-based permissions system to allow, as well as to deny, author access to certain aspects of administration. As the administrator of your blog, you can choose how much access you wish to give to a user: whether the user can post to the blog, can edit the templates for the blog, can edit the configuration, and so on.

To add an author, scroll down to the Add an Author section and fill in the form. You will need to assign a username and password to the new user. Then, from the list of blogs on the right, allow the user access to a blog by checking the checkbox next to the blog name.

Click Save to create the new author; once you have done this, the new author will be activated and will be able to log in to the system to post to the blog.

By default, new authors are given posting permissions only; in the permission-editing screen (Figure 5-26), you can modify these permissions if you wish to.

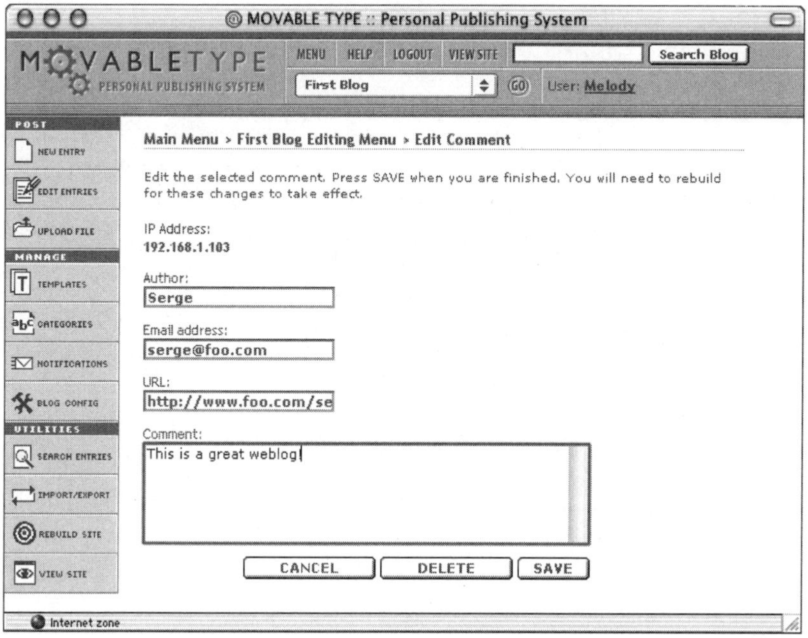

Figure 5-24. Edit comments form

Movable Type allows you to set permissions for most tasks supported by the application. For example, if you trust a certain author, you could give that author the permission to edit all posts. If you distrust the design sense of one of your authors, you might not want to give that author permission to edit the site templates.

Uploading an Image

Movable Type makes it simple to upload images to your web server and can even automatically create thumbnails of the images that you upload. For example, if you have a digital camera or a scanner, you might want to place pictures that you have taken onto your web site.

In the left-hand navigation, click Upload File. In the pop up window (Figure 5-27), click the Browse... button to select an image you would like to upload from your hard drive. Then click Upload to upload the file.

Movable Type tells you the size of the uploaded image and gives you the option to create a new entry, with either a link to the image or an embedded version of the image (Figure 5-28). In addition, the system gives you the option to create a thumbnail. To do so, click the Create a Thumbnail checkbox, and adjust the size of the thumbnail using the form. For example, to create a thumbnail that is half as wide and half as tall as the original image, select Percent from the Width pull-down menu, then enter "50" into the input box.

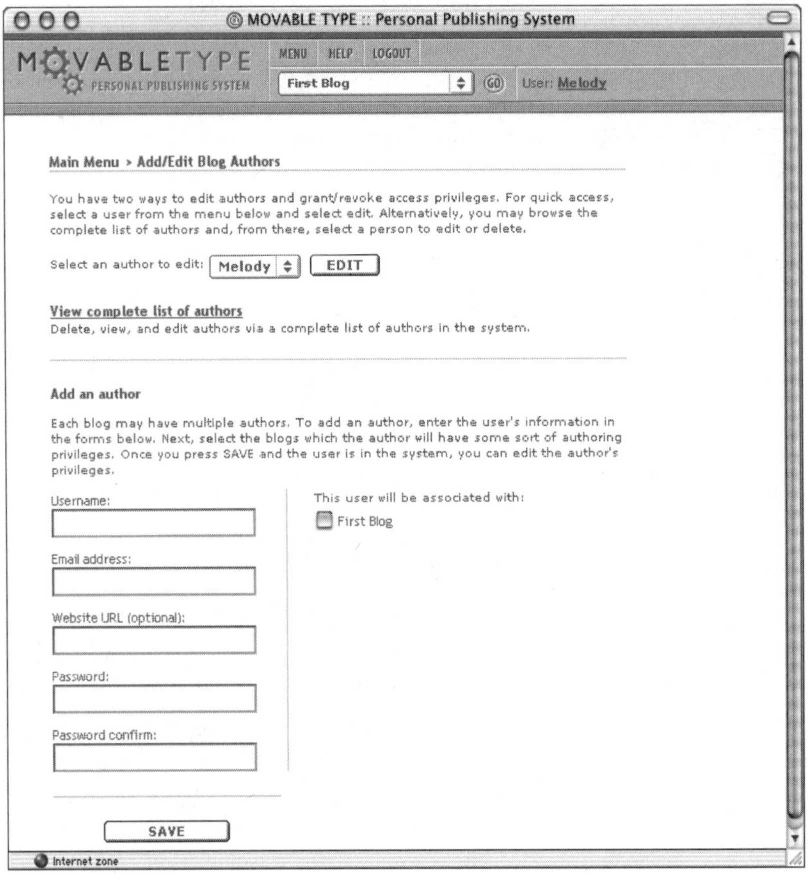

Figure 5-25. Add/edit blog authors

Click Pop-up Image to create a link to the full-sized image in a pop-up window. The system displays the new entry screen (Figure 5-29), and the HTML needed to include your thumbnail is automatically included in the entry body.

You can type in some text below the HTML that the system has inserted, and save the entry by pressing Save. The thumbnail appears on your public site (Figure 5-30), and visitors can view the full-size image in a pop-up window by clicking on the thumbnail.

Syndication

Movable Type's default installation provides RSS syndication. Thus, with no extra work, your Movable Type–powered blog can be easily syndicated. Two RSS files are created automatically for each of your blogs: an RSS 1.0 template and an RSS 0.91

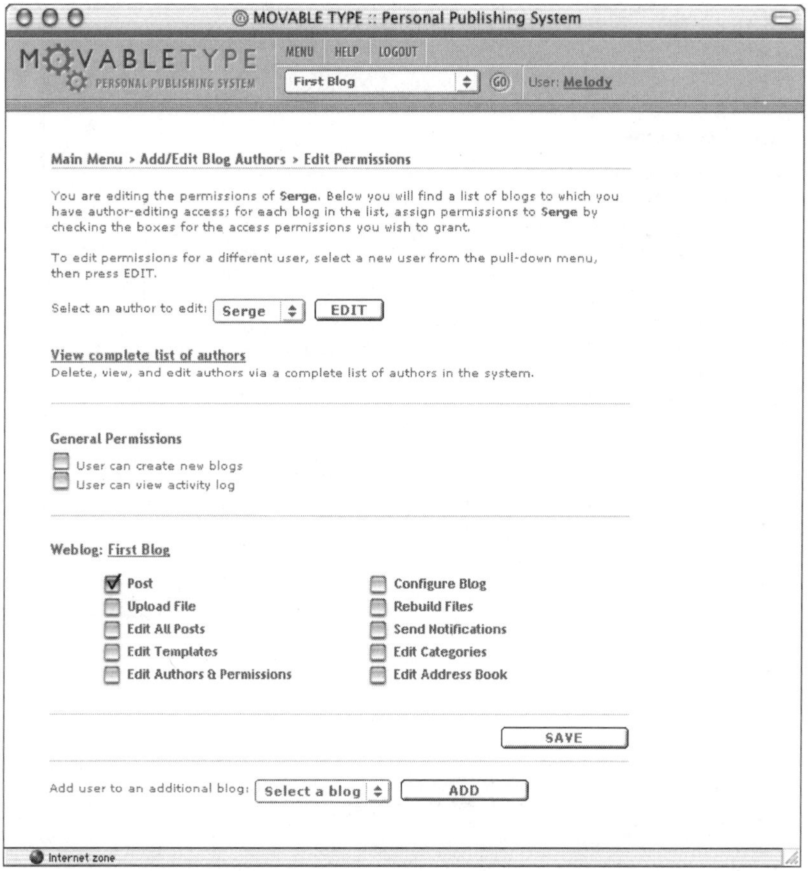

Figure 5-26. Editing permissions

template. These two files correspond to two index templates installed into each new blog in the system: RSS 1.0 index and RSS 0.91 index. By default, both templates list the last 15 entries posted to your blog, but you can change this by editing the templates. For more information on editing the default templates, see Chapter 8.

Your RSS files will be located in your *Local Site Path* directory and will be accessible through the web at your Site URL. For example, if your main site is located at *http:// www.foo.com*, your RSS 1.0 index is located at *http://www.foo.com/index.rdf*.

Syndicating the headlines from your blog allows you to notify your readers when you create a new post, using either a dedicated RSS reader or by visiting a centralized syndication service like syndic8. See Chapter 1 for more on syndication.

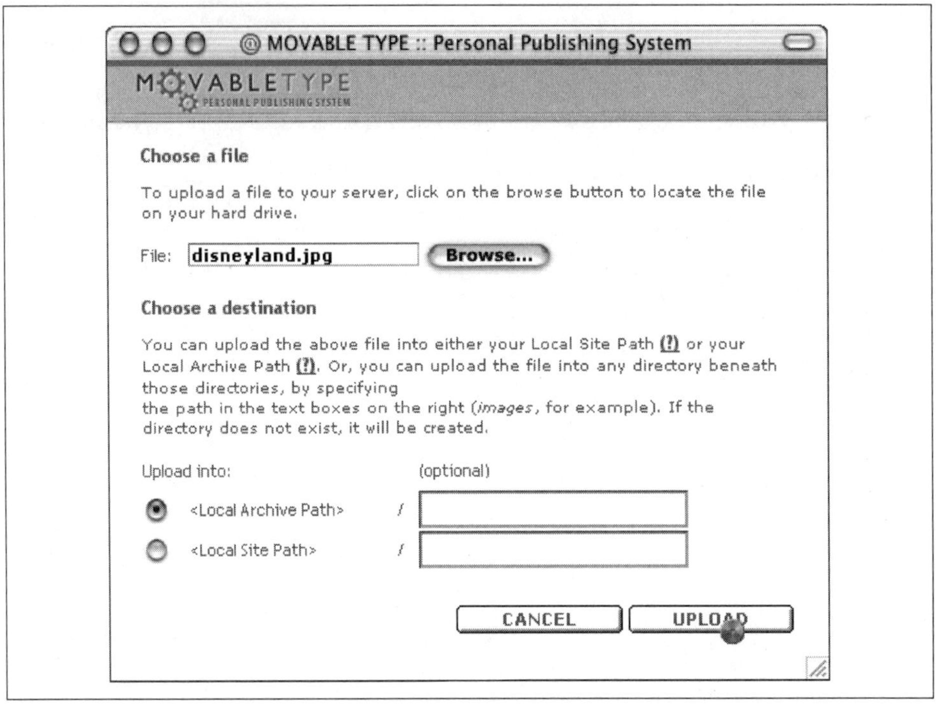

Figure 5-27. Uploading a file

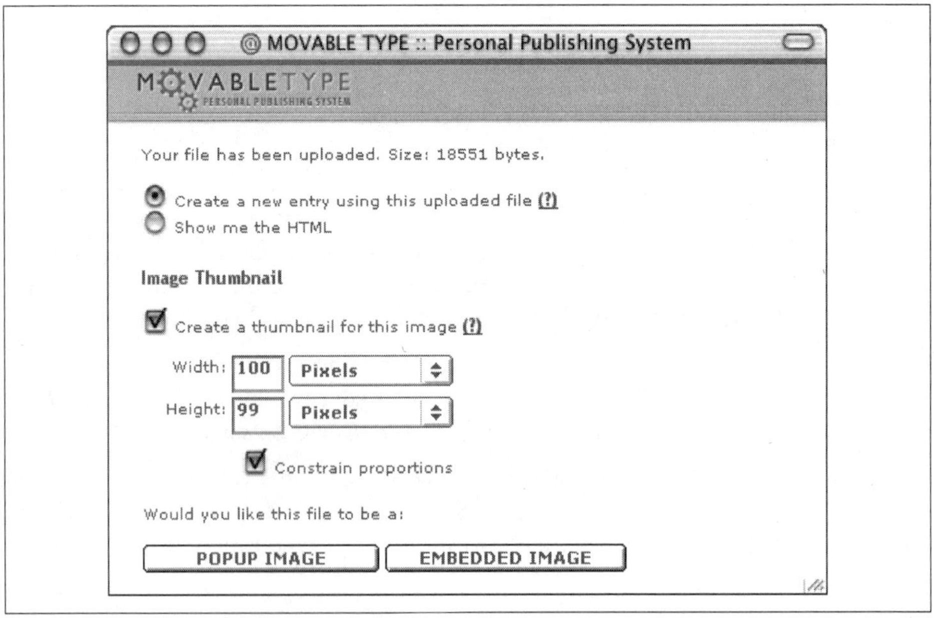

Figure 5-28. Image thumbnail screen

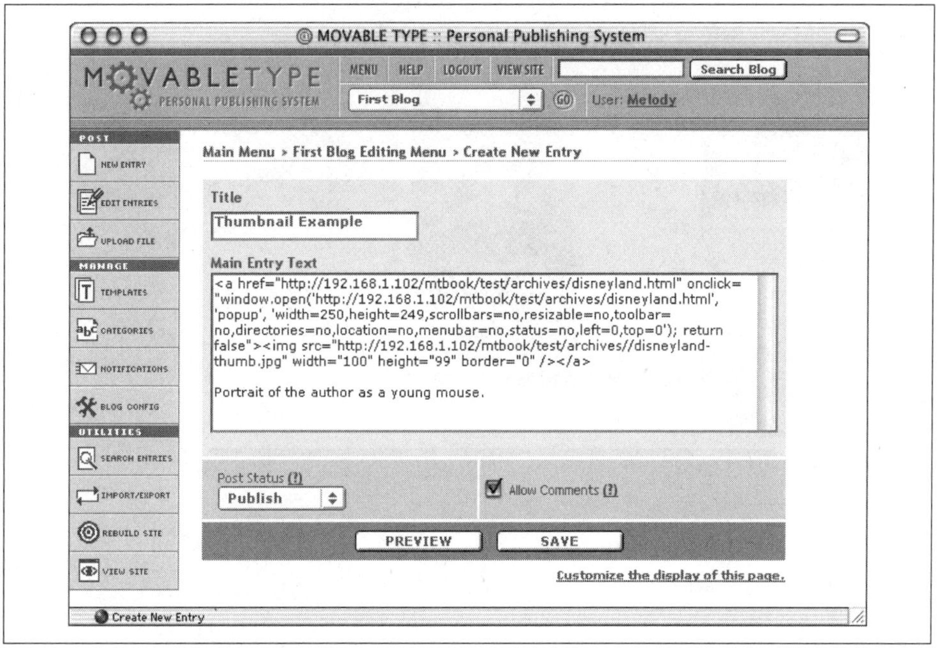

Figure 5-29. New entry linking to thumbnail

The Future of Movable Type

Version 1.0 of Movable Type was released in October 2001, and Version 2.0 was released in March 2002. As such, the system is still young, but it is still developing very quickly.

Features for future releases of Movable Type include:

Enhanced data storage
> In addition to using Berkeley DB for your data storage, the system will support the MySQL and PostgreSQL databases.

Remote operation
> Currently Movable Type works best when you run the system on the same server where you host your public web site. In the future, the system will support automatic distribution of your site to a remote server through FTP or SFTP.

Posting via email
> Post to your blog simply by sending email to a specific email address. Digital signatures will be used for secure authentication, therefore, your username and password never need be passed through an email message.

Figure 5-30. Entry, image, and thumbnail

Peer-to-peer pinging

> Track and list posts from other blogs that reference a specific category or post.

Localization

> The entire Movable Type application interface is available in multiple languages. The application has been restructured so that adding support for a new language is as simple as dropping in a plug-in module with the new language support.

Also in the works: an official service that provides turnkey solutions for users who wish to use Movable Type, want affordable web hosting, and do not want to worry about the hassles of installation or upgrading the system. This service will likely be launched by the time of this book's publication, so be sure to keep an eye on *http://www.movabletype.org* for further details.

CHAPTER 6

Advanced Blogger

Blogger's primary advantage is its simplicity—if you accept the default settings and host on BlogSpot, you can be up and running within five minutes. Once you have your blog, you'll find it's just as easy to customize it.

You can begin with any one of the built-in templates, and then you can change the fonts, colors, layout, and order of contents. Also, you can start without technical embellishment and add comments, web statistics, and support for RSS and other specialized XML. If you host your pages, you can integrate your blog into your preferred development environment by converting the standard HTML output of Blogger into your preferred application type, such as ASP or PHP.

In this chapter, we cover some features specific to Blogger Pro. We take a look at some of the most popular customizations for Blogger, including template customization, adding comments, and statistic reporting. In addition, we discuss blog modifications you can make to integrate your blog into an external application environment, as well as generating RSS for participation in aggregation.

Though most of these changes can be applied whether your blog is hosted on BlogSpot or not, the examples are demonstrated with a blog that's hosted on an individual server. In addition, all the examples are also demonstrated with Blogger Pro. We note any dependencies based on Blogger version location.

Basics of Blogger Pro

The examples in Chapter 3 used the free version of Blogger. If Blogger is your long-term blogging solution, consider upgrading to Blogger Pro, the subscription version of the product. Blogger Pro has additional features such as email blog posting, RSS generation, and spellchecking. Also, the Blogger Pro system isn't hosted on the same servers as the standard Blogger system, providing more reliable and faster service.

A Blogger Pro subscription is for the individual or organization that signed up, rather than any particular blog. You can still work with multiple blogs. To switch to

Blogger Pro, go to the Pro web site at *http://pro.blogger.com* and follow the instructions. Figure 6-1 shows the Blogger Pro page after making your switch.

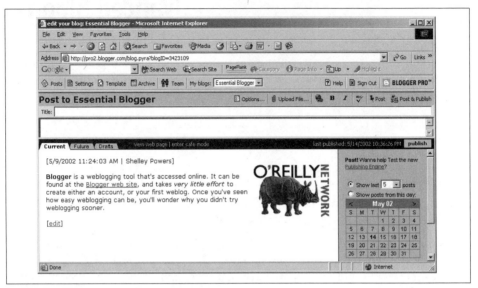

Figure 6-1. After moving your blog to Blogger Pro

If it looks like your archive files didn't move when you made the switch, turn archiving off, then back on and republish all the archives. This should solve the missing archive file links.

Once switched, try out the features of this expanded version of Blogger.

Spellchecking

Unless you're one of those unusual people who seems to naturally know how to spell every word correctly, you'll misspell words in your posts. Blogger Pro provides help for bloggers in the form of easy access to a spellchecking service you can use to check your content before you post it for public consumption.

To demonstrate the spellchecker, create a new post and add the following text containing misspelled words:

```
This post is goin to demonstrte how to spellcheck your weblog. You'll find that
the Blogger spll checker is very similar to that of Microsoft's spellchcker.
```

Before you post, click the ABC icon on the Blogger toolbar—this opens up access to the spellchecker, as shown in Figure 6-2.

Each suspect word is underlined in the page, with the first suspect word bolded. You can choose to change the word to a suggested alternative, ignore it, or add it to your personal dictionary. This latter is particularly helpful with words such as "weblog,"

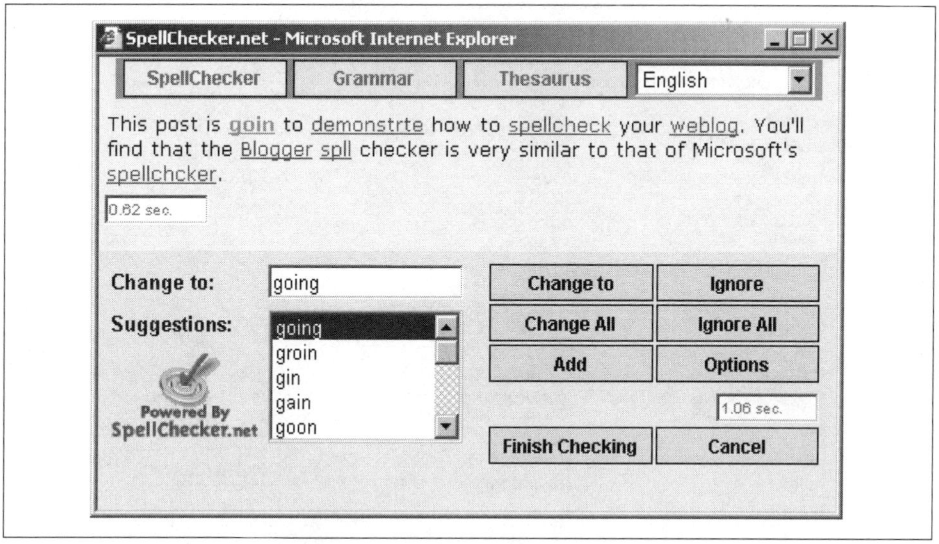

Figure 6-2. Spellchecker accessible through Pro Blogger

which you'll use a lot but isn't a "real" word—at least outside of the blogging world. Once you've made the decision on the current word, the spellchecker then moves on to the next word.

The spellchecker has individual options you can set, such as being able to ignore domains (a must!) and mixed-case words, common in technology posts. You can also ignore words with numbers and all-cap words or upload a file with your own vocabulary to enhance the built-in one. Clicking the Options button opens a page with the options listed, a checkbox next to each; check those options you prefer.

Once you're finished with the spellchecker, try the associated grammar tool accessible via the second tab. For the example text, the tool suggests not using contractions, such as "you'll," within formal writing. However, blogs are anything but formal writing—feel free to disregard the grammar changes to suit your own particular style.

The thesaurus tool highlights several of the words in the example and provides recommendations for possible replacements, as shown in Figure 6-3.

Posting via Email

You don't always have access to a browser or to Blogger, but with the advent of PDAs and web-enabled cell phones, you almost always have access to email. Because of this almost universal access to email, blogging tools have been adding support for posting by email.

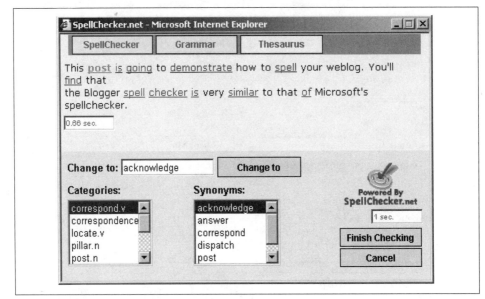

Figure 6-3. Blogger Pro thesaurus checking

Posting by email is a new feature in Blogger. The delivery isn't always timely or consistent, but this should improve over time.

To enable posting by email, access the Settings viewpoint and then click the Email tab. Within the page that opens is a field for adding a "secret" word that verifies that the email is legitimate and allows the email posting to take place. Because anyone deducing this word could post to your blog, take the time to make this a hard-to-guess word.

Once you've added the secret word, any email sent to the derived email address is posted to your blog. For demonstration purposes, we used a secret word of "tomatoe," misspelled deliberately. The email address then became *burningbird. tomatoe@blogger.com*, burningbird being our username. (The secret keyword was changed after this was written in case you were thinking of having a little fun with the demonstration blog!)

The email content will only be posted to Blogger, not published, unless you check the Publish checkbox. If you're self-hosting your blog and you want to publish immediately to your web site, you need to add your web site username and password to the Publishing settings. Otherwise, the system won't be able to publish the email text when it arrives. You'll have to judge if email posting is worth the extra security risk of storing your username and password within Blogger.

The subject line of the email will become the title of the posting, and the content of the email, the body. You'll want to remove any email signatures and make sure not to send the email in HTML format. You can include HTML tags, but the email itself should be sent as plain text. Finally, spacing can get a bit weird with the posts, so you might not want to rely on this too much; keep email posts reserved for short, one paragraph posts as much as possible.

To try this, we created an email with the following content:

```
Subject: Testing email posting
This is a test of email posting
```

This eventually showed up in the blog as shown in Figure 6-4.

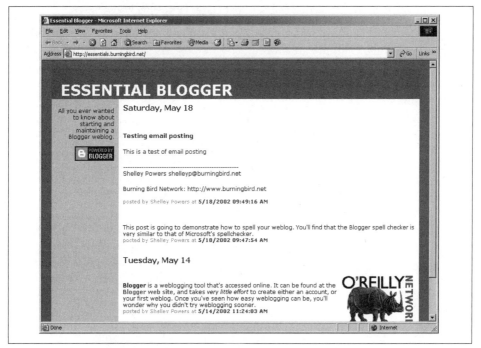

Figure 6-4. Blog posting via email

As you can see, we didn't remove the email signature, which ended up being appended to the post.

Another email feature with Blogger Pro is the ability to send an email to a given email address when new material is posted. The email address is also supplied in the Settings Email view, in the field labeled BlogSend Address. When set, new posts are sent to the specified email address—either an individual's email address or an email list.

Future and Draft Posting

Another very nice new feature of Blogger Pro is the draft posting. With this, you can work on a draft of a blog posting, save it, and then return to it to finish at a later time.

If you want to save a posting as a draft but not publish it, create the posting as usual but before you post it, access the Options icon from the Blogger toolbar. In the window that opens, click the checkbox that says the posting is a draft. When you save the posting, you'll find that it's been placed into Drafts rather than the current window in the Posts view at the bottom of the Edit view page.

The draft will remain as a draft until you edit it again and uncheck the draft checkbox. Note, though, that the date the draft was created will be the one used for publication. If you want it to be "current," remove the date- and timestamp, or overwrite it with one of your own and click the Set Post Date/Time checkbox.

You can also create a future posting by, again, editing a post, accessing the Options, and then supplying a future date and time of the post, as shown in Figure 6-5. Any posts with a posting date past the current time appear in the Future posts window until that time is met or past. Once the time is met, they're moved to the Current post window.

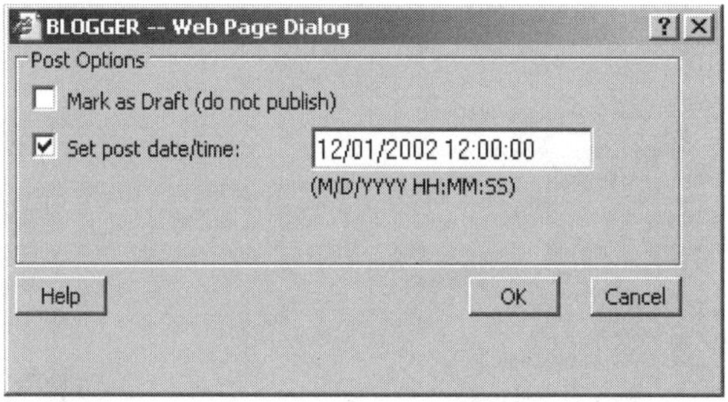

Figure 6-5. Setting a future posting date

Future blog postings won't actually post when the time of the posting comes around. They'll only post when you next do a manual blog publication after the posting date has passed.

Image Uploads

It's fairly common to include images within your blog posts. You've already tried this manually in Chapter 3. Blogger Pro provides a technique that allows you to upload images through the tool rather than having to upload them through an FTP program and then work with them in Blogger.

To upload an image or any other file type, click the Upload File option on the Blogger toolbar. In the window that opens, shown in Figure 6-6, enter the name of the file you want to upload, or click on the Browse button and access the file from your directory. In the demonstration, the upload location is equivalent to the location of your blog pages; if you want something different, edit the Upload path. In addition, you can change the remote name of the file.

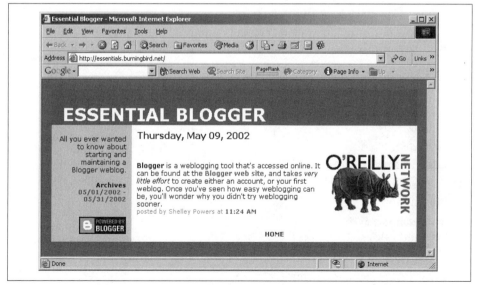

Figure 6-6. *Uploading an image*

After clicking on the Upload button, a second window opens, if the system determines that you're uploading an image, such as a GIF or JPEG file. This window asks whether you want to add an inline or link to the new image. If you choose the inline option, HTML to add the image to the page is added to the edit text box and you can then add additional content. If you choose the hypertext link route, HTML for the link is added instead.

The Blogger Template

The basic blog created in Chapter 3 used a default Blogger design without any customization, as shown in Figure 6-7.

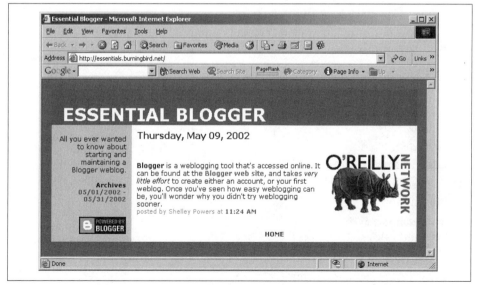

Figure 6-7. *Default blog design with Chroma blogger template*

Though functional and accessible to all the key elements of a blog—postings, archives, date, and person making the posting—at some point you'll most likely want to customize the template, if only to add a blogroll or implement Blogger Pro titles (discussed in a later section). The more you want to individualize the look and the behavior of the blog, the more customization required.

Blogger templates such as Chroma, used in Figure 6-7, are HTML and CSS bundled into a particular design, with Blogger template tags inserted to incorporate your individual blog postings, archive files, name, and so on.

The Template Tags

Blogger template tags act as placeholders for generated content. When the blog page is published, Blogger retrieves the writing for the postings, as well as other information unique to the blog, from its internal database and generates HTML from the data. This generated HTML is then used to replace the appropriate template tags within the template. The merged result is then FTP'd to the blog location.

The format of the template tags is:

```
<$tag name$>
```

The tag names themselves determine what type of content is embedded in place of the tag. The following is a list of currently supported Blogger tags and the content they represent:

`<$BlogTitle$>`
 Title of the blog

`<$BlogArchiveFileName$>`
 Name of the Blogger archive index filename

`<$BlogDateHeaderDate$>`
 Daily date header

`<$BlogItemNumber$>`
 Individual posting item number

`<$BlogItemBody$>`
 Posting body

`<$BlogItemDateTime$>`
 Date- and timestamp of posting

`<$BlogItemAuthor$>`
 Blog author

`<$BlogItemAuthorEmail$>`
 Blog author's email address

`<$BlogItemArchiveFileName$>`
 Individual post archive name

`<$BlogItemAuthorNickname$>`
    Nickname of blog author, if any (usually not shown)

`<$BlogItemAuthorURL$>`
    URL for blog author (usually not shown)

`<$BlogItemSubject$>`
    Subject (title) of the posting

`<$BlogURL$>`
    URL of the blog

`<$BlogArchiveLink$>`
    In archive template, link for archive page

`<$BlogArchiveName$>`
    In archive template, link for archive name

In addition to the template tags, Blogger also supports custom XML elements that act as containers for individual postings, or a footer that's placed at the end of a day's content. The elements are:

`Blogger`
    Container for all postings and related date and footer content

`BlogDateHeader`
    Container for date displayed in daily header

`BlogDateFooter`
    Container for content displayed in daily footer

`PostSubject`
    Container for posting title (Blogger Pro only)

Not all Blogger template tags must be enclosed within container elements—`<$BlogTitle$>`, `<$BlogArchiveFileName$>`, and `<$BlogDescription$>` can be used anywhere within the Blogger template. However, tags requiring enclosure within container elements and placed outside of those elements are ignored by the Blogger generator and displayed as regular HTML content on the blog page.

The Template View

The Blogger template can be examined in the Template view window, opened by clicking the Template button on the Blogger toolbar. At the top of the Template view page is a large text edit box that contains the actual template itself, as shown in Figure 6-8.

In the Figure, the `<$BlogTitle$>` template tag is used to name the blog page. Scrolling down through the template text, you'll quickly spot the other Blogger template tags that control the archive and posting.

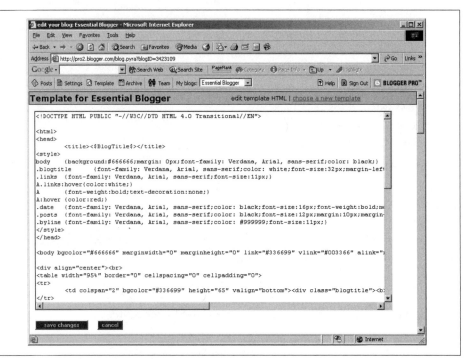

Figure 6-8. Blogger template view window with template

As a good rule of thumb, once you've modified the template, make a backup of it before saving it to the Blogger database. This way if a problem occurs, you won't lose your work. Additionally, you'll have a copy of the template as a backup in case of future problems.

Once you're comfortable with the template and the placement of the tags, you're ready to start the template customization, detailed in the next section.

Template Customization

Customizations to the blog template can take many forms. Some change the blog's overall design and layout; others are primarily focused on adding new content to the page, such as a blogroll. We'll focus on the latter type of customization in this chapter, because discussions about design can literally fill books, and the customization basics are the same for both categories of change.

First, as a precaution, always make a backup of your blog template before you modify it in any way—even simple modifications. You can do this by selecting the text and copying it into a text file. Additionally, if your changes are fairly significant, you'll want to make a second copy after the modifications and before saving them. Problems can occur when transmitting text across the Internet and if you don't have a local copy of the changes, you could lose them and then have to reedit the template.

Adding a Blogroll

Adding a blogroll isn't a customization to the template as much as it is an addition. You're not changing the underlying format of the template—just adding a bit of text to one side.

To demonstrate adding a blogroll, we'll modify the Essential Blogger blog, created in Chapter 3. After opening the Template view page, find the occurrence of the `<$BlogArchiveFileName$>` template tag within the template. You'll add the blogroll just above the archives and contained within the same `div` block (class name of "links") to take advantage of the CSS styles applied to the block.

The blogroll is nothing more than standard HTML copied or typed into the template, as shown in Example 6-1. This particular blogroll contains the locations of the blogs of the authors of this book.

Example 6-1. Adding a blogroll to the blog

```
<div class="posts">
<$BlogDescription$><br>
<br>
<div class="links">
        <h5>Blogroll:</h5>
        <a href="http://radio.weblogs.com/0103807/">J. Scott Johnson</a><br>
        <a href="http://boingboing.net">Cory Doctorow</a><br>
        <a href="http://www.movabletype.org">Ben and Mena Trott</a><br>
        <a href="http://www.oreillynet.com/~rael/">Rael Dornfest</a><br>
        <a href="http://weblog.burningbird.net/">Shelley Powers</a><br>
        <br>
<b>Archives</b><br>
<script type="text/javascript" src="<$BlogArchiveFileName$>"></script>
<br><br>
</div>
```

The new blogroll HTML is indented in the example. After modifying the template, save the changes and publish the main blog page. The page should look similar to that shown in Figure 6-9.

When you're satisfied with the change, republish all the archives to pick up the template change.

This example just has plain HTML added to the template. The example in the next section manipulates works with the Blogger template tags to add titles to the blog posts.

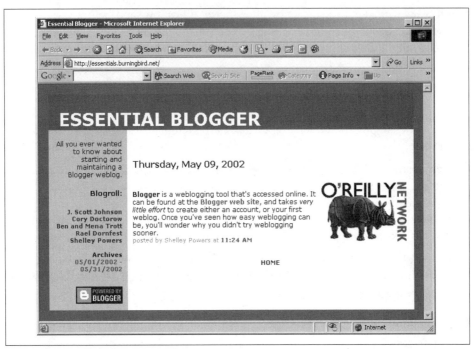

Figure 6-9. Blog page with new blogroll

Adding a Blogger Pro Title

One difference between Blogger Pro and standard Blogger is a Title field right above the text edit box in the Edit view page. This field allows you to add titles to your post, a popular practice among bloggers and an important modification if you're interesting in using RSS and other aggregation technologies. In addition, titles give your readers something to refer to when they talk about your posts—another thing you want to encourage.

To turn the Title field on and off, access the Settings view. Click on the Formatting tab and, when the page opens, scroll down until you see the field labeled Show Title Field. Change this to Yes if you want to use the field, as shown in Figure 6-10.

After returning to the Edit view, edit the existing post and add the following title:

```
What this weblog is all about
```

Publish the page and open it for viewing. The new title won't show on the page, even though you've added it, because the template you're using doesn't implement the title tag. To add the title into the display, you'll need to add the `<$BlogItemSubject$>` template tag within its containing `<PostSubject>` elements for the title to show with each post. Example 6-2 shows the blog's Blogger template area after the new title tag has been added (the change is highlighted).

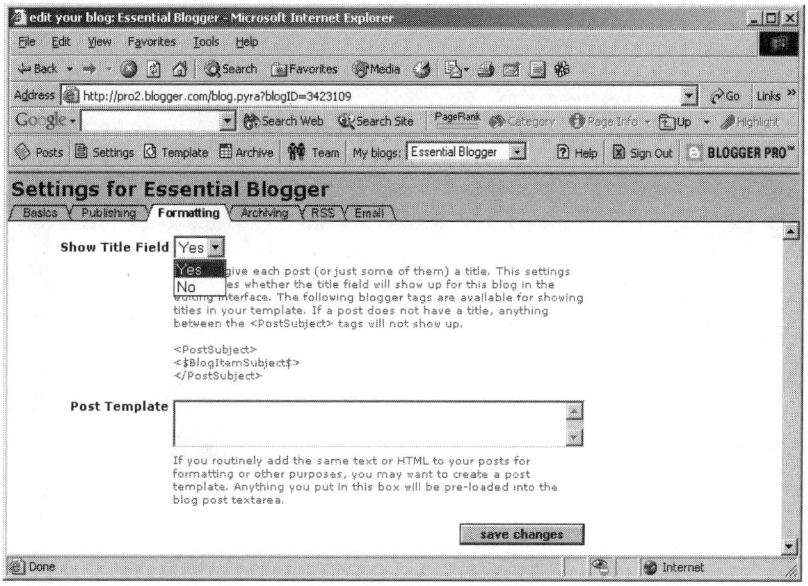

Figure 6-10. Enabling support for post titles

Example 6-2. Blog's template after adding in posting title template tag

```
<Blogger>
<BlogDateHeader>
    <div class="date"><$BlogDateHeaderDate$></div>
    </BlogDateHeader>

    <div class="posts">
    <a name="<$BlogItemNumber$>"> </a><br>

      <PostSubject>
      <h5><$BlogItemSubject$></h5>
      </PostSubject>

    <$BlogItemBody$><br>
    <span class="byline">posted by <$BlogItemAuthor$> at
    <a href="<$BlogItemArchiveFileName$>#<$BlogItemNumber$>">
    <$BlogItemDateTime$></a></span>
    </div>
<br>
</Blogger>
```

After saving the template change, republish the posting and view the results, as shown in Figure 6-11. If the change is satisfactory, republish all the archives to pick up the template modifications. Adding a title for new postings won't impact your previous postings—if no title exists, none's printed.

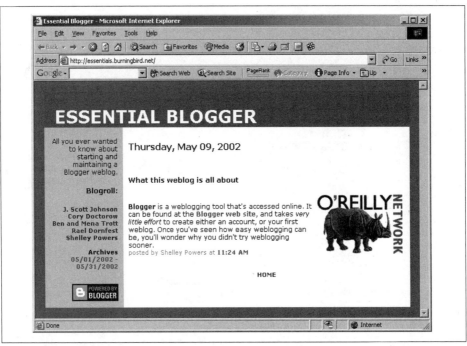

Figure 6-11. Blog page with titled post

Though the template modifications just demonstrated—adding a blogroll and a blog title—were fairly minor, hopefully they demonstrate that working with the Blogger template can be a straightforward process.

Customizing the Archive

Take a look again at the blog page screen shot in Figure 6-11. Notice the format of the archive list—a date range, with each archive accessible via a different hypertext link. Over time, this list can get quite large and take up considerable room in your page.

Rather than list each archive link within the main blog page, you can host a separate Archive index page that contains the list of archived items. Then, within the blog page, attach a link to this page rather than the individual archive items.

Creating a Custom Archive Page

To demonstrate how to create an Archive index page, within the Archive view, click the Archive template option in the upper righthand side of the page. A new page opens showing a small template used to print out the archive history links. As displayed in Example 6-3, the content doesn't contain any HTML elements.

Example 6-3. Blogger archive listing text

```
<Blogger>
    document.write("<a href='<$BlogArchiveLink$>'><$BlogArchiveName$></a><br>")
</Blogger>
if (location.href.indexOf("archive") != -1) {
document.write("<a href=\"./\">current >></a>")
}
```

The content of the Archive template is so simple because the content is normally opened within the template page, using JavaScript:

```
<script type="text/javascript" src="<$BlogArchiveFileName$>"></script>
```

When the file is opened in the blog page, JavaScript prints out the archive links.

To create a separate archive page, copy the blog template to the Archive template and then adjust the contents to display archive links rather than postings. The steps to do this are:

1. Open the Archive view and then the Archive template.
2. Make a backup of the template and then access the Template view.
3. Copy the template and then return to the Archive view.
4. Open the Archive template and paste the copied template text at the top of the file, being careful *not* to overwrite the existing text.
5. In the copied material, remove the left column by removing the leftmost td tag. You'll also need to remove colspan=2 from the top row of the table.
6. Modify the CSS for the page, changing the anchor tag style to:

   ```
   A {font-weight:bold;text-decoration:none; font-size: smaller}
   ```
7. Replace the Blogger block within the copied template with the Blogger block of the Archive template.
8. Remove the reference to Home from the newly modified template syntax.
9. Save your changes and republish all the archive files.

Once you've adjusted the archive template, change the main blog template to remove the JavaScript surrounding the archive file call and replace it within a link to the archive filename:

```
<a href="<$BlogArchiveFileName$>"><b>Archives</b></a>
```

After saving the template changes, republish the archive files and then the blog page.

When you view the blog main page, you'll now have a link to the archive file rather than a list of archive files. Clicking on this link will open the Archive index file, which should look similar to Figure 6-12.

To make this transition easier, Example 6-4 contains the complete text of the Archive template.

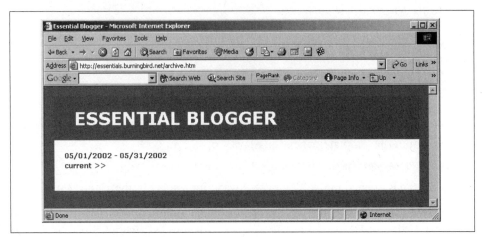

Figure 6-12. Blog archive index file

Example 6-4. Complete example text

```
<!DOCTYPE HTML PUBLIC "-//W3C//DTD HTML 4.0 Transitional//EN">

<html>
<head>
  <title><$BlogTitle$></title>
<style>
body {background:#666666;margin: 0px;font-family: Verdana, Arial, sans-serif}
.blogtitle{font-family: Verdana, Arial, sans-serif;color: white;
    font-size:32px;margin-left:20px;margin-bottom:1px; text-transform:uppercase;}
A {font-weight:bold;text-decoration:none; font-size: smaller}
A:hover {color:red;}
</style>
</head>

<body bgcolor="#666666" marginwidth="0" marginheight="0"
      link="#336699" vlink="#003366" alink="red">
<br>
<div align="center">
<table width="95%" align="center" border="0" cellspacing="0" cellpadding="20">
<tr>
<td bgcolor="#336699" height="65" valign="bottom">
<div class="blogtitle"><b><$BlogTitle$></b></div></td>
</tr>
<tr>
<td bgcolor="white">
<Blogger>
<script type="text/javascript">
    document.write("<a href='<$BlogArchiveLink$>'><$BlogArchiveName$></a><br>");
</Blogger>
if (location.href.indexOf("archive") != -1) {
document.write("<a href=\"./\">current >></a>")
}
</script>
```

Example 6-4. Complete example text (continued)

```
<br>
<br>
</tr>
</table>
</body>
</html>
```

You can get more creative with this file if you wish. A good place to see variations of handling archive script is at Phil Ringnalda's Archive Script web site at *http://www.philringnalda.com/archivescripts/*.

Changing the Location of the Archive Files

Archive files are stored in the same directory as the blog files by default. If you prefer to have the archive files located in a subdirectory, such as one named *archives*, you'll need to change the archive file location and adjust the main blog page template.

Before proceeding with changes to the Blogger templates and settings, create an *archives* subdirectory. If you don't have one already created, you'll get an error when you attempt to generate the archive files. Once the subdirectory is created, open the Archive view, and then the archive settings.

Within the archive settings, change the FTP Archive path to add the new subdirectory. For instance, in the Essentials blog, we changed the path to:

```
/usr/local/www/vhosts/essentials.burningbird.net/htdocs/archives
```

Once you've made this change, save it and then open the Template view.

In the Template view, add the subdirectory in front of the Archive filename in the link:

```
<a href="/archives/<$BlogArchiveFileName$>"><b>Archives</b></a>
```

You'll also need to adjust the permalink for each posting. In the Template view, modify the permalink text to the following:

```
<span class="byline">posted by <$BlogItemAuthor$> at
<a href="/archives/<$BlogItemArchiveFileName$>#<$BlogItemNumber$>">
<$BlogItemDateTime$></a></span></div>
```

Once these changes are saved, republish all your archive files first, and then the main blog page. If all goes well, your archive files appear in the new subdirectory and you'll be able to access them from your blog page. You'll have to manually remove the previously generated archive files—this action doesn't clean up the existing files. Additionally, don't forget to change the "current" reference in the Archive template to point to the main blog page directory.

Adding Comments

Unlike more traditional web pages, blogging is highly interactive, with the blog reader responding directly to the blog writer. This process is facilitated with blog comments—functionality to allow your blog readers to add comments to each posting.

At this time, Blogger doesn't have a built-in comment system, but you can use any number of commenting software packages, particularly if you host your blog pages yourself and are comfortable with incorporating some coding into your blog. One PHP-based comment system called dotcomments (accessible at *http://groups.yahoo.com/group/dotcomments-support/files/*) works well.

 Another freely accessible comment system is SnorComments, available for download at *http://www.snorland.com/scripts/snorcomments2/*. This application works if you host your own blog pages and your system supports CGI.

However, if you're not interested in server-side coding, or if you aren't hosting your blog pages on your own server, you can still incorporate comments by using a JavaScript client–based comment system such as YACCS.

YACCS commenting is an online service that works with several blogging tools including Blogger and Radio UserLand. You begin the process of using YACCS by signing up for an account at *http://rateyourmusic.com/yaccs/*, providing information such as blogging tool used (this is important as it impacts the code incorporated into your blog), your name, the URL for the blog, and so on. You'll also provide some basic operating instructions for the comments, such as ordering comments in descending order (recent comments on top), whether the blog is public, and so on.

Add the information for your blog, making sure to pick the Pop-up Window option for opening the comments. Also change the "No Comments" text to "Comments?", as shown in Figure 6-13.

One you're finished providing information on the page, clicking the Modify Your Comments button will open a second window providing two options for installing the comments: either manually using copy and paste, or automatically.

Automatic comment installation uses the Blogger API to update your template, as is demonstrated in the next section when you add a statistics counter to your blog page. For now, you'll add the Comment code directly yourself.

The generated code is shown in Example 6-5. To manually add this to your blog, we select and copy all of it.

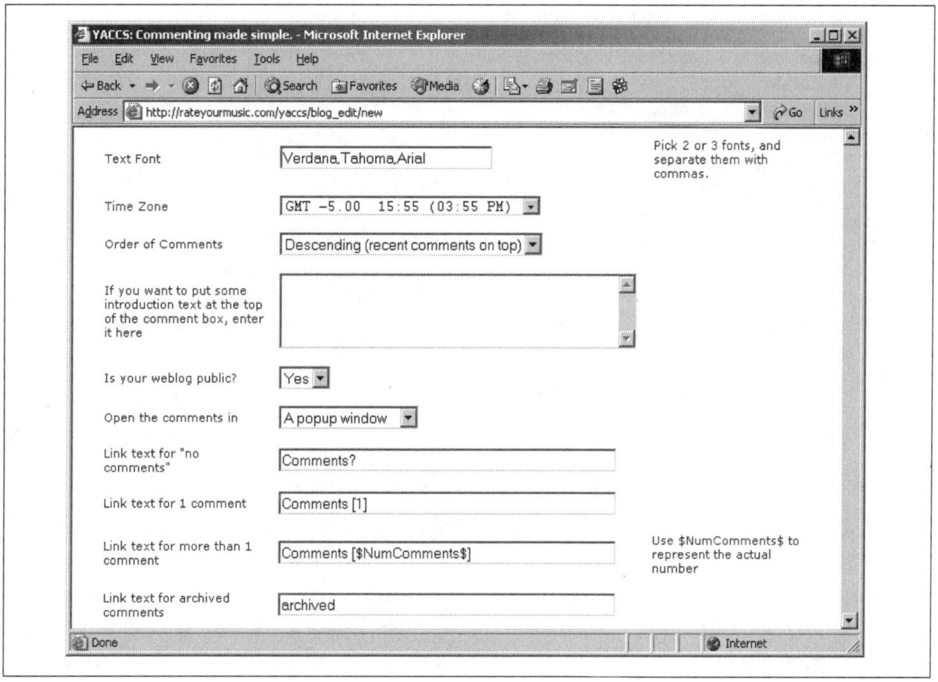

Figure 6-13. Providing basic comment information

Example 6-5. Generated YACCS code

```
<!-- Begin YACCS Code (part 1) -->

<script type="text/javascript"
src="http://rateyourmusic.com/bclw?b=90000020370"></script>
<script type="text/javascript">
function yaccs_c() {
    document.write(ycso[0]);
}
function ycs(e) {
    for(i=0;i<ycso[2];i++)
    {if(ycsx[i*2]==e){return ycsx[(i*2)+1];}
}
if(e<ycso[3])if(ycso[2]>=ycso[1])
    {return -1} else{return 0} else return 0
}
function get_comment_link(e){
 cc=ycs(e);if(cc==0){yfs=ycso[9]}
 if(cc==1){yfs=ycso[10]}if(cc>1){yfs=ycso[11];
 if(ycso[13]){yfs+=cc}yfs+=ycso[12]}if(cc==-1){yfs=ycso[14]}
 if(ycso[5])
 {
```

Example 6-5. Generated YACCS code (continued)

```
    document.write('<a target=\"'+ycso[4]+
        '\" class=\"yaccslink\" href=\"javascript:void(0)\" ' +
        'onmouseover=\"window.status=\'Comment on this post\'; return true\" '+
        'onMouseout=\"window.status=\' \'; return true"
            onclick=\"window.open(\'http://' + ycso[8] +
            'commentsn?blog_id=' + ycso[15] + '&blog_entry_id='+e+'\',\'intags\',\
'scrollbars=yes,resizable=yes,height=' +
            ycso[6]  + ',width=' + ycso[7]  +',left=80,top=80\');\">'+yfs+'<\/a>')
    } else {
        document.write('<a class=\"yaccslink\" href = \"http://' + ycso[8] +
        'commentsn?returnurl=' + document.URL + '&blog_id=' + ycso[15] + '&blog_entry_
id='+e+'\">'+yfs+'<\/a>')}}
</script>

<!-- End YACCS Code (part 1) -->
```

The code gets added to the Blogger template directly after the opening head tag.

In the next step, code to handle the individual post comments is copied and added to the template area contained within the Blogger tags. The actual placement of the code can vary and depends on your preferences as to where you want the comment link to appear. In the Essentials blog, we placed it right next to the `<$BlogItemDateTime$>` template tag, within the posts div block, with a couple of dashes preceding it as shown in Example 6-6.

Example 6-6. Modification of Essential Blogger template to incorporate YACCS comment

```
<Blogger>
<BlogDateHeader>
  <div class="date"><$BlogDateHeaderDate$></div>
</BlogDateHeader>

<div class="posts">
  <a name="<$BlogItemNumber$>"> </a><br>
    <PostSubject>
    <h5><$BlogItemSubject$></h5>
    </PostSubject>
  <$BlogItemBody$><br>
   <span class="byline">posted by <$BlogItemAuthor$> at
    <a href="/archives/<$BlogItemArchiveFileName$>#<$BlogItemNumber$>">
      <$BlogItemDateTime$></a></span>
    -- <SCRIPT language="javascript">get_comment_link(<$BlogItemNumber$>)
      </SCRIPT><noscript>
      <a href =
    "http://rateyourmusic.com/yaccs/commentsn?b=90000020370&e=<$BlogItemNumber$>">
      Add a comment</a></noscript>
</div>
<br>
</Blogger>
```

Save the template change and republish the blog page to add the comment capability to the blog. If you click on the Comments? link, the comment window opens, as shown in Figure 6-14.

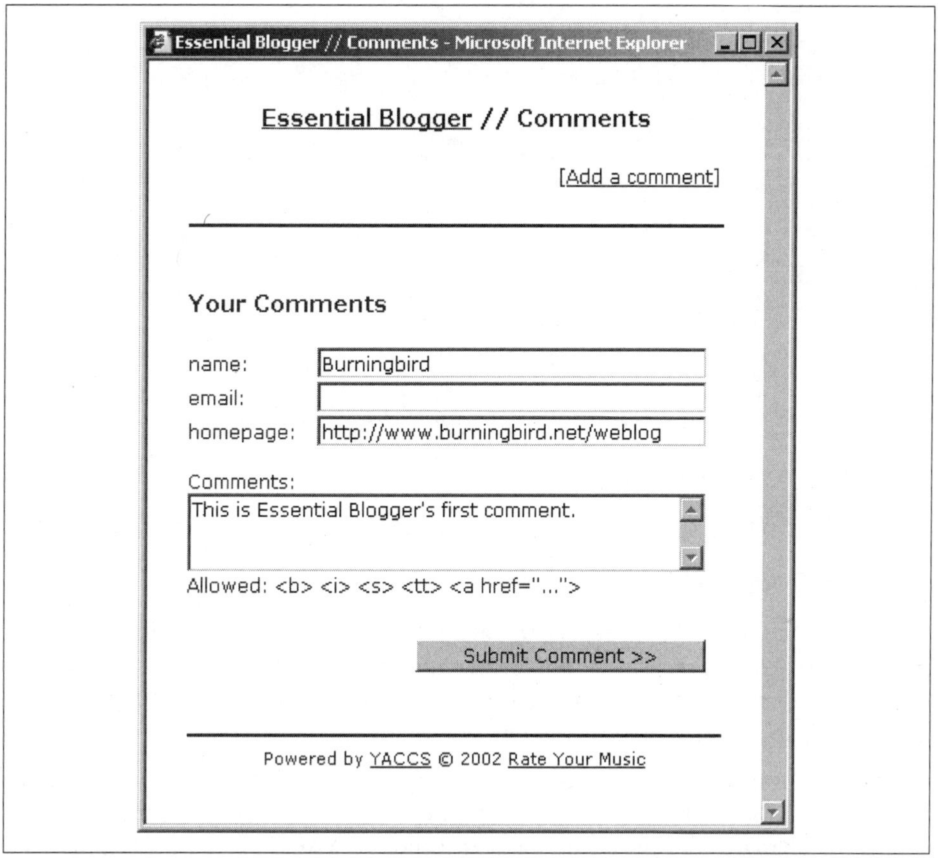

Figure 6-14. Comment window supported by YACCS and attached to Essential Blogger blog

Typing and submitting a comment adds it to your comments; refreshing the blog page shows that the comment count is now at one. Clicking the Comments link opens the comments window and the saved message is displayed.

If you wish to try a different look for your comments, you can access the YACCS control panel and select one of the public templates or create one of your own. The best thing about this is you don't have to modify your Blogger template again—the comment template is separate from the Blogger template.

For the Essential Blogger blog, we picked the Movable Type template because of its simplicity and ease of reading. After previewing it, click the Copy link associated with it. A new page opens giving you a chance to preview the template and modify it if you wish. Clicking on the link to modify the template, opens the template modification page, as shown in Figure 6-15.

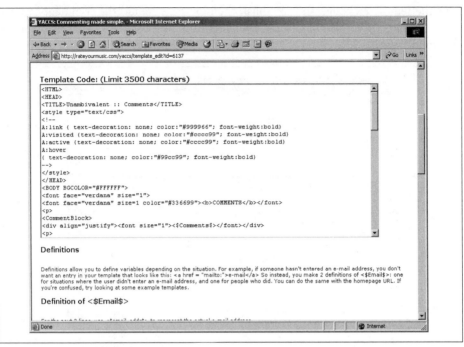

Figure 6-15. Template page for YACCS comment

As you can see, the YACCS template page is quite similar to the Blogger template page—a top text box for editing the template, as well as individual fields for modifying specific elements of the template such as how to handle the email field when a user doesn't specify an email, and so on.

For now, the only change we made to the template is to change the comment window title from "Unambivalent::Comments" to "Essential Blogger::Comments." After saving the changes, the next step is to incorporate YACCS functionality into the Blogger template.

Returning to the YACCS control panel, the comment account shows in the top of the page. Click the More>> associated with the account to open the detailed information page for the comments. In this page, you can select the new template from a drop-down box. Click the Apply button to apply the change.

Incorporating Statistics

Over time, you're going to be curious about the people who visit your blog. In particular, you'll want to know if anyone is linking to you and which particular blog archive files seem to be the most popular. Though this information isn't going to improve the quality of your writing, it does give you some useful feedback.

If you FTP your Blogger-generated files to a server, chances are you have a log statistics package already in place to track visitors. However, if you don't have a package in place, or if you're hosting on BlogSpot, you'll need a web statistics package that can be embedded into the blog page itself, rather than being integrated with your web server.

One popular web statistics package is Site Meter, accessible from *http://sitemeter.com*. The basic service is free, and, because it's a client-side process, it doesn't require any server-side support. To get access to this service, go to the site and sign up for an account following the site instructions.

Eventually, you'll get directed to a page that contains the HTML to add to your blog, or you can use the pre-built service Site Meter provides by supplying your Blogger ID. You can find your Blogger ID by looking at the URL when you open your blog in Blogger. Once you provide the ID and your username and password, as shown in Figure 6-16, click the Add Site Meter to Template button.

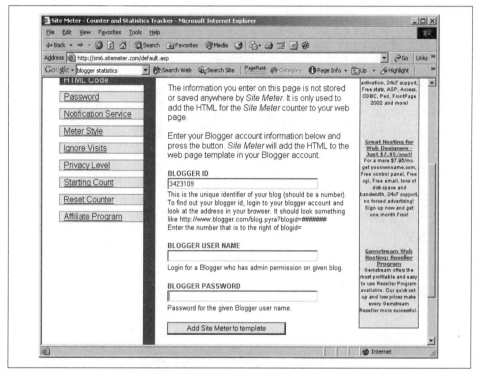

Figure 6-16. Service to add Site Meter support to the blog

The Site Meter service invokes the Blogger API to embed the Site Meter code within the template without any intervention on your part. The code it adds is shown in Example 6-7.

Example 6-7. Generated Site Meter code, embedded using XML-RPC based Blogger API

```
<!--WEBBOT bot="HTMLMarkup" startspan ALT="Site Meter" -->
<script type="text/javascript" language="JavaScript">var
                                            site="s13essential"</script>
<script type="text/javascript" language="JavaScript1.2" src="http://s13.sitemeter.com/js/
counter.js?site=s13essential">
</script>
<noscript>
<a href="http://s13.sitemeter.com/stats.asp?site=s13essential" target="_top">
<img src="http://s13.sitemeter.com/meter.asp?site=s13essential"
                                            alt="Site Meter" border=0></a>
</noscript>
<!-- Copyright (c)2002 Site Meter -->
<!--WEBBOT bot="HTMLMarkup" Endspan -->
```

After publishing the blog page, you'll see the Site Meter indicator at the bottom. Click on the icon to open the Site Meter statistics for the page, shown in Figure 6-17. The statistics are accessible only with a code name and password—sent by Site Meter to you in an email when you signed up for the account.

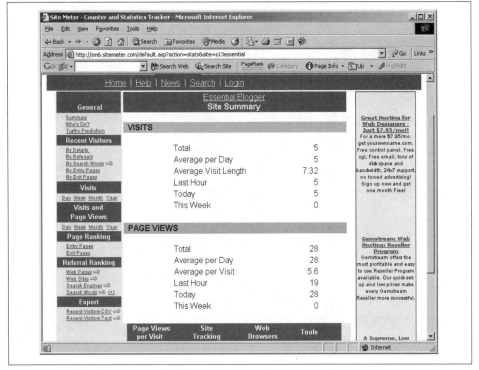

Figure 6-17. Site Meter statistics for blog page

If you're not comfortable supplying your Blogger account name and password, you can copy the generated HTML and paste it into your blog yourself.

Automated Blogrolling

Automated blogrolling is another JavaScript-enabled technology you can incorporate into your blog. This service is available once you sign up for an account at *http://blogrolling.com*. With automated blogrolling, rather than make a change in your Blogger template every time you add, remove, or update a blogroll link, you make the change to the service and it's automatically reflected in your blog.

To create an automated blogroll, you must first provide a Blogroll name and URL location at Blogrolling. Next, add links to the blogroll, as shown in Figure 6-18, using the Add Links option on Blogrolling's member page.

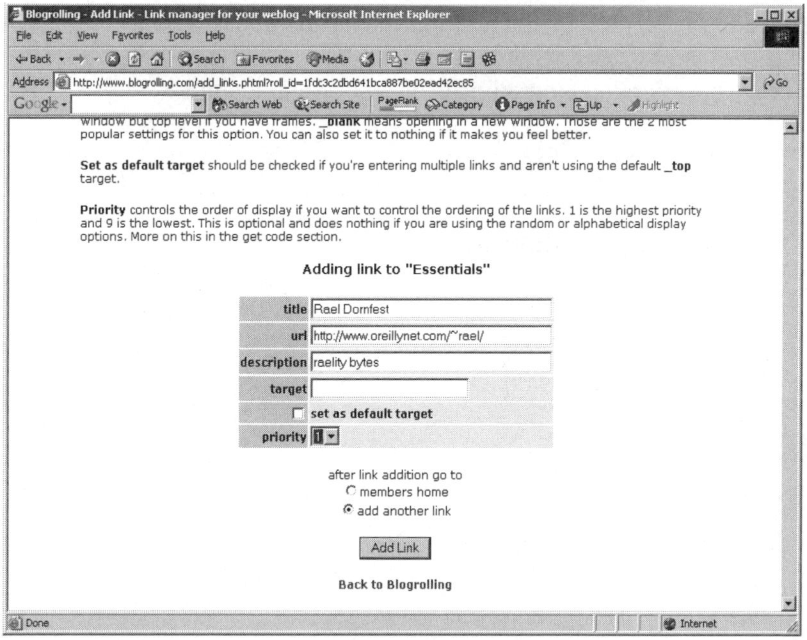

Figure 6-18. Adding a link to Essential Blogger's automated blogroll

Continue adding links until all the existing blogroll links are added. In this example, the target field is left blank so that the page opens in the existing browser window. Instead of leaving target blank, you can use _top to set the target to the top window in a frame or _blank to open a new window.

The priority is set at 1 for each entry as all entries are of equal importance—no one entry has priority over the others. The description you provide in the form is used as the title attribute of the hypertext link and displays when the mouse is over the link.

Once the entries are added (additional entries can be added later), accessing the Get Code link from Blogrolling's member page gets the generated code for displaying the blogroll. You can choose to display links randomly, by priority, or alphabetically. You can also add custom text to signal freshly updated blogs. (The information used to signal fresh blog postings is pulled from weblogs.com)

For presentation, you control if the blogroll appears in a `div` block (which you can then supply presentation characters for using CSS), within an HTML table, and even if the links are contained within blocks of links (for larger blogrolls to break them up a bit). Finally, one field is provided whereby you can put anything to be prepended or appended to a link.

For the Essential blog, the blogroll is ordered alphabetically, and the word "Recent!" is appended to the blogroll item if it has been recently updated on weblogs.com. The blogroll entries are enclosed within the default `div` block and no other customization is provided. The generated Blogrolling code is shown in Example 6-8.

Example 6-8. Generated Blogrolling code

```
<!-- Hide script
//<![CDATA[
var r = "1fdc3c2dbd641bca887be02ead42ec85";
var o = "alpha";
var xb = "";
var ut = "0";
var pb = "1";
var tb = "";
var tw = "";
var tcs = "";
var tcp = "";
var sr = "1";
var srp = "";
var sra = "Recent";
var lpp = "";
var lap = "";
var url = "http://blogrolling.com/br/js.php";
url += "?r="+r+"&o="+o+"&xb="+xb+"&pb="+pb+"&ut="+ut;
url += "&tb="+tb+"&tw="+tw+"&tcs="+tcs+"&tcp="+tcp;
url += "&sr="+sr+"&srp="+srp+"&sra="+sra+"&lpp="+lpp+"&lap="+lap;
document.write("<script language='JavaScript' src='"+url+"'>");
document.write("<\/script>");
//]]> End script hiding -->
</script>
```

Automated Blogrolling is incorporated into your Blogger blog by replacing the existing blogroll HTML with the generated code.

You can edit, add, or delete new blogroll entries, customize the generated code, as well as changing the ordering. If you change your blogroll frequently, Blogrolling is quite handy. Even if you don't adjust your blogroll that often, the service's ability to highlight freshly updated blogs is very useful.

Any reliance on third-party software makes your blog vulnerable to system problems at more than one location. In addition, using JavaScript fails for any browser that turns scripting support off. These potential problems apply to YACCS, Site Meter, as well as Blogrolling. However, for the most part, these services respond quite nicely. The fun of using the services usually compensates for occasional problems.

Adding Support for Syndication

Syndication gives your readers the ability to subscribe to an XML extraction of your blog information. This can be used within aggregation products such as Syndic8 (*http://www.syndic8.com*) or Radio UserLand.

Just as we finished writing this chapter, automatic support for RSS generation was added to Blogger Pro. The process does require that you use titles for your entries, but again, this is automatically supported with Blogger Pro. If you have access to Pro and self-host your blog (RSS isn't currently supported on BlogSpot), enable RSS generation by selecting the Settings view and clicking the RSS tab.

In the page that opens, turn RSS generation on by changing the entry in the drop-down box labeled Publish RSS from No to the version of RSS you wish. At this time, the only version supported is RSS .91. You can also choose whether a description is added for each entry in addition to the link and the title. You can choose a short description—approximately 255 characters or the first paragraph—or a full description (complete posting). We strongly recommend that you use the short description; long RSS entries play havoc with the usability of aggregation tools.

Finally, if you host your blog on your server, provide the RSS server path, RSS filename, and URL; these are most likely based on the same location as your blog page path. The RSS file for the Essential blog is named to *rss.xml* and is colocated with the blog page. Figure 6-19 shows the entries for this form.

Once the changes are saved, publishing new blog postings or republishing the archives also publishes new entries to the RSS file.

All you need to do at this point is add a link to your template to point to your newly generated RSS file. This is usually labeled Subscribe, or marked by an orange button with XML in it, but you can use whatever you wish.

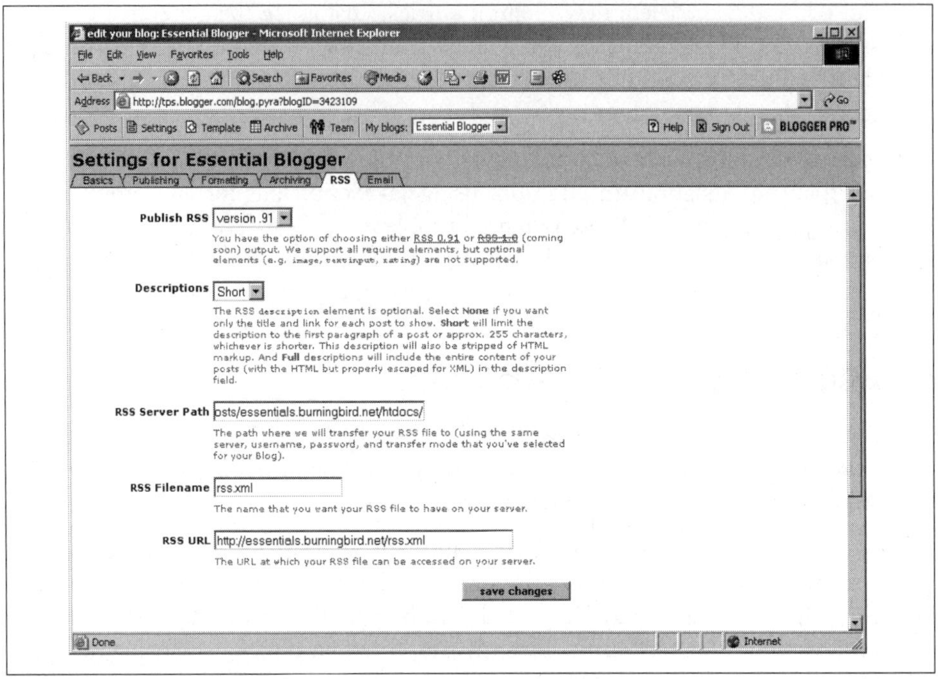

Figure 6-19. Adding RSS support to the Essential Blogger blog

Integrating Blogger into an External Application Environment

By default, Blogger generates the main blog page and supporting archives as HTML extensions, but this is easy to change if you want to include ASP or PHP, or any other type of server-side script. For instance, as mentioned earlier, we use a comment system called dotcomments that's based on PHP. We've also added a PHP date and time function, showing our current date and time (handy when you have blog readers from around the world). To support this functionality, we need to save our files as PHP-based files.

To change the blog to generate files with a *.php* extension, access the Settings view and the Publishing tab. In the page, you'll want to change the blog filename to *index.php* instead of *index.htm* or *index.html*, whichever you already have. Save this change. If the archives also need the extension changed, access the Archive view next. Again, change the archive filename to a *.php* extension. The same extension will be used for all archive files. (Though the Archive index file won't usually need to have the extension change—it won't have server-side script—the filename is used as the basis for all other archive files, which is why you'll need to make the extension name change.)

Republish the archives and the main blog page. The files are now saved as PHP files rather than HTML. At this point, you can open the blog template and add your server-side script as you would a regular file.

Exporting Blogger Data

When you publish within Blogger, you are, in actuality, exporting Blogger data in a templated format, which just happens to be readable in a browser. However, there's no reason why you can't export the data using any other template.

As an example of this process, if you eventually decide to move from Blogger to another blog tool such as Movable Type, you can export your existing posts and all associated information into a format that Movable Type can then import.

To demonstrate exporting the Blogger Data, we'll use the Movable Type Blogger Export template. To download and learn about this, visit:

> *http://www.movabletype.org/docs/mtmanual_importing.html*
> *#exporting%20blogger%20entries*

This template is shown in Example 6-9. As you can see, it's much smaller than your existing template.

Example 6-9. Movable Type blogger export template

```
<Blogger>
AUTHOR: <$BlogItemAuthor$>
DATE: <$BlogItemDateTime$>
-----
BODY:
<$BlogItemBody$>
--------
</Blogger>
```

Once you've backed up your existing template, copy the Movable Type export template over it and save the change. Next, access the Settings view and the Publishing tab and change the name of the generated file to *export.txt*, to prevent overwriting your existing blog page. Save this change. Access the Formatting tag next and change the count of postings to cover the number that you want to export. At this time, the value is set to seven days' worth of posts, which we'll leave as is.

 If you want to export all your data, just make sure you pick the Latest Posts option, and set the number of posts to be greater than the number you know you have.

Finally, access the Archive tab and turn archiving off, so that you don't override the archived pages. Publish the page.

The results of the exportation of the data are:

```
AUTHOR: Shelley Powers
DATE: 11:24 AM
-----
BODY:
<img src="http://www.oreillynet.com/images/javascript/javascript_logo.jpg"
align="right" vspace="10px" hspace="10px"><br><b>Blogger<
/b> is a weblogging tool that's accessed online. It can be found at the
<a href="http://blogger.com">Blogger web site</a>, and takes
 <i>very little effort</i> to create either an account, or your first weblog.
Once you've seen how easy weblogging can be, you'll wonder
why you didn't try weblogging sooner.
--------
```

Because there's only one posting, there's only one entry in the exported file. If there were more postings, there would be more entries.

Once you're finished, return your blog filename back to the original, turn archiving back on again, and change the number of posts back to what you normally display. Any format can be used to export the data. You can export into a spreadsheet format, a plain text format, or even a specialized XML format.

CHAPTER 7

Advanced Radio UserLand

Radio UserLand (Radio) is a sophisticated, rich product. Radio goes far beyond simple blogging, with powerful features such as macros, object databases, outliners, a built-in web server, a full development environment, a scripting language, support for the Blogger API, and the ability to build your own web services. In this chapter, we start with a description of the products related to Radio: UserLand Frontier and Manila. After that, we continue with Radio techniques such as shortcuts and categories and then move into more advanced topics such as macros and UserTalk.

Radio, Frontier, and Manila

Blogger and Movable Type are pure server-side products. They run on a server only and all authoring is done through a web browser. Radio, by contrast, runs on your desktop or notebook computer and publishes to a server.

UserLand Software also offers UserLand Frontier (*http://frontier.userland.com*) that includes another tool called Manila (*http://manila.userland.com*). Manila provides equivalent functionality to a Blogger- or Movable Type–style blogging system.

Radio UserLand
  A desktop blogging tool for a single blog.

UserLand Frontier
  An overall web content management system for any type of web publishing including large web sites.

Manila
  Like Movable Type and Blogger, Manila runs on a server and all authoring is done through a web browser. Manila differs from Radio in that it is really targeted at applications beyond the level of individual blogs. Manila, for example, lets you build your own community of blogs. Though Frontier and Manila are technically separate, Manila is heavily used by virtually all Frontier customers.

Both Manila and Frontier run purely on a server (e.g., Windows NT, Mac OS, or Mac OS X) and all authoring is done through a web browser. Like Radio, Frontier includes a full object database, scripting language, script editor and debugger, outliner, multithreaded runtime, search engine, integrated HTTP server, full XML support, full RSS support, and distributed computing protocols, such as XML-RPC and SOAP.

Radio, Frontier, and Manila all interoperate. For example, you can use Radio as an authoring tool for your Manila site, taking advantage of Radio's enhanced editing features. While this is in no way required, it is a powerful combination.

Radio Techniques

This section explains some of the quick things you can do with Radio. Among the topics covered in this section are shortcuts, publishing to your blog via email, learning to use Radio's automatic updating, republishing your entire blog, and backing up your Radio data.

Shortcuts

Shortcuts are a unique feature in Radio that makes entering content into your blog postings easier, faster, and more accurate. Shortcuts replace quoted text (e.g., "tds") with other, generally longer, text ("The Daily Show with Jon Stewart"). The text in quotes is the shortcut's *name*.

Shortcuts can include full HTML content, such as an image reference, a URL, or both. When you are writing or editing a blog post, you see the name of the shortcut not its value. When Radio publishes your posting to your blog, the shortcut's name is replaced with its value. Shortcuts can be changed globally across all blog entries just by completely republishing your blog. Instructions on how to republish your entire blog are at the end of this section.

Automatic shortcuts

An automatic shortcut is created when you publish a blog entry with a title. Radio automatically takes that title and makes a shortcut out of it. For example, if you published a book review of Perl programming books that had a title of Perl Books you could always create a link to that post by putting "Perl Books" into a blog entry.

To prevent the "Perl Books" shortcut from being expanded, put backslashes in front of the quotes:

```
\"Perl Books\"
```

Radio treats backslashed quotes as literal quotes, so the string that appears in your final blog is simply "Perl Books" and not a link to the Perl Books post.

Creating your own shortcuts

You can also create your own shortcuts. Your own shortcuts can, for example, convert text into URLs, insert boilerplate, and even insert the HTML code for images. For example, my shortcut "virgil" inserts a picture of my cat Virgil and the shortcut "fuzzyweb" inserts a link to my web site, *http://www.fuzzygroup.com.*

To create your own shortcut, click on Shortcuts in the Radio command bar. This displays the Radio Shortcuts screen, shown in Figure 7-1.

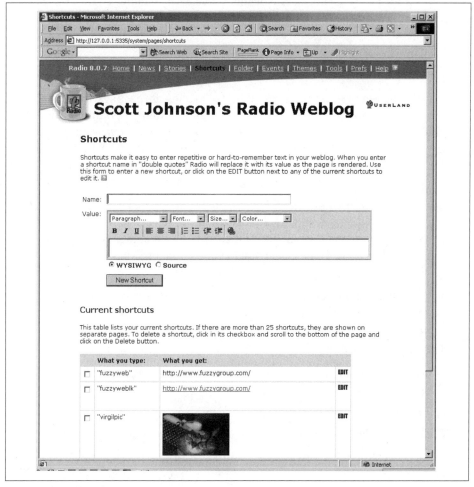

Figure 7-1. Adding shortcuts

In the Name field, enter the name of the shortcut. This is the text you type, enclosed by quotation marks, that inserts the body of the shortcut in your web page when it is published. You do not need to type the quotes.

In the Value field enter the body of the shortcut. This can include URLs, pictures that you paste into the WYSIWYG editor, plain text, and more. You can also customize the HTML code for the shortcut by source editing the entry.

To save the shortcut, click the New Shortcut button. This saves your shortcut and displays the list of all shortcuts below the value field. If you need to change the shortcut, click the Edit button. If you need to delete a shortcut, select the checkbox on its left and click the Delete button.

A useful tip for creating shortcuts is using a consistent naming style. For example you might use "donkeypic" for a picture of a donkey and "donkeylk" for a link to the Donkey site.

Using Mail-to-Weblog to Post to Your Weblog

Mail-to-Weblog lets you update your blog by mailing in postings from any email account, or even a Yahoo! Mail or Hotmail account. Within corporations, many firewalls block FTP, so if your blog isn't hosted at *radio.weblogs.com*, your only option may be Mail-to-Weblog. Be careful with this, though, and make sure you understand it completely before you begin to use it with Radio—if you configure Mail-to-Weblog incorrectly, you can lose email messages from your mailbox.

You need a POP compatible email account that can be dedicated to the Mail-to-Weblog feature. Radio retrieves and deletes any messages in the account that it monitors. If you use your main email account for Mail-to-Weblog, you *will* lose email messages (don't do that). Here's what you need to configure Mail-to-Weblog:

The account name
> This is usually either *accountname* or *accountname@somedomain.com*. We recommend that you call it something easy to remember like *myblog@domain.com*.

The POP server
> This is often something like *mail.somedomain.com*. Check with your ISP.

Once your mail account is set up, follow these steps to configure Radio to publish to your blog via email:

1. Click on the Prefs link in the Radio command bar.
2. Click on the Mail-to-Weblog option. You should see a screen like Figure 7-2.
3. Check the checkbox to turn on this feature.
4. Security for Mail-to-Weblog is handled by a "Secret Subject" approach. What this means is Radio will only post your email to your blog if the subject line matches your "Secret Subject." Don't pick something obvious or anyone who knows the account name can publish to your blog.
5. Fill out your Radio password in both fields.
6. Click Submit.

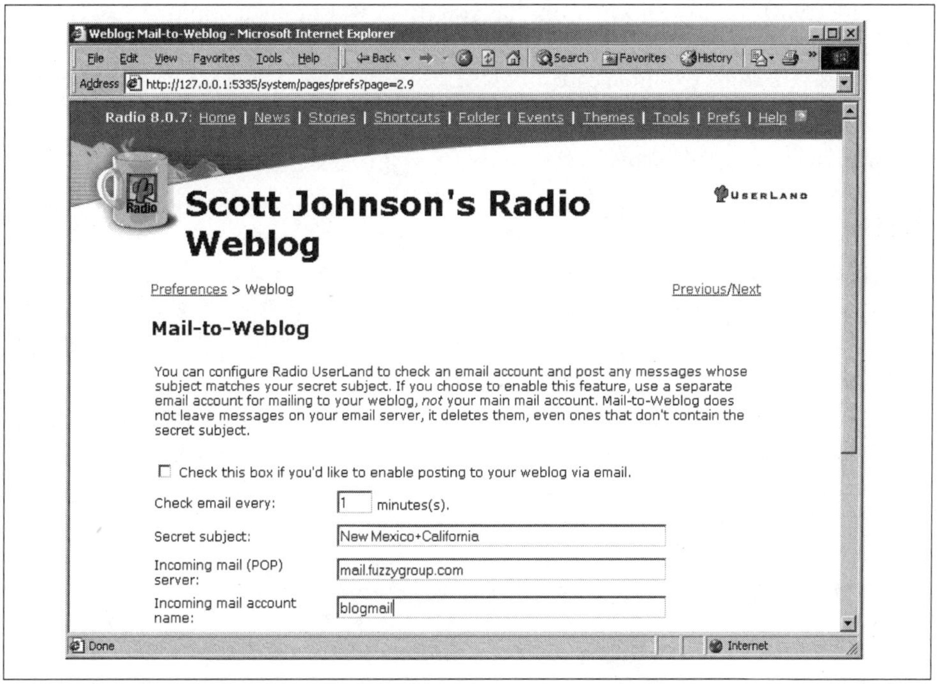

Figure 7-2. Mail-to-weblog form

To submit a blog entry via email, send a message to the account you set up. The subject line of the message must be your secret subject.

Until you have used this feature several times, you should check your blog carefully to ensure that the correct information and formatting is posted to your blog. Mail software can add footers and headers to messages, or even mangle them as attachments, so it pays to confirm that your blog isn't garbled.

Categories

The Categories feature, which is disabled by default in Radio, lets you segment and organize your blog into different types of content. For example, you might write a blog that mentions your work but also talks about your personal life and your hobbies. You could create categories for Work and Play, then assign each blog post to one category or the other. Radio then automatically creates separate index pages (which can be separately themed) for each category.

Although you can create your own categories, Radio includes several predefined categories: Home Page, My Hobbies, My Organization, My Friends, My Interests, and My Profession. By default, everything is tagged for Home Page. You can turn it off if you want, but the custom for categorized blogs is to have the home page include everything.

If you are trying to blog information that you don't want most people to see, turn off the Home Page category and send people that need the contents the URL of the category. These are some example category URLs:

http://www.fuzzyblog.com/categories/
http://www.fuzzyblog.com/categories/marketing101/

Enabling categories

By default, categories are turned off in Radio. The Prefs screen lets you turn them back on. Click on Prefs in the Radio command bar. Under the Blog grouping, click on Categories, then check the box for categories. Click Submit, then reload the new blog entry page.

At the bottom of the editing area, above the Post to Weblog button, are six checkboxes that, when selected, assign something to one or more categories. You will also see that the Home Page category is selected by default. This is shown in Figure 7-3.

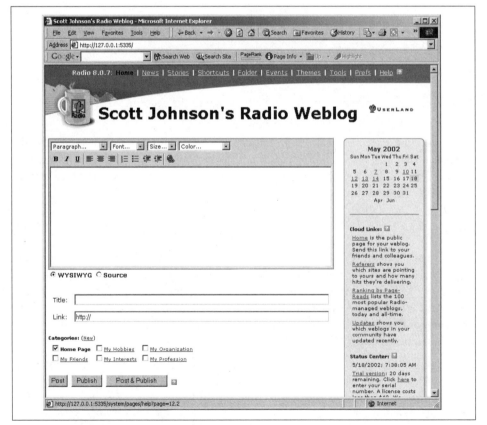

Figure 7-3. Categories for new blog entries

Creating your own categories

Although Radio has built-in categories, you probably want to create your own that are better suited to the needs of your blog. To create a new category, click on Prefs in the Radio command bar. Under the Blog grouping, click on Categories, and then follow the New Category link. This gives you the New Category options page shown in Figure 7-4.

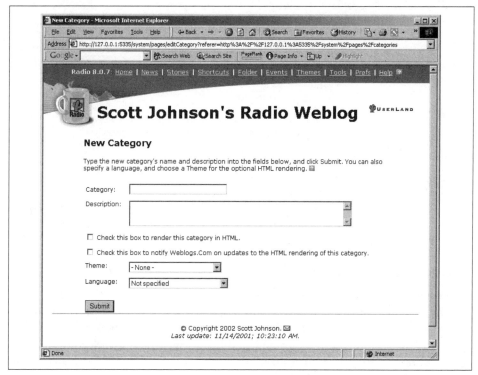

Figure 7-4. Creating new categories

Enter the name of the category. This can be anything you like, including multiple words, provided that it doesn't conflict with an existing category. It is recommended that you use only letters, numbers, and spaces for category names. Fill out the category description.

Turn on the Render as HTML option as needed. This controls whether or not Radio builds a full home page and calendar entries for your category. This really treats your category as a blog within a blog. You generally turn this on only when you want people to go directly to your category and see the rolling group of entries. In other words, you turn this on when people use a category as a destination within your blog in and of itself. If you just want people to see your category from an RSS feed or linked to from your home page, leave this option off.

Turn on the Notify option as needed. Normally, whenever you post an entry to your blog, Radio notifies the central server at weblogs.com of your update, allowing others in the blogging community to see your update. If you are using categories to segment your blog so that material stays private, you want to leave this option off.

Select a theme for the category. Radio defaults all new categories to the default theme, so if you aren't using the default theme for your blog then you probably should select a theme for the category.

Select the language in which your blog is written. Click Submit to create the category.

When you refresh the New Blog Entry page, you should see a new category at the bottom of the screen listed with the other existing categories that Radio supplies by default.

 There is a New link above the categories, listed on the home page. You can also use that link to create a new category with fewer steps.

Assigning posts to categories

If you have Categories turned on, before you publish your post, select the categories to which you want to assign the post and click Publish. Edit old posts to assign them to the new category.

Advanced categories

Although additional information on categories is beyond the scope of this chapter, you should be aware that Categories is a very powerful, very extensible feature. Categories are how you make multiple blogs from Radio. Each blog can be represented by a category, and postings can be routed to different blogs just by selecting the category that represents the destination blog. This is a powerful content management feature built into every copy of Radio.

Using the Blogger API in Radio

Radio fully supports the Blogger API standard so you can take advantage of any tool that supports it. Not only can you post to other blogs from Radio (see the Manila-Blogger Bridge tool describe in Chapter 2), but you can also use any of the desktop blogging clients in Chapter 2 to post to your Radio UserLand blog.

To use the Blogger API in Radio, click on the Prefs link in Radio's command bar. Under Internet and Server Settings, choose the Blogger API in Radio option. Turn on the checkbox to enable the Blogger API and click Submit. This allows your copy of Radio to accept data from a Blogger API–compatible tool. When you are using such a tool, you have to tell it where your blog is located on your local machine. Here are the normal settings: *http://127.0.0.1:5335/RPC2/* (the destination to which the tool should post blog entries), your username and password, and a blog ID of "home" (no quotes; this is required).

Please note that Blogger API support in Radio provides both import and export support for moving your blog entries between systems. This is obvious when you think about it but not apparent when you are used to a file-based approach to importing and exporting.

Backing Up Your Radio

It's always smart to back up your data in any program—even in a blogging application. For Radio, this means backing up the database of articles and configuration information. The files that Radio publishes onto the Internet don't have all features of your local copy. These files are only HTML pages, and they lack important metadata, formatting directives, and so on.

All your Radio data is stored in the *\Program Files\Radio UserLand* set of directories on Windows, and in the Radio UserLand folder in Applications on OS X.

Backing Up All Data on Windows

Here's your backup process for all your Radio data. It relies on WinZip or another archiving tool such as WinRar to make a single backup file, as Radio stores its data in many small files.

1. Shut down Radio by right-clicking the Radio icon in the Windows System Tray (bottom right, by default) and choosing Shut Down Radio. This is important because Radio normally runs in the background and regularly updates files. The main files you need to back up are the *.root* files, which contain all your Radio data, because you don't want Radio updating those files as you're archiving them.

2. Use your archiving program to make a backup file containing the following directories and files:

   \Radio UserLand\Data Files
   \Radio UserLand\www
   \Radio UserLand\Themes
   \Radio UserLand\Backups\ (yes this is redundant but it's safer)
   \Radio UserLand.root*

3. Copy this ZIP file to another hard drive or some removable medium.

More details on backup are given at *http://radio.userland.com/stories/storyReader$7010*.

Backing Up all Data on the Mac

The easiest way to back up Radio on the Mac is to copy the entire Radio UserLand folder to another disk.

1. Shut down Radio by Ctrl-clicking the Radio icon in the Dock and choosing Shut Down Radio. This is important because Radio normally runs in the background and regularly updates files. The main files that you need to back up are the *.root* files, which contain all your Radio data, because you don't want Radio updating those files as you're archiving them.

2. Copy the entire Radio UserLand folder from the Application folder to another drive. If you don't want to move the program files as well, move these folders:

    Radio UserLand: Data Files
    Radio UserLand: www
    Radio UserLand: Themes
    Radio UserLand: Backups (yes this is redundant but it's safer)
    Radio UserLand - All the .root files

 Don't forget to do this regularly. Your blog data is important!

Themes, Templates, and Macros

Themes and templates in Radio are the two features that control the presentation of your blog. Each page you see is composed of many templates. A *template* is just an HTML file with some non-HTML tags to indicate Radio-specific elements such as entries and dates. Where these elements exist, Radio, when posting your blog entry, inserts the content represented by those elements. A *theme* is a collection of templates that has a consistent look and feel.

The non-HTML tags are called *macros*. A macro corresponds to functionality within Radio, generally written in UserTalk, that is inserted into your blog when your page is published. Macros add additional functionality such as enabling comments on your blog, adding a list of recent blog posts and more. While changing your theme involves only a few mouse clicks, editing templates to add macros is much harder.

As with other blogging systems, adding macros requires that you understand HTML, because the macros are inserted directly into HTML "chunks" stored in Radio.

Using Existing Themes

Use these steps to change your overall theme.

1. Click the Themes link on the Radio command bar at the top of the screen.

2. Select a theme to use by clicking on the radio button to its left.

3. Confirm that you really do want to replace your existing theme. This is important because changing your theme eliminates all customizations to your current theme. Be careful that you don't lose something important!

To save your existing theme changes, go into each template in the Prefs section of Radio and copy each of the templates to a text file. After changing to a new theme, you can make these changes to the new theme.

1. Click Submit.

2. Click Home to return to the home page. If your new theme doesn't appear, refresh your browser and it will be displayed.

3. Check your blog to make sure you like the appearance you chose. If you don't like it, repeat this process to choose a different theme.

Radio comes with many variations on the Adult Contemporary theme, plus several exotic themes such as Soundwave, Space, Transmitter, and Woodlands. Many people have made Radio themes available for download, and a simple Google search for "UserLand Radio themes" will find them. For example: *http://radio.weblogs.com/0001246/gthemes/*.

Figure 7-5 shows a blog with the Woodland theme, while Figure 7-6 shows the same blog with the Space theme.

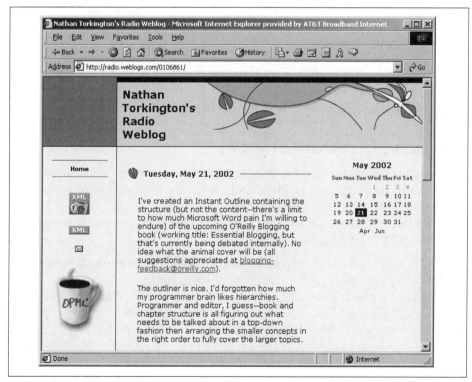

Figure 7-5. The Woodland theme

Figure 7-6. The Space theme

For additional themes for Radio or to see examples of the themes, see:

http://themes.userland.com
http://themes.userland.com/newsItems/viewDepartment$new%20radio%20theme

Customizing Templates with Macros

Radio macros are always used between the <% and %> delimiters, which tell Radio to replace the name of the macro with its action when the blog is published. The standard Radio macros, those published and documented on the UserLand web site, are listed below. Your copy of Radio will have additional macros added to it automatically when *Radio.root* is updated.

The Prefs menu has a list of templates: Main template (the basic structure of almost every page in your blog); Main template (the basic structure of your public Radio UserLand home page); Day template (view of one day's entries); Item template (the format of a single item); and Desktop Website template, which contributes the home page when you are authoring your blog in Radio. Click on a template to edit it. Let's edit your Home page template to add a reminder of how to sign your checks. Once you've selected the template to edit, you'll see a page like Figure 7-7.

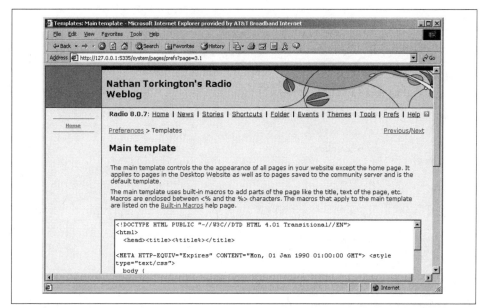

Figure 7-7. Editing the main template

The HTML template is in the textbox. Scroll down approximately halfway until you find the macro <%navigatorLinks%> in HTML like this:

```
<%navigatorLinks%>
<hr size="1">
</td>
```

Change it to:

```
<%navigatorLinks%>
<hr size="1">
<br>Don't forget to date your checks <%year%>!
</td>
```

Click the Submit button and your Main template change will be saved. On the resulting page, you can see the effect of your change (see Figure 7-8).

When Radio constructs a page from the Main template, it now finds the macro <%year%>, which is replaced with the current year.

Useful Macros

Macros for use in the Main, Home Page, and Desktop Website templates include:

<%title%>
    Title of the page (e.g., "Stories").

<%siteName%>
    Name of your blog (e.g., "Sherlock Holmes' Casebook").

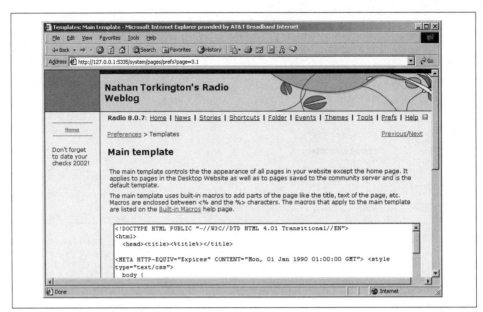

Figure 7-8. Main template with change

`<%description%>`

Description of your blog (e.g., "Elementary, Dear Watson").

`<%bodytext%>`

Body of the page. The Main template is used to generate every page you see from Radio, from Create New Entry to Prefs. The content specific to the Create New Entry and Prefs pages is represented by the `<%bodytext%>` macro.

`<%year%>`

Current year (e.g., 2002).

`<%authorName%>`

Your name (e.g., "Dr Watson").

`<%authorMailAddress%>`

Your email address (e.g., *watson@example.com*).

`<%navigatorLinks%>`

Contents of your *#navigatorLinks* file (see Chapter 3).

`<%radioBadge%>`

Image that links to the Radio UserLand home page.

`<%rssLink%>`

Orange XML button that links to the RSS version of your blog.

`<%now%>`

Time you published the page, used for Last Update message (e.g., 5/21/2002; 10:06:40 P.M.)

Macros for use in the Day template include:

`<%archiveLink%>`
> Image that links to the archive page for that day.

`<%longDate%>`
> Long version of the date for that day (e.g., "Tuesday, May 21, 2002").

`<%items%>`
> Posts for that day.

Macros for use in the Item template include:

`<%itemText%>`
> Text of a blog post.

`<%itemTitle%>`
> Title of a blog post, if specified.

`<%when%>`
> Time the post was made (e.g., 4:31:19 P.M.).

`<%permalink%>`
> Image that links to the post on the archive page (a small # sign by default).

`<%editButton%>`
> The button that appears next to blog posts in the Desktop Website.

`<%enclosure%>`
> Link to a post's enclosure—applies only to items that have enclosures. An enclosure is a binary attachment to an RSS item, such as an MP3 file.

`<%itemNum%>`
> The unique ID for this blog post.

`<%paddedItemNum%>`
> The unique ID for this blog post, padded with zeros to make it eight digits long.

`<%source%>`
> A link to the site that was the source for the item—applies only to items posted from the News page.

`<%commentLink%>`
> A link to open a pop-up page where visitors can post comments about your blog posts.

Saving Your Customizations

When you change your theme (remember a theme is a collection of individual templates), any changes you've made to your existing templates *are lost*. For example, if you customize the Woodlands theme and then decide to experiment with the Space theme, your changes to the Woodlands theme are lost. Radio warns you about this, but most users are so used to clicking right through warning dialogs that it's very easy to lose your work.

To save a customized theme, go to the Themes page. A link in the first paragraph of the Themes page lets you create your own theme. Others will be able to download your customized theme if you choose to publish it. To share a theme you create, please see the Create Theme page accessed from the main Themes page (click on the Themes link in the Radio command bar).

Enabling Comments

UserLand offers a comments service to all Radio users, which works even if you publish your blog to your own web server instead of running your blog from UserLand. Comments are disabled by default. To enable comments, add the <%commentLink%> macro to your Item template.

1. Click on the Prefs link in the Radio command bar.

2. In the Weblog grouping, click on the Comments option.

3. Click on the comments checkbox and then click Submit.

4. Now you need to modify your template to allow comments to be added. Click on Prefs again and then click on Templates.

5. Under Templates, click on the Item template.

6. Paste the text <%commentLink%> into the edit after the <%editButton%>. This places the link to the comment tool on the left hand side of the screen below your post.

7. Click Submit to save your change.

8. Reload your blog.

To disable the comments, go to the Prefs page and simply remove the <%commentLink%> macro.

The standard Radio comment tool has limitations, such as relatively slow performance, no ability to delete comments, and no notification to authors of comments. There are other services offering Radio-compatible comment engines, such as *http://rateyourmusic.com/yaccs/*.

Listing Recent Posts

People who read your blog will vary from everyday readers to occasional browsers. If you blog frequently, you may find that those occasional readers are penalized by the sequential, newest to earliest, nature of blogs. To make this easier for readers, you can add the Recent Posts macro to your blog. The Recent Posts macro lists the titles of recently added posts. You must have titles enabled (see Chapter 4) to use the Recent Posts macro. Figure 7-9 shows the Recent Posts macro in action.

Like many Radio macros, the Recent Posts macro (actually called radio.macros. recentTitledBlogPosts) can be called with parameters. In the case of this macro, the parameters specify how many posts to display, whether to truncate titles, and so on.

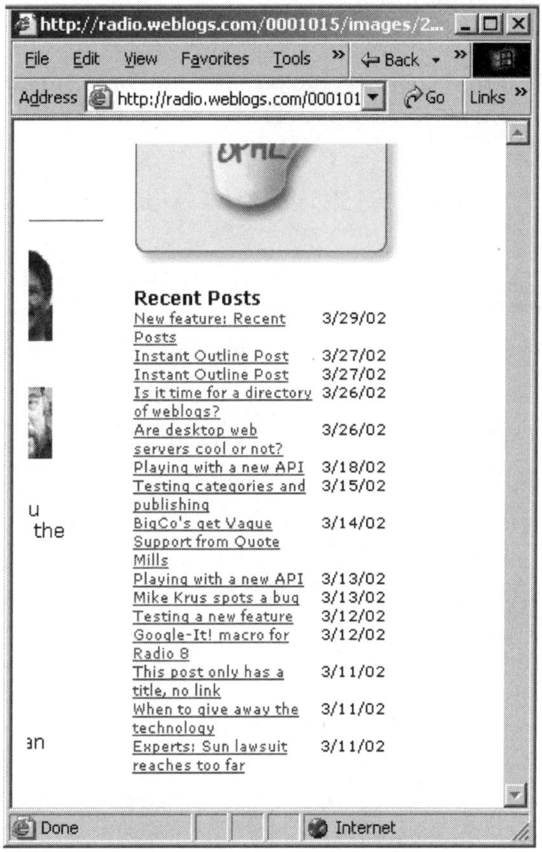

Figure 7-9. Recent Posts macro

The five parameters, all of which are optional, are listed with their default values in Table 7-1.

Table 7-1. Parameters to the Recent Posts macro

Parameter	Default Value	Meaning
maxPosts	25	Maximum number of posts to display
maxTitleLength	(infinite)	Maximum length of title (titles will be truncated to this length)
flIncludeWhen	true	List the dates of the posts as well as their titles
Catname	""	Category of posts (empty string means all)
cellSpacing	0	Cell spacing for the table

So to display a Recent Posts list, but truncate the titles at 50 characters, you'd use:

```
<%radio.macros.recentTitledBlogPosts (maxTitleLength:50)%>
```

To raise the number of posts to 50:

```
<%radio.macros.recentTitledBlogPosts (maxPosts:50)%>
```

To add 5 pixels between each line in the post lists and between the title and the data (i.e., set the cellspacing attribute of the HTML table that displays the posts):

```
<%radio.macros.recentTitledBlogPosts (cellSpacing:5)%>
```

To give 10 posts a title length of 50 characters, with no dates and 5 pixels of cell spacing:

```
<%radio.macros.recentTitledBlogPosts (maxPosts:50, maxTitleLength:50,
  flIncludeWhen:false, cellSpacing:5)%>
```

To add this macro to your template underneath your calendar:

1. Update your Radio.root file as described earlier in Chapter 3.
2. Click on the Prefs link in the Radio command bar.
3. In the Templates group of links, click on the Home Page template.
4. Find the call to `<%drawcalendar ( )%>`.
5. Add the Recent Posts macro after the call to `drawcalendar`. Exactly where to put it in the HTML depends on the template you're using. For example, in the Default template, the calendar is part of a table with your navigation links and various Radio and XML icons. In this case, it's best to put the Recent Posts list outside that table. In the Woodlands theme, the icons and links are elsewhere, so you can simply put the Recent Posts macro call immediately after the drawcalendar call.

    ```
    <%radio.macros.recentTitledBlogPosts (maxTitleLength:50)%>
    ```

6. Click on Submit to save your template.

Reload your blog's home page and you should see the Recent Post list. Figure 7-10 shows the Recent Posts list added to the Default theme.

If you find that the macro's output doesn't appear on your blog, one of two things is probably wrong. An error message from Radio probably indicates a syntax error—check that you haven't mistyped the % characters or mistyped the macro or its arguments. If you just don't see a change, your changed post probably hasn't been upstreamed yet—wait a few seconds and try again. If it still doesn't work, check your network connectivity and look at the Events log in Radio.

Additional Macros

There are many different macros for Radio templates: some from UserLand, some from individual developers, and some from third parties. Different types of macros include the very popular GoogleBox, picture galleries, image uploaders, and more. Locate these macros via these directories:

> *http://radio.userland.com/directory/6742*
> *http://ruminations.weblogger.com/directory/143*

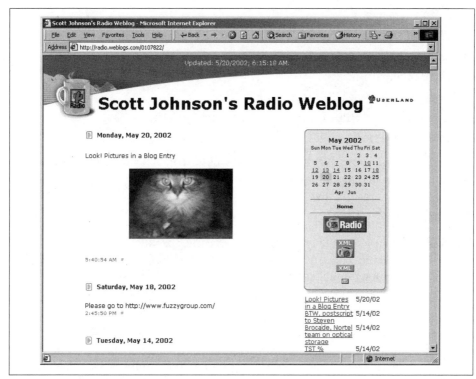

Figure 7-10. Calendar and recent posts

Creating and Downloading Themes

Although adding macros to an existing Radio template is relatively easy if you are comfortable with HTML, it is actually quite difficult to create an entire theme. A third-party product for Radio, themeTool, lets you create your own themes using standard web development tools such as DreamWeaver or FrontPage. More information is available from:

> *http://radiotools.evectors.it*
> *http://radio.userland.com/stories/storyReader$7024*

Understanding How Radio Works

At its core, Radio is a very sophisticated piece of software—as sophisticated as you can purchase from any vendor today including Microsoft, IBM, and Sun. Here are some of the key components that make up Radio:

- Overall content management system
- Object database

- Scripting language
- Network engine
- Content publishing preprocessor
- XML engine
- Logical, consistent URL structuring
- SOAP and XML-RPC server and client engines
- Open architecture

Each component is discussed below. Please note that depending on your level of "geekiness," you may want to skip this section.

Overall Content Management System

The Radio blogging tool really began life as an earlier product from UserLand called Frontier, a powerful content management system (CMS). A CMS is designed to make web publishing much easier and more powerful. At the simplest level, a CMS isolates content from presentation. This lets you alter your web publishing with a few clicks of the mouse rather than hours or days of HTML changes.

For example, a CMS lets you globally change your web site's look and feel just by applying a theme or style to it. A CMS also lets you globally manage and fix broken links. If this sounds like Radio, you're correct—Radio is a full CMS and has features normally found in larger, more complicated, more expensive products.

Object Database

One of the problems with typical web publishing is the huge number of individual files involved. Radio's object database, the *.root* files it uses, takes care of managing all the files involved in your blog. Additionally, if you are a developer, you can use Radio's object database in your own applications where you need storage of variable length objects.

Scripting Language

Although it's not covered in this book, Radio has a full scripting language, UserTalk, which you can use to build custom applications. Much of Radio, in fact, is actually written in UserTalk. This means that if you need to change how a built-in Radio function works, you generally can. Additionally, Radio has a full development environment for UserTalk, including a debugger and a unique outline-based scripting environment. For more on UserTalk, see *http://www.fuzzygroup.com/go/?usertalk*.

Network Engine

Radio is fundamentally a network application that is always in contact with the Internet. This means that Radio is regularly uploading content, downloading news, and even updating itself with new features over the Internet. This network functionality is also available to your own programs if you want to develop within the User-Talk environment.

RSS and Content Syndication

As described in Chapter 1, RSS allows you to both accept content and broadcast content (assuming that some users subscribe to your blog). This means that your blog content can get very widely distributed without any additional work on your part. Additionally, your blog can incorporate rich content from a vast number of sources.

Logical, Consistent, Permanent URL Structuring

By this time, you have seen at least some of Radio's URLs such as:

A home page
  http://radio.weblogs.com/0103807/

A daily posting
  http://radio.weblogs.com/0103807/2002/05/01.html

A list of all stories
  http://radio.weblogs.com/0103807/stories

An individual story
  http://radio.weblogs.com/0103807/stories/2002/05/06/
  marketing101ItsAllAboutTrust.html

Radio automatically generates these consistent, permanent URLs for all your blog entries. This makes your blog posts very accessible to search engines because they represent just straight HTML, not complicated CGI URLs. Additional examples of Radio's URLs are covered in the next section.

Web Services, SOAP, and XML-RPC

Web services, SOAP, and XML-RPC are three of the hottest technologies in the computer industry today. A full description of these could take pages, not just a paragraph. In short, not only does Radio let you create web services, those web services are fully standards-based and support both SOAP and XML-RPC (in fact, UserLand software helped define both of these very important standards).

For more on using XML-RPC and SOAP in Radio, please see:

> *http://www.fuzzygroup.com/go/?radioSOAP*
> *http://www.fuzzygroup.com/go/?radioXML-RPC*
> *http://www.fuzzygroup.com/go/?radioWebServices*

Open Architecture

Software products from vendors differ in their degree of "open-ness". This is not only their support of an API or a standard, but it's the ability for a user to "get under the hood" of a product and fix it if there is a problem. The single most sophisticated feature in Radio is that its architecture is both open and understandable. It can be a bit inconsistent at times, like all products, but its very, very open. The meaning of this for you, the user, is that Radio doesn't lock you in. If you need to figure out how to do something, you can. If you need control of your blog data, it's available.

For a detailed look underneath the hood of Radio and how a user can examine it, see:

> *http://www.fuzzygroup.com/go/?radioExposed*

Important Radio URLs

Radio provides standard URLs to many different aspects of your blog. These are listed below so that you understand them. All these URLs are available to anyone who knows they exist.

URL	Explanation
http://yourblog/rss.xml	RSS feed for your blog.
http://yourblog/stories/	Master list of all your stories in Radio.
http://yourblog/categories/	All your categories.
http://yourblog/gems/mySubscriptions.opml	URLs to all the RSS feeds to which you subscribe.
http://yourblog/year/	Access to all months of your posts. Substitute "2002" or the specific year.
http://yourblog/year/month/	Access to all months of your posts. Substitute "04" for the month or the desired month.
http://yourblog/year/month/day.html	Access to all postings for a specific day. Substitute "03.html" for the third day of the month.
http://yourblog/images/	All the images in your *images* directory. You might also have another directory for images to separate your blog-specific images from images that Radio uses.

Upstreaming

Upstreaming is the process by which Radio moves information from your local computer to the server where your blog is located. The overall upstreaming process is controlled by an XML file named *#upstream.xml* stored in your *www* folder. This file contains configuration information specifying where your rendered HTML files are to be placed. Passwords are never placed in this file—they are stored in the *radio.prefs.passwords* table in Radio's object database.

There are three types of *#upstream.xml* files: xmlStorageSystem, FTP, and none. An xmlStorageSystem upstream file moves blog postings off to the *radio.weblogs.com* destination or to a Radio Community Server. An FTP upstream driver transfers files via FTP. A none type prevents information in the folder where it is located from being upstreamed at all.

The none type seems confusing but consider this example: you want to have a */www/images/photos* directory that has all your photos; but there are two versions of photos—the high-resolution versions for print publication and the low-resolution version for on screen use. If you use an upstream of type none, you can prevent the high-resolution files from going up to your blog.

Here's a sample upstream file for FTP:

```
<?xml version="1.0"?>
<upstream type="ftp" version="1.0">
 <username>fuzzygroup.com</username>
  <passwordName>ftp</passwordName>
  <server>ftp.fuzzygroup.com</server>
  <path>htdocs/ftpblog/</path>
  <url>http://www.fuzzygroup.com/ftpblog/</url>
  <mode>passive</mode>
</upstream>
```

Here's a sample upstream file for xmlStorageSystem:

```
<upstream type="xmlStorageSystem" version="1.0">
  <usernum>1015</usernum>
  <name>Dave Winer</name>
  <passwordName>default</passwordName>
  <server>radio.xmlstoragesystem.com</server>
  <port>80</port>
  <protocol>xml-rpc</protocol>
  <rpcPath>/RPC2</rpcPath>
  <soapAction>/xmlStorageSystem</soapAction>
</upstream>
```

Here's a sample upstream file for none:

```
<upstream type="none" version="1.0">
</upstream>
```

The real power of the upstreaming architecture becomes apparent when you use multiple upstream files concurrently. You can have *#upstream.xml* files in multiple locations in your *www* folder, and mix the three different built-in types to have one folder upstreamed with xmlStorageSystem, another upstreamed to an FTP server, and another folder with an *#upstream.xml* using the none type so it isn't upstreamed. This is a powerful content management feature in Radio.

For more on upstreaming, see:

> *http://radio.userland.com/stories/storyReader$6926*

Online Resources for Advanced Users

As this chapter has shown you, Radio is a very sophisticated product that this chapter only begins to address. The following lists suggests additional online resources.

The radio-dev mailing list
> *http://groups.yahoo.com/group/radio-dev/*

The developers section of the Radio UserLand directory
> *http://radio.userland.com/directory/6742/developers/*

Andy Sylvester's directory
> *http://ruminations.weblogger.com/directory/143/*

The Radio community server
> *http://rcs.userland.com*

soapware.org (directory for SOAP 1.1 developers)
> *http://www.soapware.org*

APIs, formats, and protocols supported by Radio include:

RSS 0.92
> *http://backend.userland.com/rss092/*

OPML 1.1
> *http://www.opml.org*

XML-RPC
> *http://www.xml-rpc.com*

Blogger API
> *http://plant.blogger.com/api/index.html*

MetaWeblog API
> *http://www.xmlrpc.com/metaWeblogApi/*

XmlStorageSystem
> *http://www.soapware.org/xmlStorageSystem/*

CHAPTER 8

Advanced Movable Type

Once you have mastered the management of entries, comments, and the other topics discussed in Chapter 5, you are ready to move on to the more advanced customization options of Movable Type. You may find that you would like to change the look and feel of your blog; make use of Movable Type's powerful archiving features; personalize your blog by modifying its configuration to suit the way you use the tool; display a random entry from your blog somewhere on your site; or one of many other advanced topics described in this chapter.

Changing the Look and Feel of Your Blog

Movable Type is a template-based tool. To change the look and feel of your blog, you edit templates. These templates give you complete control over the look and feel of your blog; the system will never produce output where you have not explicitly instructed it do so.

Templates are composed of special Movable Type tags embedded within standard chunks of plain text (or HTML, or XML, or any other markup language you wish to use—see the later section "Advanced Template Manipulation" for more details). When you rebuild your pages, the application processes your templates, fills in the tags with data, and generates static pages on your web server.

Modifying Default Templates

When you install Movable Type and create your first blog, the blog will be initialized with a set of default templates. These templates are laid out using CSS, because with CSS, changing the design of all your templates is as simple as editing one stylesheet—as opposed to editing each template in the system. Of course, you do not have to use CSS in your Movable Type templates. Movable Type places no restrictions on the type of formatting you use.

If you tire of the default templates, you may wish to try one of the other flavors of Movable Type default template. Alternate templates are located at *http://www.movabletype.org/default-styles.html*. To choose one of these templates, copy the CSS into the Index template named Stylesheet, then rebuild. Your site will now take on the new layout.

Or, if you prefer, you do not need to use the default templates at all; you can remove all the default templates from the system and start from scratch, if you wish. If you're not sure what tags to use and where, you might consider starting with the default templates as a base, and modifying all the markup around the Movable Type tags.

To edit your blog templates, log in to Movable Type, and select your blog. Then click the Templates link in the left navigation to display the list of templates in your blog (Figure 8-1).

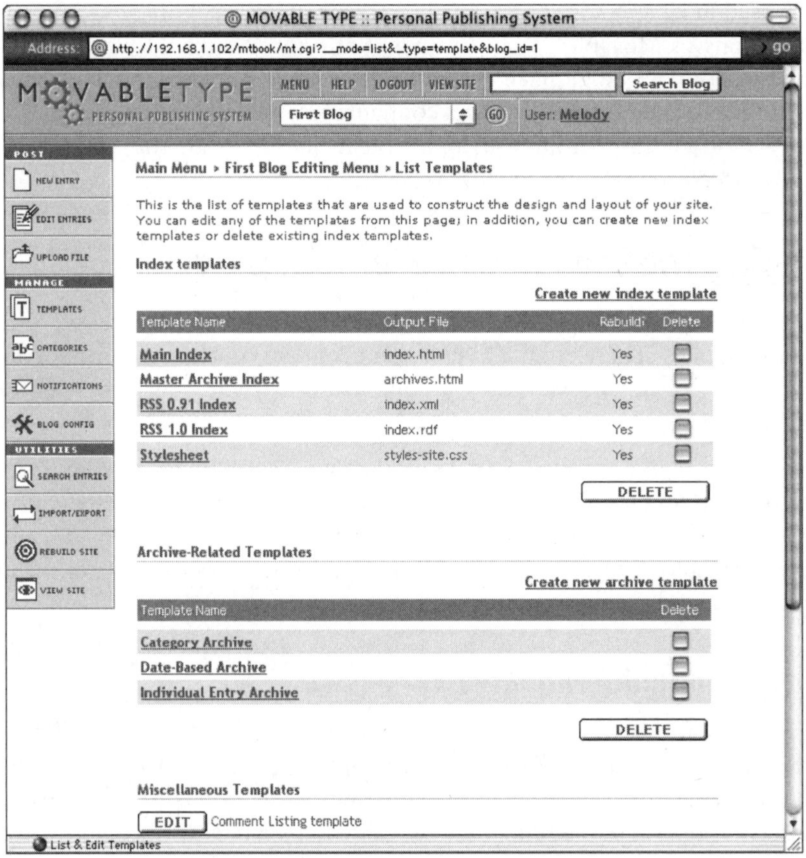

Figure 8-1. Templates list

There are two main types of Movable Type templates: Index templates and Archive templates. Index templates are used for one-off pages, such as the Main index of your web site, or the RSS-syndicated list of the last 15 headlines on your site. Archive templates describe the display of your site archives, where your entries are stored after they are no longer displayed on your Site index.

Your list of links

The *index.html* file on your site is generated from the Main index. One reason you might wish to edit this template is to change the list of links in the right navigation. To do so, edit the Main Index template (Figure 8-2) and find this HTML in the template body:

```
<a href="">Add Your Links Here</a><br />
```

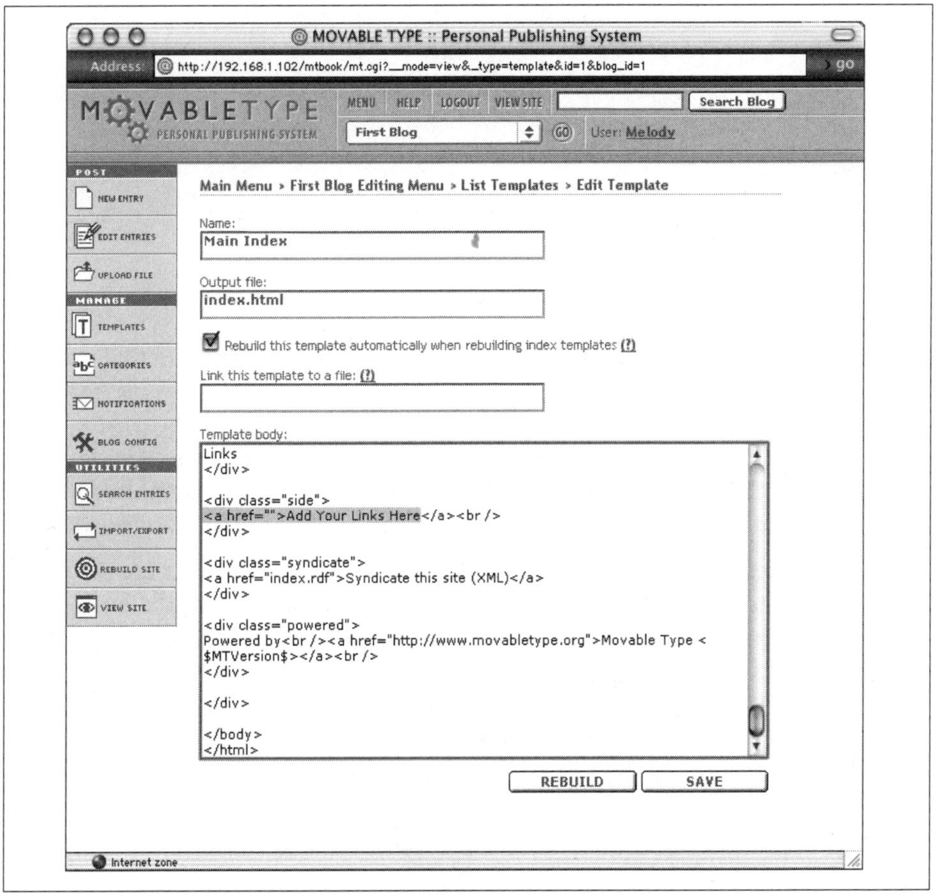

Figure 8-2. Editing the links list in the Main template

You can add links to this section by editing the HTML of the template. First, remove the above line. Then, for example, to add a link to *movabletype.org*, you could add this HTML:

```
<a href="http://www.movabletype.org/">movabletype.org</a>
```

Save the template using the Save button, and rebuild your indexes to update your public site. Instead of the Add Your Links Here text, you see a link to Movable Type (Figure 8-3).

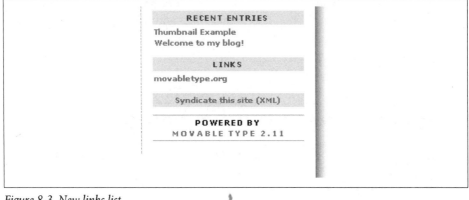

Figure 8-3. New links list

Public display of categorization

If you categorize your entries and have instructed Movable Type to build category archives, you might wish to display to your visitors the category that you have assigned to each entry on your index. The name of the category can be used as a link to the category archive. This works well as "what's related" navigation for your site, because when visitors read an entry whose subject matter they are interested in, they can click the name of the category to read more entries about similar subjects.

In the default templates, the category you have assigned to an entry is not displayed. We will add the name of the category to the metadata line below the entry body, which currently contains the name of the author, the timestamp, and (optionally) a link to the comments (Figure 8-4).

WELCOME TO MY BLOG!

This is my first blog entry using Movable Type.

Posted by Melody at 02:31 AM | Comments (0)

Figure 8-4. Default entry

From the main Templates menu, select the Main Index template for editing by clicking on its name. Then find the following markup:

```
<div class="posted">Posted by <$MTEntryAuthor$> at <a href="<$MTEntryLink$>
#<$MTEntryID pad="1"$>"><$MTEntryDate format="%I:%M %p"$></a>
```

Change it to this:

```
<div class="posted">Posted by <$MTEntryAuthor$> at <a href="<$MTEntryLink$>
#<$MTEntryID pad="1"$>"><$MTEntryDate format="%I:%M %p"$></a> in category: <a
href="<$MTEntryLink archive_type="Category"$>"><$MTEntryCategory$></a>
```

Then save the template and rebuild your indexes to update your public site (Figure 8-5).

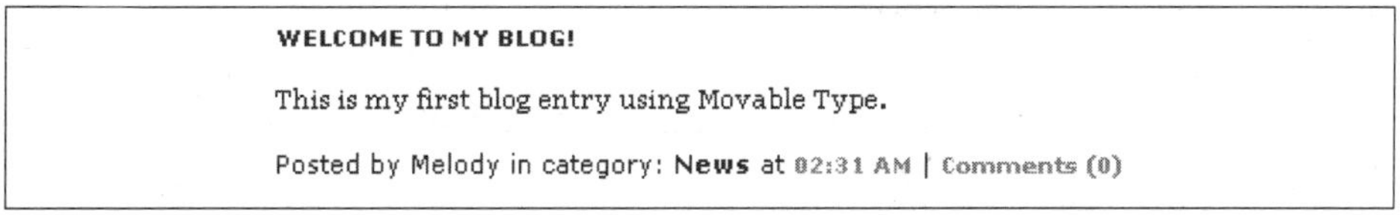

WELCOME TO MY BLOG!

This is my first blog entry using Movable Type.

Posted by Melody in category: **News** at 02:31 AM | Comments (0)

Figure 8-5. Entry with category

The metadata line for each of your entries now contains the name of the category assigned to the entry, which is a link to the category archive for that category.

Movable Type Tags

As mentioned earlier, templates in Movable Type are composed of special tags embedded within standard, static markup. All Movable Type tag names start with MT. Tags come in two flavors: variable tags and container tags.

Variable tags are simple substitution tags. They represent, and are placeholders for, dynamic pieces of data. For example, wherever the <$MTEntryTitle$> tag appears in your templates, it is replaced with the title of the entry.

Container tags, on the other hand, represent either a list or a conditional. They contain a subtemplate, a chunk of markup and Movable Type tags between two other tags: the start of the container and the end of the container. The start and end tags look like standard HTML tags.

If a container tag represents a list, the subtemplate within the container will be applied to item in that list. For example, when you use an <MTEntries> tag, the markup between <MTEntries> and </MTEntries> is applied to each in the list.

If a container tag represents a conditional, the markup between the start and end tags will be displayed only if a certain condition is met. For example, in the case of the <MTEntryIfExtended> tag, the markup will be displayed only if the entry has extended entry data.

The Movable Type User Manual contains documentation on all the available tags. This manual is part of the distribution that ships with Movable Type and can be reached by clicking the Help button in the top navigation. Then select Template Tags from the table of contents.

Advanced Template Manipulation

The markup in Movable Type templates is simple pass-thru data; as opposed to Movable Type tags, which represent a slot to be filled with data, all other markup in the templates is passed through untouched. This means that you can use any kind of markup that you wish: HTML, XML, etc. In addition, you can use templates to generate code that will be processed by another post-processing tool such as PHP, Server Side Includes, or Mason.

In fact, the RSS pages that Movable Type produces are provided as default templates using standard Movable Type tags. In their case, the markup language surrounding the tags is XML. The body of the RSS data—the list of the last 15 items—is generated using these tags:

```
<MTEntries lastn="15">
    <item>
        <title><$MTEntryTitle encode_html="1"$></title>
        <description><$MTEntryExcerpt encode_html="1"$></description>
        <link><$MTEntryLink$></link>
    </item>
</MTEntries>
```

The encode_html attributes encode any special characters in the Movable Type data into entities suitable for use in the XML feed.

Blog Configuration

Movable Type has many configuration options that you can set for each blog, controlling archiving, notifications, comments, and so on. When you set up a new Movable Type blog, these options are all given suitable defaults. This means that you can set up a new blog without worrying about setting the configuration options, which works well if the configuration options are what you would have chosen anyway.

But if you would like to edit your configuration options, do so by logging in, selecting the blog you wish to edit, then clicking the Blog Config button in the left navigation. Then select Preferences from the navigation on the right side.

Following are descriptions of some configuration options you may be interested in:

Blog description
> Your blog description is displayed in the Movable Type main menu, as well as in the header of the default templates, under the blog name.

Language for date display

If you write your blog in a language other than English, for the sake of consistency, you may wish to display the dates in the other language, as well. The system currently supports 10 languages for date display.

Convert line and paragraph breaks

When you turn on line and paragraph break conversion, all paragraphs (blocks of text separated by two line breaks) are surrounded by <p> and </p> tags, and all single line breaks will be replaced by <br> tags.

Welcome message

When authors of your blog view the main editing menu, by default, they are presented with a message welcoming them and providing a link to the manual and some introductory text. You can edit this welcome message to say anything you would like, including notes to yourself or to other authors, announcements, and so on.

Notify weblogs.com of updates

weblogs.com is a centralized site run by UserLand that tracks updates to blogs. Users can visit this site to find out when their favorite blogs have updated, or they can use specialized tools that use the weblogs.com feeds to track a subset of the sites listed on weblogs.com. If you would like your blog to be listed on weblogs.com whenever you add a new entry, turn on the Notify Weblogs.com Updates setting.

Google API key

Movable Type features integration with the Google API to include the results of search queries on your site. Of particular interest is Google's ability to list "related sites." You can use this tool to display a list of sites related to yours. To use the Google API functionality, you need to obtain a Google API key and tell it to Movable Type.

Allow anonymous comments

By default, the system will not allow visitors to your site to leave comments unless they also leave their name and email address. If you would rather let visitors leave comments without a name and email address, you can turn on the Allow Anonymous Comments setting.

Email new comments

When visitors leave comments on your site, it can be useful to be notified via email. This might be useful if you expect to receive "controversial" comments on your site, which you will need to edit or delete.

Archiving Options

One of Movable Type's greatest strengths is the number of different archiving options it offers. When you post an entry to your blog, it generally appears both on the front page of your site (your index), as well as on any archive pages you have designated. For example, if your site has an archive of all your entries by month any new entry that you post is added to the archive for the newest month, automatically. The system takes care of all the work of creating the archive files and filling them with the correct data.

Movable Type allows you to archive your entries by day, week, and/or month, by category and by individual entry. This last option means that each entry that you post has a page dedicated to displaying only that entry in the archives. This works well for sites with long entries or article-based sites, in particular.

Archiving by Category

Category archives are a flexible way to manage your archives. Because categories can represent any sort of structure you wish to impose, your category archives can be used to emulate that structure on your public web site. This allows Movable Type to act as more than just a blogging tool; for example, it can be used to manage:

- A news site, where categories might be standard newspaper sections (Local News, Politics, Entertainment & Media)
- A movie review site, where categories might be genre names (Action/Adventure, Comedy, Drama)
- A magazine, where categories might be column names (Question & Answer, Letters to the Editor, Arts & Entertainment)
- A project site, where categories might be project names (Revolt Dress, Merry Wife Apron)

In addition, Movable Type allows you to assign multiple categories to one entry. So in the case of the movie review site, you might even wish to use two different types of category archives: one categorized by genre and one categorized by the first letter of the movie title (A, B, C, etc). Or, in the case of the magazine, one set of categories could be section names and the other issue names; so you could categorize your entries by column name ("All Arts & Entertainment Stories") or by issue name ("All Stories from the May 2002 Issue").

In all these cases, the only work you have to do is to create the categories, and assign each entry to one or more categories; Movable Type will manage your archives for you.

Multiple Archive Templates

An archive template defines the layout of your archive pages and the "slots" into which your archived entries will be placed. For each archive type that you use, you can associate one or more archive templates with that archive type. This allows you to create multiple views of the same set of archived entries. For example, you might wish to provide a standard set of HTML archives, along with a printer-friendly set of archives; or perhaps you wish to cater to an older readership so you also might provide a large-font set of archives.

In any case, creating multiple archive templates is a simple matter of defining a new archive template, and associating it with the archive type of your choosing.

For this example, we will create an RSS feed for each category in the Movable Type system. As discussed in the "Syndication" section of Chapter 5, syndicating your entries to an RSS feed allows users to easily determine when you have added a new entry. Suppose your site discusses several programming languages (Perl, Python, and Ruby) and devoted readers interested in your Perl stories may not wish to read your syndicated Python stories (in fact, they may become upset when you even *mention* Python). Therefore, you wish to create separate RSS feeds for your content—one RSS feed each for Perl, Python, and Ruby.

Assuming you have already categorized your entries into Perl, Python, and Ruby categories, this is easy.

1. Log in to Movable Type and select the blog containing your entries.
2. Click the Templates button to manage your templates.
3. Click on the Create New Archive Template link.
4. Set the name of the archive template to RSS Archives, and set the body of the template to the following:

```
<?xml version="1.0"?>
<!-- generator="Movable Type/<$MTVersion$>" -->
<rss version="0.91">
  <channel>
    <title><$MTBlogName encode_html="1"$>: <$MTArchiveTitle$></title>
    <link><$MTArchiveLink$></link>
    <description>My <$MTArchiveTitle$> Entries</description>
    <language>en-us</language>
    <webMaster></webMaster>
    <lastBuildDate><MTEntries lastn="1">
<$MTEntryDate format="%Y-%m-%dT%H:%M:%S"$><$MTBlogTimezone$>
</MTEntries></lastBuildDate>
<pubDate><$MTDate format="%Y-%m-%dT%H:%M:%S"$><$MTBlogTimezone$>
</pubDate>
<MTEntries lastn="15">
    <item>
      <title><$MTEntryTitle encode_html="1"$></title>
      <description><$MTEntryExcerpt encode_html="1"$></description>
      <link><$MTEntryLink$></link>
    </item>
</MTEntries>
  </channel>
</rss>
```

5. Save the template.
6. Click on the Blog Config button to edit your blog configuration.

7. Click the Archiving link in the top right subnavigation.

8. Click the Add New... button, which will open a pop-up window in which you can add a new archive template.

9. In the pop-up window, for the Archive Type select Category, and for the Template select RSS Archives (the template you created in Step 4).

10. Click Add.

11. After the pop-up window closes and the page refreshes, you see that the new archive template has been associated with your Category archives. Now we just need to create a unique page name for each archive file to distinguish it from your standard HTML category archives.

12. In the Archive File Template column, for the RSS Archives template, paste in the following:

```
<$MTArchiveCategory dirify="1"$>.rss
```

The `dirify` attribute means that the category label (for example, "Perl") will be transformed into a string suitable for use in a directory or filename. This doesn't matter if your categories are single words, but if one of your categories had been named "Common Lisp," it wouldn't do to have the space in the filename; therefore, it would be transformed into *common_lisp*, and the archive filename would be *common_lisp.rss*.

13. Click Save.

That's it! Whenever you rebuild your category archives add a new entry, the RSS file for the appropriate category will automatically be rebuilt. The RSS file is named based on the name of the category, with the extension *.rss*; the generated files will be placed in your Local Archive Path (the setting from the Blog Config screen), and the URL will be your Archive URL (also in the Blog Config screen) plus the filename. For example, if you have a category called "Perl", and your Archive URL is *http://www.foo.com/archives/*, the RSS file containing your syndicated Perl stories will live at *http://www.foo.com/archives/perl.rss*.

Archive File Templates

Archive File templates allow you to customize the URLs used for the archive pages on your site using standard Movable Type tags. We saw Archive File templates briefly in the previous section when we assigned a filename to the RSS Archives template. In that case, we were using Archive File templates to distinguish the RSS archive files from the standard HTML archive files. But Archive File templates can also be used to impose a hierarchical directory structure on your archives.

Date hierarchy

For example, suppose you blog daily and you have been writing your blog for two years. In the course of these two years, you are keeping daily archives of your blog, which means that in your archive directory, you have 730 (365 * 2) daily archive files. You are starting to feel overwhelmed by the large number of files in the directory.

Instead of storing all your daily archives in one directory, Archive File templates allow you to create a hierarchy for your archive files to populate. This makes your directory structure much more manageable, and it can also make your archive URLs prettier; instead of *http://www.foo.com/archives/2002_05_04.html*, you could have *http://www.foo.com/archives/2002/05/04/*.

To create this structure using Archive File templates, follow these steps:

1. Log into Movable Type and select the blog containing your entries.
2. Click on the Blog Config button to edit your blog configuration.
3. Click the Archiving link in the top right subnavigation.
4. In the Archive File Template column, for the Date-Based Archive template for Daily archiving, paste in the following:

   ```
   <$MTArchiveDate format="%Y/%m/%d/index.html"$>
   ```
5. Click Save.

That's it! When you rebuild your daily archives, Movable Type will now automatically create the proper directory structure in your filesystem.

Categorized individual entries

By default, individual archive filenames are generated as a padded form of the numeric entry ID (*000002.html*, for example) and are stored directly in the *Local Archive Path* directory. You may wish for more descriptive filenames, however. For example, if you are using Movable Type to power a music review site, it would be useful if the filename corresponded to the name of the album being reviewed. And it would be even better if the archive file were located in a directory named based on the genre of the review. Instead of *http://www.foo.com/archives/000002.html*, you would like a sample archive URL to look like *http://www.foo.com/french/comic_strip.html*.

To do this, follow these steps:

1. Log into Movable Type and select the blog containing your entries.
2. Click on the Blog Config button to edit your blog configuration.
3. Click the Archiving link in the top right subnavigation.
4. In the Archive File Template column, for the Individual Archive template for individual archiving, paste in the following:

   ```
   <$MTEntryCategory dirify="1"$>/<$MTEntryTitle dirify="1"$>.html
   ```
5. Click Save.

When you rebuild your individual archives, the filenames for your reviews will now be based on the category assigned to the entry (e.g., "French") and the title of the entry (e.g., "Comic Strip").

Besides the more memorable URLs for your review archives, a side benefit of naming your individual archives using the entry title is that entry titles will not change unless you manually change them. The entry ID, on the other hand, could change if you ever need to move your entries from one blog to another using Movable Type's export and import mechanisms. Basing the filename on the entry title, rather than the ID, decreases the number of links to your site that will break if your entry IDs ever change.

Usage of existing syntax

Archive File templates use syntax that you already know to name your archive files: they use Movable Type tags. Each archive type has a set of tags that will work in Archive File templates—the working set of tags depends on the context of the archive. For example, when defining the Archive File template for category archives, you need to use the <$MTArchiveCategory$> tag to represent the name of the category being archived. A common mistake in this scenario is to use the <$MTEntryCategory$> tag, which will cause an error. <$MTEntryCategory$> does not work, because it assumes that a particular entry will be in context—that is, it is replaced with the category of the "current entry". In a category archive page, there is no "current entry"—there is only a set of entries corresponding to that particular category. So in that context, you must use the <$MTArchiveCategory$> tag.

Archiving by Calendar

Movable Type's calendar is completely customizable; it can be used as navigation through the most recent month's entries, as it is in the default templates; it can be used to power a calendar of events; it can be used to lay out an entire site, as it is by A Day Late (*http://www.dollarshort.org/days/*, as depicted in Figure 8-6); and it can even be used to emulate the output of the Unix *cal* program.

A Day Late uses a combination of Movable Type and PHP to generate a calendar of daily links. On each day, there can be zero or more links, and all the links appear in the calendar square corresponding to that day. This behavior differs from more traditional web calendars, where each calendar square links to a listing of posts from that day or the latest post from that day. In this case, the entries are displayed directly in each calendar square.

In this example, we will create a template for an event calendar similar in style to the calendar at A Day Late, to demonstrate the use of the Movable Type calendar tags. If you run a news site with a list of events for each month, you might wish to generate your archives in calendar form rather than in the standard entry listing form used in the default templates. This example will generate event calendars for all of your monthly archives.

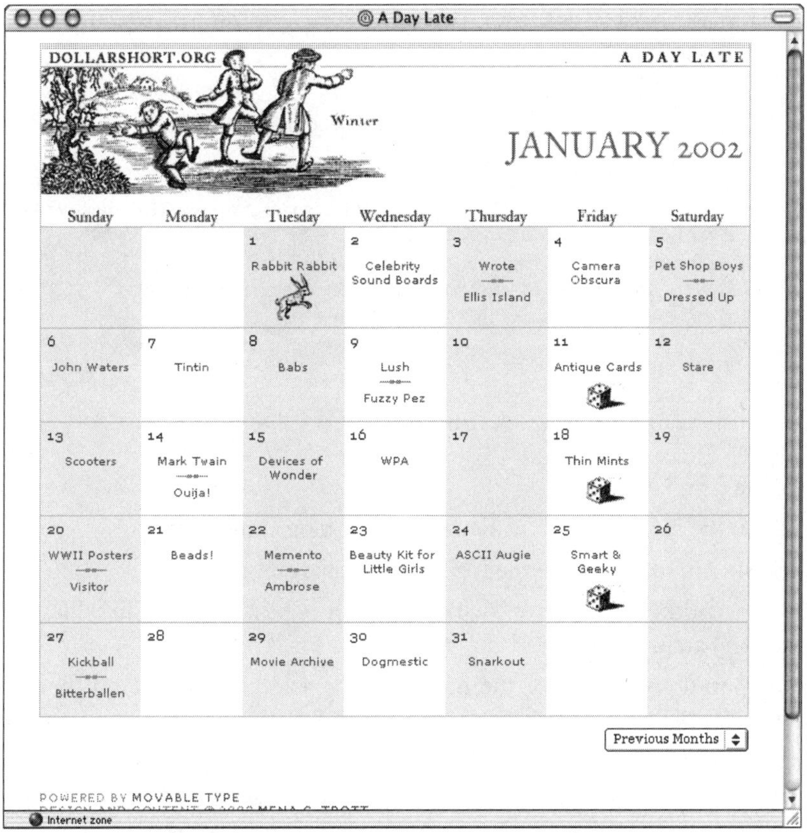

Figure 8-6. A Day Late calendar

1. Log in to Movable Type, and select the blog containing your entries.

2. Click the Templates button to manage your templates.

3. Click on the Create New Archive Template link.

4. Set the name of the Archive template to Monthly Calendar, and set the body of the template to the following:

```
<table border="1" cellspacing="1" cellpadding="0">
<tr>
<td colspan="7" align="center"><$MTArchiveDate format="%B %Y"$></td>
</tr>
<tr>
<td align="center">Sunday</td>
<td align="center">Monday</td>
<td align="center">Tuesday</td>
<td align="center">Wednesday</td>
<td align="center">Thursday</td>
<td align="center">Friday</td>
<td align="center">Saturday</td>
```

```
</tr>
<MTCalendar month="this"><MTCalendarWeekHeader><tr></MTCalendarWeekHeader>
<td valign="top">

<MTCalendarIfEntries>
    <table border="0" cellspacing="0" cellpadding="5">
    <tr><td><$MTCalendarDay$></td></tr>
    <tr><td valign="bottom"><MTEntries><span class="excerpt"><a
href="<$MTEntryLink$>"><$MTEntryTitle$></a></span><br /></MTEntries></td></tr>
    </table>
</MTCalendarIfEntries>
<MTCalendarIfNoEntries><$MTCalendarDay$></MTCalendarIfNoEntries>
<MTCalendarIfBlank> </MTCalendarIfBlank>
</td>

<MTCalendarWeekFooter></tr>
</MTCalendarWeekFooter></MTCalendar>
</table>
```

5. Save the template.

6. Click on the Blog Config button to edit your blog configuration.

7. Click the Archiving link in the top right subnavigation.

8. Click the Add New... button, which opens a pop-up window in which you can add a new archive template.

9. In the pop-up window, for the Archive Type select Monthly, and for the Template select Monthly Calendar.

10. Click Add.

11. After the pop-up window closes and the page refreshes, the new archive template has been associated with your Monthly archives. Now just need to create a unique page name for each archive file, to distinguish it from your standard HTML category archives.

12. In the Archive File Template column, for the Monthly Calendar template, paste in the following:

```
<$MTArchiveDate format="cal-%m-%Y"$>.html
```

13. Click Save.

That's it! Whenever you rebuild your monthly archives, or whenever you add a new entry, the monthly events calendar is rebuilt automatically. The calendar filename is based on the month and the year. For example, for the month of May 2002, the calendar filename is *cal-05-2002.html*.

Using the XML-RPC API

Movable Type supports the Blogger XML-RPC API, the metaWeblog XML-RPC API, and several XML-RPC methods of its own. Because of this, you can use client tools such as those described in Chapter 2 to post to your Movable Type blog.

Although the Movable Type web application is more full-featured than any existing desktop clients, there are reasons you might rather use a desktop client for adding or editing entries. For one thing, desktop clients can provide a richer editing environment than a web application: a WYSIWYG editing environment and tools, automatic spell-checking, word counts, and integrated search and replace. Of course, Movable Type offers some of these tools (tools to embolden, italicize, and underline text; search and replace), but as a web application, support for these tools are browser-dependent. And what's more, the speed of response that you might expect from a desktop client is difficult to provide in a web application.

Configuration of the tools will differ slightly depending on the tool. In all cases, however, you will need the same three pieces of information: the XML-RPC Server URL, your Movable Type username, and your Movable Type password. Your Movable Type username and password are simply the username and password that you use to log into the web interface. The XML-RPC Server URL (also called the XML-RPC endpoint) is the URL that you use to access *mt.cgi*, but instead of *mt.cgi* at the end, it's *mt-xmlrpc.cgi*.

For example, if you typically use the URL *http://www.foo.com/cgi-bin/mt/mt.cgi* to access *mt.cgi*, you would use *http://www.foo.com/cgi-bin/mt/mt-xmlrpc.cgi* as the XML-RPC Server URL.

Security Issues

Any application has security issues of which you, the user, should be aware. Because Movable Type is a server-based application, you and your hosting provider should be aware of web server security issues due to running CGI scripts (not just Movable Type, but any CGI script). In addition, as someone who is publishing personal information readable by the entire world, you may be interested in blog security or the ability to create private blogs readable only by your close friends.

Web Server Security

As a web application, Movable Type is more vulnerable to security problems than is a desktop application. The system is a series of CGI scripts. When the web server executes CGI scripts, in most configurations they are executed as a non-privileged user on the system. That is, as a user who does not have privileges to write to files in your home directory, where your web-accessible files are stored. Because Movable Type needs to write files into your directories to publish your blog, you must make some of your files and directories world-writable. This is a security risk on a shared server. The web server user can now write files to your directories but so can any other user on the system! This is a real problem, because most hosting servers are shared between many users.

To prevent this security hole, many providers have installed *cgiwrap* and/or *suexec*. These systems both use the same technique: instead of running CGI scripts as the web server, they run the CGI scripts as you. Because the scripts are running as you, the files and directories that they manage do not have to be world-writable—they need be writable only by you, which they will be anyway, because you created them. When using *cgiwrap*, you usually need to invoke your CGI scripts using a specially formatted URL; *suexec* usage is generally transparent to you. Your hosting provider's support pages should have more information on how to use either of these tools.

When you first run *mt-check.cgi* on your system, you should be able to determine whether or not your server is running *suexec*. When you invoke the CGI script from your browser, the output may contain a line like this:

```
(Probably) Running under cgiwrap or suexec
```

If the output contains this line (which will be under the line beginning "Perl version:"), you will know that your server is set up to use *suexec*. In this case, you should configure Movable Type so that the files and directories it creates are created with the proper permissions (that is, so that they are not world-writable). To do so, follow these steps:

1. Open the file *mt.cfg* in a text editor.

2. Add the following lines at the end of the file:

```
DBUmask 0022
HTMLUmask 0022
UploadUmask 0022
DirUmask 0022
```

3. Save the file.

If your hosting provider does not support running CGI scripts under *cgiwrap* or *suexec*, you may wish to put pressure on them to do so. Ultimately, your provider has the most to lose if the web server is hacked and files are compromised. It is in their best interest to prevent this by installing *cgiwrap* or *suexec*.

Private Blogs

We've covered security on the web server level. But what about security on the blog level? If you post an entry to your blog that you only want certain people to read, how can you control who can access that entry?

Movable Type itself does not possess the functionality to post private entries to your blog and protect them from viewing by anyone other than a select group of people. However, your web server probably does possess this functionality: all web servers implement Basic HTTP authentication, which allows you to set up a list of users who can access specific sections of your site. When a visitor to your site requests a page protected by this form of authentication, the web server firsts tell the user to authenticate himself by entering a username and password. If the username and password match those of a user who you have allowed access to your blog, the web server will then send the protected file to the browser, where it will be displayed like a normal page.

The method of setting up this authentication depends on your web server. With the Apache web server, for example, you use *.htaccess* files to configure the web server and set up password protection. In addition, your hosting provider may have an online control panel that will allow you to set up password protection; you may wish to consult your provider's support manual for more information on setting up a password-protected directory.

To set up password protection using *.htaccess* files, you first need to create a file containing the list of users who can access your blog. You do this using the *htpasswd* command from the command line:

```
% htpasswd -c ~/htpasswd.blog friend
New password: <password>
Re-type new password: <password>
Adding password for user foo
```

This will create a file *htpasswd.blog* in your home directory to set up the user "friend."

The next step is to set up an *.htaccess* file in the private directory, allowing in only the users who you wish to allow to read your blog. In the directory that you wish to make private, create a new file called *.htaccess*, and paste the following text into it:

```
AuthUserFile <path/to/home/directory/htpasswd.blog
AuthName "My Private Blog"
AuthType Basic
Require user friend
```

Once you have saved this file, your blog will be password-protected. When visiting your private blog, visitors will be presented with a standard HTTP authentication dialog, into which they will have to enter one of the usernames that you have allowed in your *.htaccess* file.

Tips and Tricks

Movable Type is a complicated application, and as you may have guessed from some of the sections earlier in this chapter and in Chapter 5, a very powerful application. This section contains some tips and tricks that may not be readily apparent via the Movable Type manual: how to display a random entry from your blog, how to display the last *n* non-consecutive days of entries on your blog, and so on.

Displaying a Random Entry

A common request from users is the ability to display a random entry from their blogs on one of their pages. This can be useful in driving traffic to your site archives. By providing visitors with a teaser of one of your older entries, you could hook them for hours as they trawl through your archives, looking for similar gems.

Because Movable Type produces completely static pages, there is not a built-in set of tags for displaying a random entry on your public site. It is fairly simple, however, to add this feature using a post-processing tool such as PHP or server-side includes. Following is an example of using PHP to include a random entry:

1. Log in to Movable Type and select the blog containing your entries.
2. Click the Templates button to manage your templates.
3. Click on the Create New Index Template link.
4. Set the name of the template to Random Entry Pool, set the Output file to *entry-pool.dump*, and set the body of the template to the following:

```
<MTEntries lastn="100">
<$MTEntryTitle$>
<$MTEntryLink$>
<$MTEntryExcerpt$>
--------
</MTEntries>
```

5. Save the template.

Now that you have created the index template, whenever you post a new entry, the file *entry-pool.dump* will be rebuilt. It will always contain the last 100 entries that you have posted to your blog.

All that is left now is to write a script that will grab a random entry out of the random entry pool (the file *entry-pool.dump*) and display it. This can be done in PHP, Perl, or any other language. Here is a sample PHP solution, which can be pasted directly into your template if you are already using PHP:

```
<?php
$filename = "entry-pool.dump";
$posts = explode('--------', implode('', file($filename)));
srand((double) microtime( ) * 1000000);
list($num, $it) = each($posts);
$it = trim($it);
while (list($num, $line) = each($posts)) {
    $line = trim($line);
    if ($line != '')
        if (rand(0, $num+1) < 1)
            $it = $line;
}
list($title, $url, $excerpt) = explode("\n", $it, 3);
echo "<a href=\"$url\">$title</a> - $excerpt<br />";
?>
```

Displaying the Last N Nonconsecutive Days of Entries

In your blog configuration, you can set the number of days of entries that you'd like to appear on your index template. You can also customize the entries listed using either the days or lastn attributes to <MTEntries>. For example, <MTEntries days=10> will list the last 10 days of entries, and <MTEntries lastn="10"> will list the last 10 entries, no matter when they were posted.

However, suppose that you wish to display the last 10 days on which you actually posted an entry to your blog. This is covered by neither of the above options, but there is a way to do it.

1. Turn on Daily archiving, if you do not already have it turned on; this technique currently requires that you use Daily archiving as one of your archiving methods.

2. In your Index template, instead of using

```
<MTEntries>
...
</MTEntries>
```

where ... is all the markup between the two tags use:

```
<MTArchiveList archive_type="Daily" lastn="10">
<MTEntries>
...
</MTEntries>
</MTArchiveList>
```

3. Save your Index template and rebuild.

This works because `<MTArchiveList archive_type="Daily" lastn="10">` always lists the last 10 days in your archives; and if you use the `<MTEntries>` container within `<MTArchiveList>`, it lists all the entries from that archive page (in this case, all the entries posted on that day).

Blog Locally, Publish Globally

If you have a server account where you do not have the ability to run CGI scripts, you still may be able to use Movable Type to publish your blog. The caveat is that users will not be able to leave comments on your site, because comment functionality requires that the server where you host your site have CGI script access.

To do this, you will need to set up your home computer as a web server, enable CGI scripting, and install the Movable Type application on your own system. Installing a web server on your home computer is beyond the scope of this tutorial, but note that for almost every platform that you may be running, the Apache web server is available to install on your computer. In fact, on many systems (OS X and Linux/Unix systems) it may already be installed. If you are on a Windows system, you can use either IIS or the Windows version of Apache.

Once you have installed your web server, install Movable Type as usual (see Chapter 5). Then use the system as you would if it were installed on your public web server. When you publish your blog, however, you will need to manually copy the files over to your public web server. You can do this by using an FTP client to upload the files. Or, if you have the *rsync* tool installed on both your home computer and on your public server, you can use *rsync* to copy the files. For example:

```
rsync -a -v -essh source username@hostname:destination
```

This command looks complicated, but it is actually fairly straightfoward. *-a* tells *rsync* to run in "archive" mode, meaning that it should try to preserve all the file metadata between the source and the destination. *-v* tells *rsync* to be "verbose" about the operations it takes and the files it transfers. *source*, *username*, *hostname*, and *destination* are what you would expect (*source* and *destination* are directories).

Here is a sample invocation of *rsync*:

```
rsync -a -v -essh /Users/foo/Sites/blog/ bar@myhost:public_html/blog
```

Copying your files using *rsync* will be faster than using FTP, because *rsync* transfers only the pieces of the files that have changed. Thus, using *rsync* means that less data must be sent over the network.

Customizing the Entry-Editing Screen

By default, the entry-editing screen contains all the possible fields that can be associated with an entry: title, extended entry box, excerpt, and so on. This may be overkill for your particular use of Movable Type. For example, if you only use the title, the post status, and the entry body, you might want to display only those fields when editing entries.

Movable Type allows you to customize the fields that appear on the entry-editing screen. When you are on that screen, click the Customize the Display of This Page link. The customization window (Figure 8-7) gives you the option of Basic, Advanced, or Custom configurations. In a Custom configuration, you can choose the exact fields that you would like to appear. Try changing the configuration to Basic by checking the button next to Basic, then clicking Save. You now see a much simpler new entry screen (Figure 8-8).

Using this same technique, you can enable or disable certain fields from appearing by choosing a Custom configuration. You can even choose where to display the button bar with the Delete, Preview, and Save buttons.

Multiple Blogs, One Movable Type Installation

As mentioned earlier in Chapter 5, Movable Type easily supports running multiple blogs on one installation of the system. Running multiple blogs is a good way to create a complicated site containing different sources of content. For example, the site Sew Wrong (*http://www.sewwrong.com*) uses one blog to manage the news section on the main page and another blog to manage the projects (projects themselves are sorted using categories).

To create a new blog, log in to Movable Type, then select the Create a New Blog link. You need to name your blog, and fill in the paths and URLs for the new blog. These values can be determined in the same way as when configuring your first Movable Type blog. See the "Installation Directories" section of Chapter 5 for more

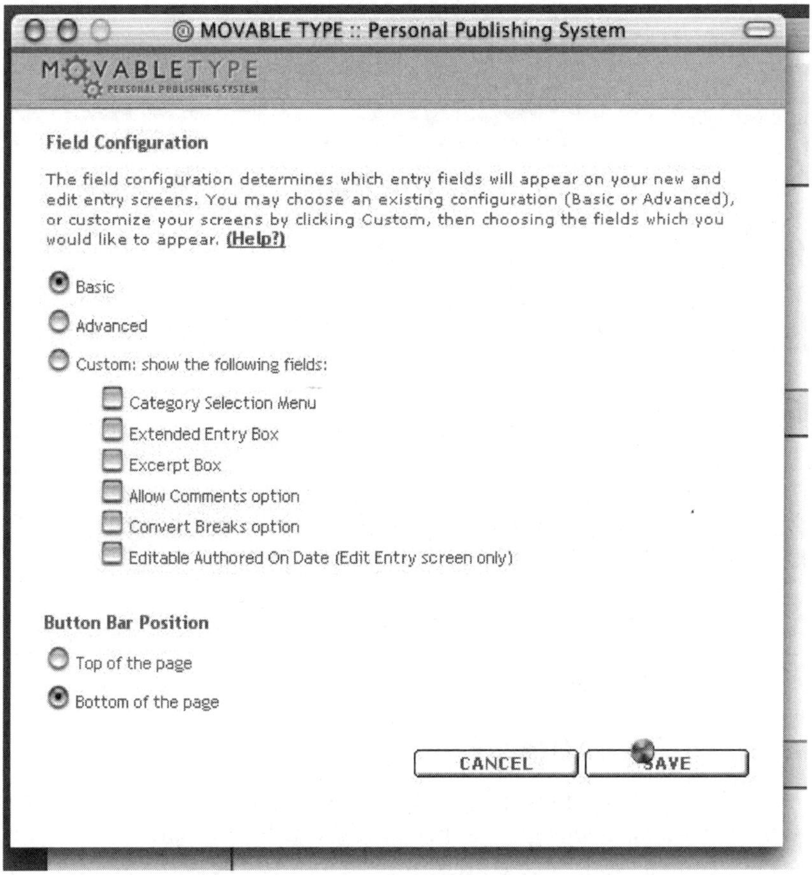

Figure 8-7. Field configuration

information on selecting your blog directories, and the "Configuring Your Blog" section of Chapter 5 for information on setting these values.

For example, if you have a blog whose Local Site Path is currently */home/foo/public_ html/news/*, the Local Site Path for the new blog that you create might be */home/foo/ public_html/projects/*. This might correspond to the URL *http://www.foo.com/ projects/* for your Site URL.

When you create a new blog, you, as the author who created the blog, are given full permissions to the blog. This means that you can post, manage templates, rebuild, edit authors, and so on. Other authors currently in the system will not, by default, be allowed access to the new blog you have created. You can grant permission to existing authors by editing their permissions and associating them with the new blog.

Because you may not wish to grant all your authors the ability to create new blogs in the system, the permission to "create a new blog" can be disabled for an author.

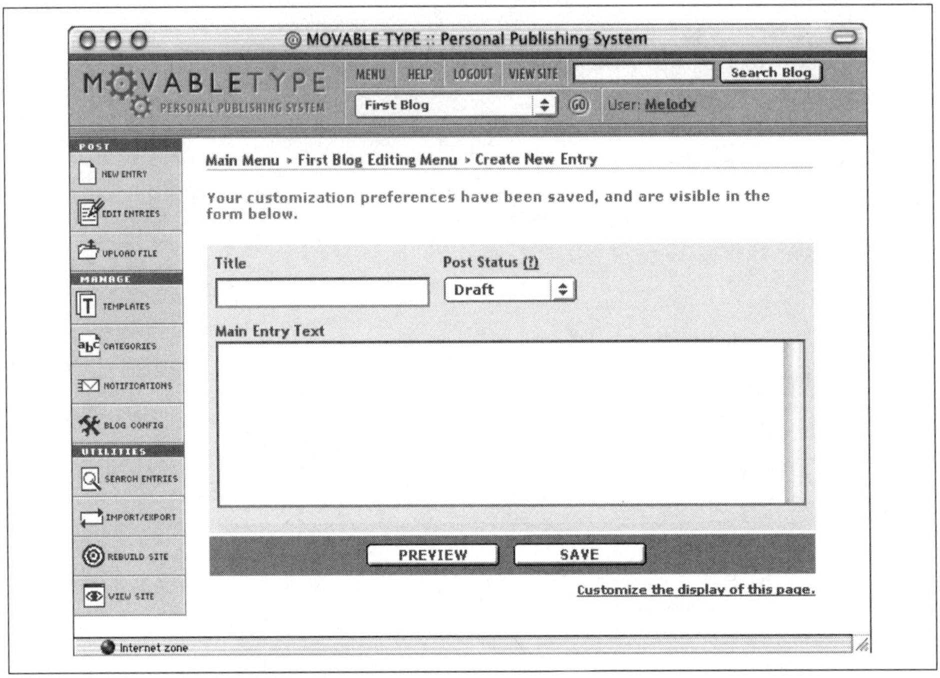

Figure 8-8. Saved customization preferences

Displaying Entries on Other Pages

A common scenario is one in which you have a personal site *http://www.foo.com* and a blog *http://www.foo.com/blog/*. In other words, this is a scenario where your main site does not contain your blog entries; instead you have a separate index of those entries. However, you would like to display the most recent entry from your blog on your main site, to draw visitors into your blog, and to keep your site timely.

You can use Movable Type's index templates to easily distribute your blog content out to different pages of your site, even if those pages are not otherwise connected with the Movable Type system. Index templates are essentially output channels for your content. You can use them to push your blog content into syndicated format (RSS templates), into a pool of entries for random selection ("Displaying a Random Entry," earlier in this section), into your standard site index (your Main Index template), and so on.

To include the most recent entry on your blog in a page unconnected to Movable Type, you first need to set up an index template containing only the most recent entry. (Note that this technique still applies if you would rather display the 2, 3, or however many most recent entries. All that needs to be changed is the number below in the lastn attribute.)

1. Log into Movable Type, and select the blog containing your entries.
2. Click the Templates button to manage your templates.
3. Click on the Create New Index Template link.
4. Set the name of the template to Most Recent Entry, set the Output file to *recent.html*, and set the body of the template to the following:

```
<MTEntries lastn="1">
<a href="<$MTEntryLink$>"><$MTEntryTitle$></a>
<$MTEntryExcerpt$>
</MTEntries>
```

5. Save the template.

This template will produce a small chunk of HTML with your most recent entry, which can then be inserted into another page on your site using server-side includes (SSI), PHP, or another post-processing technology.

For example to include this file in a page using PHP, you would use this code:

```
<?php include('recent.html') ?>
```

To include the file in a page using SSI, use this code:

```
<!--#include virtual="recent.html"-->
```

Whenever you post a new entry to your site, your index templates will be rebuilt, including the Most Recent Entry template. The chunk of HTML will then be dynamically inserted into the main page of your personal site and will thus always reflect the most recent entry on your blog, without any manual work on your part.

More Information

The above tutorials have given you some sense of the power and customization abilities of Movable Type. Of course, there is much more that the system can do. Some of these features were described in the introduction to Chapter 5 and others are described in the online documentation.

The definitive reference guide to Movable Type is the manual, available in the distribution through the Help button in the top navigation. It is also available at *http://www.movabletype.org/docs/mtmanual.html*.

If you are having trouble with the system, support forums are available through *http://www.movabletype.org/support/*.

For some of the features that will be in future versions of Movable Type, see the section of Chapter 5.

CHAPTER 9

Minimalist Blogging with Blosxom

Blosxom (pronounced Blossom) is a lightweight, yet feature-packed, weblog application designed from the ground up with simplicity, usability, and interoperability in mind.

Fundamental is its reliance upon the filesystem—folders and files—as its content database. Blosxom's weblog entries are plain text files. Write from the comfort of your favorite text editor and hit the Save button. Create, edit, rename, and delete entries on the command line, via FTP, WebDAV, or anything else you might use to manipulate your files. There's no import or export; entries are nothing more complex than title on the first line, body being everything thereafter.

Despite its tiny footprint—at the time of this writing, a mere 61 lines of Perl code—Blosxom sports the majority of features one would find in any other weblog application: multiple weblogs under just one installation; multiple authors—anyone with access to the filesystem may be a full-fledged blogger; daily, monthly, and individual entry ("permalink") archives; and RSS content syndication, to name but a few.

Blosxom's simplicity brings with it great flexibility. Customize your weblog's look and feel with any HTML, stylesheets, and the like you're accustomed to using. Incorporate Blosxom output into your existing template or web development framework. Blosxom is simple, straightforward, minimalist Perl affording even the dabbler an opportunity for experimentation and customization. And last, but not least, Blosxom is open source and free for the taking and altering.

Requirements

Designed for use on all operating systems and web servers, Blosxom has little in the way of requirements. You need:

- A web server, running either on your local desktop or an account at your local service provider
- The ability to run CGI scripts

- Perl
- Command-line or FTP access to the server
- To aggregate RSS feeds using Blagg, you also need a command-line application capable of fetching a remote resource over the Internet; typically available are Curl, Lynx, or Wget

Any Internet service or web hosting provider worth its salt makes this base level of functionality available to users.

Downloading

Blosxom lives at *http://www.raelity.org/lang/perl/blosxom/*, the Blosxom home page. Here you'll find the latest happenings on the Blosxom front, release notes, links to related projects, and Blosxom-based blogs of particular interest.

The latest version of the script itself is always available for download at *http://www.raelity.org/lang/perl/blosxom/download/blosxom/*.

Download Blosxom by visiting the Blosxom home page, right-clicking (that's Ctrl-clicking if you're on a Macintosh) the download link and saving the file to your hard drive. Alternately, from the OS X or Unix command line, you can make use of *cURL* or the like and simply say:

```
% curl -O http://www.raelity.org/lang/perl/blosxom/downloads/blosxom
```

With the ubiquitous *wget*:

```
% wget http://www.raelity.org/lang/perl/blosxom/downloads/blosxom
```

Or via the Lynx text-based web browser:

```
% lynx -source  http://www.raelity.org/lang/perl/blosxom/downloads/blosxom  > blosxom
```

Installing Blosxom

Now that you have Blosxom, you're just a few short steps away from your first blog entry. Customizing Blosxom for your particular environment requires just a couple of simple configuration changes. Open the *blosxom* script in your favorite text editor.

First make sure the first line of the script (`#!/usr/bin/perl -w`) correctly identifies the location of your Perl interpreter. If you're unsure and have access to the command line, type:

```
% which perl
/usr/local/bin/perl
```

Copy and paste the resulting output after the #! in the *blosxom* script (e.g., `#!/usr/local/bin/perl -w`). If you don't have access to the command line, ask your service provider or system administrator for help. Be sure there's no space between the #! and the path to Perl.

About the only thing Blosxom really needs to know is where you keep your blog entries. Change the $datadir line from:

```
my $datadir = '/Library/WebServer/Documents/blosxom';
```

to the appropriate directory path. For Mac OS X and Unix users, we recommend something alongside your web server's document directory:

```
my $datadir = '/Library/WebServer/Data/blosxom';
```

or:

```
my $datadir = '/usr/local/apache/data/blosxom';
```

Under Windows, somewhere like:

```
my $datadir = 'c:\Inetpub\wwwdata\blosxom';
```

If you'll be running Blosxom on your service provider's web server, somewhere in your home directory will do nicely:

```
my $datadir = '/home/sam/blosxom';
```

Wherever you choose, just be sure the directory is readable by the web server.

That said, you probably don't want to put Blosxom's data anywhere web-accessible (your server's document root or *public_html* directory). While, of course, your entries will end up being publicly viewable anyway, you may want to keep drafts or other assorted files that might end up in your Blosxom directory private.

Save the *blosxom* script, then move the it to your *cgi-bin* or other directory out of which you're able to run CGI scripts.

Mac OS X
  /Library/WebServer/CGI-Executables

Unix with typical Apache installation
  /usr/local/apache/cgi-bin

Windows
  `c:\Inetpub\wwwroot\Cgi-bin`

Fairly typical service provider's web server
  /home/sam/public_html/cgi-bin

You can do this either via your operating system's graphical file manager or on the command line; if your CGI directory were */home/sam/public_html/cgi-bin/*, you'd say:

```
% mv blosxom /home/sam/public_html/cgi-bin
```

You may need to rename the *blosxom* script to *blosxom.cgi* so it's recognized by your web server as a CGI script. Again, you can do this via graphical file manager or on the command line:

```
% cd /home/sam/public_html/cgi-bin
% mv blosxom blosxom.cgi
```

Make sure your web server has permission to run the *blosxom.cgi* script by saying:

```
% chmod 755 blosxom.cgi
```

Note: Permissions vary from situation to situation; if you're unsure, ask your local administrator or service provider. That said, 755 is a reasonably safe bet.

Next, create the directory you specified as the `$datadir` to hold your blog entries. This directory and its contents must be readable (writable is not necessary) by the web server. If you chose */home/sam/blosxom*, for instance, you'd say:

```
% mkdir /home/sam/blosxom
% chmod 755 /home/sam/blosxom
```

Your Blosxom weblog is ready to go.

Optional Configuration Directives

Blosxom has a few optional configuration directives that might be worth your while to set. These are in the same Configuration section of the Blosxom CGI script as the `$datadir` directive you set just a moment ago.

Your weblog's title and description are used in outgoing RSS feeds for syndication. Set them by changing the `$blog_title` and `$blog_description` variables as follows:

```
# What's this blog's title?
my $blog_title = 'My Blosxoms';
# What's this blog's description?
my $blog_description = 'Not your garden variety Blosxom blog.';
#What's this blog's primary language (for outgoing RSS feed)?
my $blog_language = 'en';
```

Entries are presented on your weblog's home page in reverse-chronological order, with the latest rising to the top and older entries falling off the bottom. Control how many appear by setting the `$num_entries` directive:

```
# How many entries should I show on the home page?
my $num_entries = 40;
```

Blogging

Blogging with Blosxom is no more complex than editing a text file from the comfort of your favorite text editor—be it BBEdit, Notepad, Emacs, or Word. No cramped, featureless, browser-based checkboxes here!

Weblog entries themselves are rather free form. The only rule is that the first line becomes the entry's title, so keep it short and sweet. Format the rest of the entry to your heart's content using text and garden-variety HTML.

When you're ready to publish your new blog entry, simply save it to Blosxom's data directory, the location you specified in the `$datadir` configuration directive during installation. Name it anything you'd like, as long as it ends with *.txt*, a hint to Blosxom that it's to be picked up and included in your weblog.

Let's give it a whirl, shall we? Fire up your favorite text editor and type something inspired like:

```
First Post
Howdy, and welcome to my Blosxom blog.
```

Save the file as *first.txt* to Blosxom's data directory.

To get the full effect, create another entry and save it as *second.txt*.

```
Second Post
It worked twice in a row; we certainly are off to a good start :)
```

That's all there is to it.

 Here's a helpful hint: save partially complete drafts with a *.txt-* extension, ensuring Blosxom won't pick them up until you're ready. When you're ready to publish, rename the entries with *.txt*.

Viewing Your Blog

Point your web browser at the Blosxom CGI script. If you're running Blosxom on your local machine, the URL will probably be something like: *http://localhost/cgi-bin/blosxom.cgi/*. On a service provider's web server, you'll most likely find Blosxom at *http://www.myprovider.com/~sam/cgi-bin/blosxom.cgi/*, where *myprovider.com* is your provider's domain and *sam* is your username.

If all goes as planned, you should see something along the lines of Figure 9-1, your first two blog entries in Blosxom's default look and feel—such as it is.

Each day begins with the date, followed by weblog entries for that day in reverse-chronological order—the latest entries rise to the top. Each entry consists of a title, body, time of posting, and a permalink (the # bit) to the entry itself for easy reference.

The look and feel is completely customizable (see the "Customizing and Styling" section later in this chapter).

The Archives

Of course, pointing at your weblog's URL provides only the latest view with only the last few postings. Blosxom provides automatic virtual archives for your posts as well.

Appending a slash, the four-digit year, another slash, and the three-letter month abbreviation or two-digit month number transports you back to a particular month. For example, appending */2002/May* displays only entries for May 2002, */1999/01* those for January 1999.

Figure 9-1. Viewing your blog

Appending to the month view yet another slash, followed by the two-digit day (padding the 1st through the 9th with a 0), displays entries for a particular day. For instance, /2002/May/22 shows entries for May 22, 2002, /1999/Jan/01 those for New Years Day, 1999.

To zoom in on a single entry, append a slash, pound (#), and the entry's filename without the .txt extension. Thus, /2002/05/22#second or /2002/May/22#second displays entries for May 22nd and scrolls down to the "second" blog entry—the contents of the file, second.txt (see Figure 9-2). The URL for a specific entry is known as the entry's permalink and is the preferred form of referring to an entry rather than the day as a whole or the weblog's home page.

Editing and Deleting Entries

Because a blog entry is nothing more than a text file, editing is just a matter of opening it back up in a text editor, making whatever changes are needed, and saving. Deleting is equally simple; delete an entry's text file and it's gone.

One note of caution: editing an entry alters its file's modification date, used by Blosxom to determine under which date to display it. So editing yesterday's entry today means that it now shows up under today's date in your weblog.

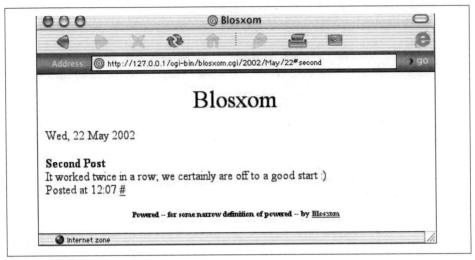

Figure 9-2. Viewing a particular entry by its permalink URL

Creating Another Weblog

Blosxom supports any number of weblogs from a single Blosxom installation. Until now, you've been editing the default weblog, placing entries into the main data directory. Additional weblogs are just subdirectories, completely independent of the default weblog and any sibling weblogs.

Let's create a new weblog on gardening. Create a new directory named *gardening* under your specified $datadir, whether via your graphical file manager, FTP, or on the command line. For instance, if your $datadir were */home/sam/blosxom*, on the command line, type:

```
% cd /home/sam/blosxom
% mkdir gardening
```

You can name a weblog just about anything you wish. The only restrictions are that weblogs must begin with a letter and contain only letters and numbers (e.g. yetanotherblog, blog2, SamIAm, gardening).

Blog as usual, saving all entries meant for your new gardening weblog in the *gardening* subdirectory. To view your gardening weblog, point your browser at the same URL as before, and append */gardening* as shown in Figure 9-3.

Repeat these steps for any number of weblogs, saving entries to the appropriate directory, and appending the blog name to that of the Blosxom script.

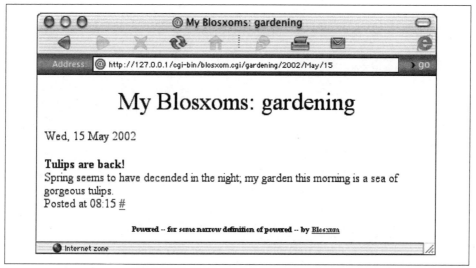

Figure 9-3. Gardening weblog entries for May 15, 2002

Syndicating with RSS

Blosxom makes creating an RSS feed a snap. Blosxom keeps the RSS representation at your weblog's URL suffixed by *?flav=rss*. You can point your browser at this (see Figure 9-4) but it's most useful as fodder for aggregators or syndication services.

Appending *?flav=rss* to any Blosxom URL—default blog, particular blog, even month or day archive view—gives an RSS representation of that blog. For example, the following URL produces an RSS view of April 1, 2002, on your gardening blog:

> *http://example.com/~sam/cgi-bin/blosxom.cgi/gardening/2002/Apr/01?flav=rss*

Customizing and Styling

Blosxom's default style is more than a little drab, and purposefully so in the hope it will influence you to add your own look and feel. This section shows you how to do that.

First, let's do away with that rather flat header and silly footer. In your text or HTML editor, create a new file containing any HTML you wish to add to the top of the document, before the actual weblog entries themselves. This might be a masthead, your site's standard toolbar, or simply a nicer looking title. Save the file to the $datadir directory as *head.html*. Example 9-1 shows a sample custom header.

Figure 9-4. An RSS representation of the default blog

Example 9-1. A custom header

```
<html>
<head>
<title>My First Blosxom</title>
<link rel=stylesheet type="text/css" href="/blogbook.css">
</head>
<body bgcolor="#ffffff" text="#333333" link="#000000"
alink="#000000" vlink="#000000">
<table border="0" width="100%" cellpadding="0" cellspacing="0">
 <tr>
  <td colspan="3">
   <span class="title">My First Blosxom</span>
  </td>
 </tr>
 <tr>
  <td colspan="9" bgcolor="#000000" height="1" ></td>
 </tr>

<tr valign="top">
 <td bgcolor="#dddddd" width="15"></td>
 <td bgcolor="#dddddd" width="100%">
  <br />
```

Do the same for the HTML to be displayed after the weblog entries. Save the file as *foot.html*. Example 9-2 shows HTML for a custom footer.

Example 9-2. A custom footer

```
<br />
  </td>
  <td bgcolor="#dddddd" width="15"></td>
 </tr>
 <tr>
  <td colspan="9" bgcolor="#000000" height="1"></td>
 </tr>
 <tr>
  <td colspan="3" align="right">
   Powered by
   <a href="http://www.raelity.org/lang/perl/blosxom/">Blosxom</a>
  </td>
 </tr>
</table>
</body>
</html>
```

The above pairing of *head.html* and *foot.html* dresses up the default weblog quite nicely, as shown in Figure 9-5.

Figure 9-5. Custom header and footer HTML

Now let's change the default font. You can apply HTML and CSS stylesheet magic, not only to your weblog's header and footer but also to the individual entries and daily date-stamps as well. A Blosxom entry's HTML looks something like Example 9-3 by default.

Example 9-3. Blosxom's default weblog entry format

```
...
<SPAN CLASS="blosxomDate">Wed, 22 May 2002</SPAN>
<p class="blosxomEntry">
<a name="second"><span class="blosxomTitle"><b>Second Post</b></span></a>
<br />
<span class="blosxomBody">It worked twice in a row; we certainly are off to a good start :
)</span>
<br />
<span class="blosxomTime">Posted at 12:07</span>
<a href="http://127.0.0.1/cgi-bin/blosxom.cgi/2002/May/22#second">#</a>
</p>
...
```

You'll notice standard CSS class calling for: blosxomEntry, blosxomTitle, blosxomBody, and blosxomTime. By pulling in a CSS stylesheet containing style definitions for these classes, you can control the look of weblog entries. Example 9-4 is the custom header from Example 9-1 with an inline stylesheet to change the entry font.

Example 9-4. A custom header with style

```
<html>
<head>
<title>My First Blosxom</title>
<!--<link rel=stylesheet type="text/css" href="/blogbook.css">-->
<style>
body,td { font-family: Verdana,Geneva,Arial,Sans-serif;
          font-size: 11px; color: #666666; }
a { text-decoration: none; }
.title { font-size: 12pt; font-weight: bold; color: #336699; }
.blosxomDate {font-weight: bold; color: #336699; }
.blosxomTitle { font-weight: bold; color: #000000; }
.blosxomTime { text-decoration: italicize; color: #336699; }
</style>
</head>
...
```

Figure 9-6 shows the result of Example 9-4.

Should you wish to go beyond CSS for altering the appearance of weblog entries, you can override the default template (see Example 9-3) and define your own using HTML and CSS, again in the form of a text file, *story.html*, saved to the *$datadir* directory. Example 9-5 subtly tweaks the default, bolding and underlining the title, removing the "Posted at" bit, and replaces the "#" with "permalink," as seen in Figure 9-7.

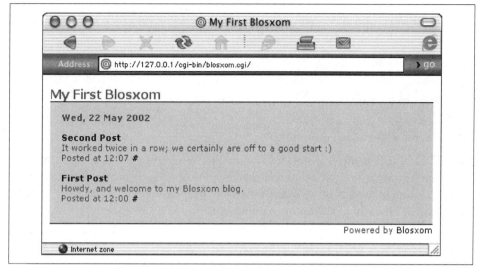

Figure 9-6. A little CSS style

Example 9-5. A custom entry format

```
<p class="blosxomEntry">
<a name="$fn">
<span class="blosxomTitle"><b><u>$title</u></b></span>
</a>
  
<span class="blosxomBody">$body</span>
<br />
<span class="blosxomTime">
$ti | <a href="$url/$yr/$mo/$da/$fn">permalink</a>
</span>
</p>
```

> **Second Post** It worked twice in a row; we certainly are off to a good start :)
> 12:07 | permalink
>
> **First Post** Howdy, and welcome to my Blosxom blog.
> 12:00 | permalink

Figure 9-7. Custom entry formatting

All the $-prepended components are variables provided by Blosxom for use in your *story.html* template. They are:

$fn

    The entry's filename

$title

    The entry's title

`$body`

   The entry's body

`$ti`

   Time of posting

`$url`

   The weblog's base URL

`$yr/$mo/$da`

   Year, month, and day of posting

In addition to the header, footer, CSS, and entry templating support Blosxom provides natively, you always have standard additional options available. You can pull a weblog's content into a server-parsed (*.shtml*) page using SSI, have your content management system pull in Blosxom output, and so on.

Aggregating RSS with Blagg

Blagg (short for Blossom Aggregator) affords Blosxom the ability to aggregate (i.e., read and blog) RSS syndicated feeds of many flavors (0.9, 0.91, 0.92, 1.0) via a simple, command-line interface. Blagg builds on the simple, lightweight framework of Blosxom, interspersing aggregated stories amongst original entries.

Blagg is maintained as a separate project from Blosxom, because while it was designed with Blosxom in mind and is indeed fully integrated, it has its own place as the basis for just about anything needing a simple, lightweight RSS reader/aggregator. Indeed, this is already the case: via plugins (Blaggplugs), Blagg is able to push aggregated RSS to email recipients, instant messenger buddies, and to weblog software such as of MovableType and Blogger.

Blagg has two modes: interactive and automatic. Interactive mode occurs when Blagg is run from the command line. It picks up, displays, and prompts you for inclusion of individual stories from elsewhere into your weblog.

The automatic mode is designed to be run untended on a regular basis from a service such as *cron*. The aggregator simply drops new stories from your favorite feeds into your weblog. One use of automatic aggregation is to create a "daily dose" of your favorite feeds in one place to be read at your leisure. A group of like-minded individuals could produce a weblog composed of entries from their individual weblogs. An author can have her main weblog reflect the writing she does across various sites and weblogs.

Requirements

Blagg doesn't need much—not even an XML-parser, for those of you who know what that means. It has only a single requirement on top of Blosxom: a command-line application capable of fetching a remote resource over the Internet; *cURL*, *Lynx*, and *wget* are good good choices.

Check for the availability of one or more of these applications—if you're running Mac OS X or some form of Unix—by typing *which* for each in turn on the command line:

```
% which curl
which: no curl in (/usr/local/bin...
% which lynx
which: no curl in (/usr/local/bin...
% which wget
/usr/bin/wget
```

Windows users can pick up a precompiled version of *wget* at:

ftp://sunsite.dk/projects/wget/windows/

Downloading

Blagg lives at *http://www.raelity.org/lang/perl/blagg/*, the Blagg home page. The latest version of the script itself is always available for download at *http://www.raelity.org/lang/perl/blagg/download/blagg*.

Download Blagg by visiting the Blagg home page, right-clicking (that's Ctrl-clicking, if you're on a Macintosh) the download link, and saving the file to your hard drive. Alternately, from the OS X or Unix command line, you can use the application Blagg will be using to grab remote RSS files. Here's how to use *wget* from the command line to download Blagg:

```
% wget http://www.raelity.org/lang/perl/blagg/downloads/blagg
--23:55:10-- http://www.oreillynet.com/%7Erael/lang/perl/blagg/downloads/blagg
           => `blagg'
Connecting to www.oreillynet.com:80... connected!
HTTP request sent, awaiting response... 200 OK
Length: 3,347 [text/plain]
    OK -> ...                                            [100%]
23:55:10 (272.38 KB/s) - `blagg' saved [3347/3347]
```

Installing Blagg

Blagg setup is all but identical to that of Blosxom—simply open the *blagg* script in your favorite text editor and adjust a few lines.

First make sure the first line of the script (#!/usr/bin/perl -w) correctly identifies the location of your Perl interpreter. This will be the same as it was in the earlier section "Installing Blosxom."

Blagg needs to know the location of your Blosxom install's data directory. Copy the $datadir line from *blosxom.cgi* and paste it in place of the default:

```
my $datadir = "/Library/WebServer/Documents/blosxom";
```

Specify which command-line application you'd like Blagg to use (the one you found in "Requirements" earlier) to retrieve remote RSS documents by changing as appropriate:

```
my $get_prog = 'curl';
```

Mac OS X users can leave the line as it is:

```
my $get_prog = 'curl';
```

Unix users should find either *lynx* or *wget* close at hand:

```
my $get_prog = '-source';
```

or:

```
my $get_prog = ' wget --quiet -O -;
```

Windows users, if you grabbed a precompiled version of *wget*, should use:

```
my $get_prog = ' wget --quiet -O -;
```

Save the *blagg* script. You won't want to put the *blagg* script anywhere beneath your web server's directory; it should live in your home directory or wherever you would usually put executables—a *bin* directory under your home directory is always a good place. Ensure that the *blagg* script is executable with:

```
% chmod 700 blagg
```

Configuring

First, you need to tell Blagg about your favorite RSS feeds. Fire up your favorite text editor and create an RSS datafile (*rss.dat*) consisting of one line per feed like so:

```
nickname  URL  [interactive or automatic]
```

These are broken down as follows:

Nickname
> A short alphanumeric nickname for the feed (e.g., raelitybytes). This nickname is prepended to the filenames of all aggregated entries (e.g., *raelitybytes.a_title. txt*).

URL
> The URL of the RSS feed to aggregate (e.g., *http://www.raelity.org?flav=rss*).

interactive or automatic
> Whether this feed should be aggregated interactively (on the command line, story by story) or automatically (on a regular basis, blogging each and every story).

Example 9-6 shows a sample *rss.dat* file that automatically blogs anything it finds on the Reality Bytes weblog, yet prompts interactively for particular stories to blog from the Boing Boing weblog.

Example 9-6. A sample rss.dat file

```
raelitybytes  http://www.raelity.org?flav=rss    automatic
boingboing  http://www.newsisfree.com/HPE/xml/feeds/33/2733.xml  interactive
```

Save the RSS datafile as *rss.dat* in your main Blosxom $datadir or subdirectory of the weblog into which you'd like to aggregate these feeds. You can add, edit, or remove feed entries at any time simply be reediting the *rss.dat* file.

Running Blagg

Blagg may be run in either interactive or automatic mode, aggregating only feeds of the same mode in your *rss.dat* file. When run in interactive mode, Blagg ignores all feeds marked as automatic and vice versa.

Interactive Blagging

To run Blagg interactively on the Mac OS X or Unix command line, type:

```
./blagg -mode=interactive
```

Under Windows, type:

```
perl blagg -mode=interactive
```

Blagg starts up, fetches each feed in turn, and asks whether you'd like to blog each story in turn. Type y for yes, n for no, or q to quit, and press the Enter key.

Figure 9-8 shows Blagg aggregating the BoingBoing feed interactively.

Figure 9-9 shows the annotated ETCON item alongside the previous two weblog entries. Notice Blagg automatically adds a parenthesized (link), linking to the original weblog entry on BoingBoing and bracketed [bOing bOing], linking to the source of the entry, the BoingBoing weblog itself.

Automatic Blagging

To run Blagg automatically on the Mac OS X or Unix command line, type:

```
./blagg -mode=automatic
```

Under Windows, type:

```
blagg -mode=automatic
```

Blagg starts up, fetches each feed in turn, and quietly adds new stories it finds to your weblog.

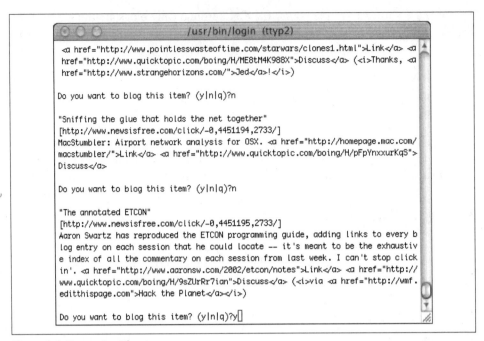

```
      /usr/bin/login (ttyp2)
<a href="http://www.pointlesswasteoftime.com/starwars/clones1.html">Link</a> <a
href="http://www.quicktopic.com/boing/H/ME8tM4K988X">Discuss</a> (<i>Thanks, <a
href="http://www.strangehorizons.com/">Jed</a>!</i>)


Do you want to blog this item? (y|n|q)?n


"Sniffing the glue that holds the net together"
[http://www.newsisfree.com/click/-0,4451194,2733/]
MacStumbler: Airport network analysis for OSX. <a href="http://homepage.mac.com/
macstumbler/">Link</a> <a href="http://www.quicktopic.com/boing/H/pFpYnxxurKqS">
Discuss</a>


Do you want to blog this item? (y|n|q)?n


"The annotated ETCON"
[http://www.newsisfree.com/click/-0,4451195,2733/]
Aaron Swartz has reproduced the ETCON programming guide, adding links to every b
log entry on each session that he could locate -- it's meant to be the exhaustiv
e index of all the commentary on each session from last week. I can't stop click
in'. <a href="http://www.aaronsw.com/2002/etcon/notes">Link</a> <a href="http://
www.quicktopic.com/boing/H/9sZUrRr7ian">Discuss</a> (<i>via <a href="http://wmf.
editthispage.com">Hack the Planet</a></i>)


Do you want to blog this item? (y|n|q)?y[]
```

Figure 9-8. Interactive Blagging

Figure 9-9. Interactively aggregated story

Figure 9-10 shows a new story on Andy Oram appearing just after the annotated ETCON story.

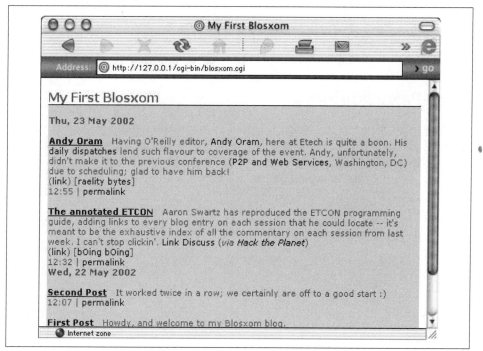

Figure 9-10. Automatically aggregated story

Blagging to Other Blogs

You can use Blagg to aggregate items in weblogs other than the default Blosxom weblog. By adding a -blog=gardening command-line switch, you can can instruct Blagg to read the *rss.dat* file in the *gardening* subdirectory under $datadir and blog any entries to your gardening weblog rather than initial weblog.

So if there were an *rss.dat* file in *$datadir/gardening* to contain a feed or three, you would interactively aggregate items to the gardening blog like so:

```
./blagg -mode=interactive -blog=gardening
```

Under the Hood

If you're curious about what's going on under the hood, it's actually rather simple. For every aggregated story, Blagg simply borrows a slightly fiddled-with version of the title (replacing all but alphanumeric characters with underscores and shortening the whole thing), prepends the feed's nickname specified in the *rss.dat* file, and pops a *.txt* extension to the end. The two aggregated items in Figure 9-10 are stored as:

```
boingboing.The_annotated_E...ETCON.txt
raelitybytes.Andy_Oram..._Oram.txt
```

Each time Blagg is run, it makes sure it doesn't already have a copy of a particular story from a particular source by checking it against the filename.

Third-Party Additions

In addition to Blosxom and Blagg themselves, users and fans have created various ports, hacks, mods, associated applications, plug-ins (Blaggplugs), tips, and tricks. Keep up to date on the latest releases and other goings on at *http://www.raelity.org/lang/perl/blosxom/*, the Blosxom home page.

CHAPTER 10

Blogging Voices

Simplest piece of advice that I was given by a former boss can be easily applied to ANY blog.

> "Re-read before you publish."

Electronic text can expose unintended meaning easily and it will also make what you say a lot more focused. If nothing else, it should help you catch spelling mistakes!

—Gordon McLean, *http://www.snowgoon.co.uk*

As well as utilizing the number of links pointing at a page to determine its overall relevance, Google also places a high emphasis on words used in title and header tags to determine its PageRank. This can sometimes have unintended consequences.

Here in the UK, a popular TV show called "Pop Idol" gripped the nation's imagination, including mine. Every week we would tune in, and vote for our favourite "Pop Idol," with the lowest-polling contestant being eliminated from the next round. After many, many weeks and a nail-biting final, I posted a (somewhat embarrassing) entry to my online journal entitled, "Will Young Wins Pop Idol 2002."

For a couple of weeks, nothing unusual happened. My friends posted a few sarcastic comments, light banter was exchanged, and everything (including my critical faculties) slowly returned to normal.

That was to be the lull before the storm. Almost two weeks after the previous-last comment was posted, came this message:

> "We all think Will is gorgeous and Chloe wants to marry him!! He has a brilliant original voice and we r gona be buying the single."

This was to be the pebble that began the avalanche. For some reason, Google had ranked my posting one place higher than the official Will Young web site, and the screaming hordes descended.

After a month or so of, "will i luv uuuuuuuuuuu" comments, my page dropped off the first page of results and (much to my relief) the postings finally came to an end. But it certainly goes to show that however few people actually visit your blog on a regular basis, you can end up being swamped in the most unexpected ways.

—Chris Carline, *http://chris.carline.org*

My blog's not all that special. I'm not an "A-lister," but my readership is decent enough—a small community of friends and a few people I don't know personally. However, one of my entries seemed to really start a fire and draw a crowd: *http://www. laze.net/fait/archive/2001_05_01_archive.php#3850765/*.

In this entry, I discuss a random charge to my credit card by "PORNOTHERAPY. NET." When I searched on the Web for information about this "company," there was nothing to be found. However, Google spidered my site shortly after I posted my experience and hosts of people started flocking to my blog entry, sharing their experiences, their hypotheses about how our credit card numbers were stolen, and who they thought was responsible (*http://www.laze.net/fait/comments.php?3850765/*). The domain was traced to an "Alex Perman," and one visitor even went so far as to post pictures to his web site of the address that was listed on the domain's WHOIS record. It amazed me how a simple entry on my blog, one that wasn't any more or less notable than any others on my site, managed to draw such a crowd. It sparked a mini-militia.

While the mystery of Alex Perman and Pornotherapy.net/Sexmedic.org was never really solved, that one entry showed me the power of blogging: random communities forming around common experiences to solve a problem. Pretty impressive, really.

—Ryan A. MacMichael, *http://www.laze.net/fait/*

Blogging isn't just a weblog. It is a way to share your opinions and thoughts to the rest of the world. If you post interesting things, share links with other bloggers, and post comments on other blogs. Linking is the way of the Web, that is the key to successful blogging.

—Greg Hard, *http://www.tssaddicts.com*

You maintain a weblog because it interests you, not because there is an audience for it. If you do it because people are watching you, then what you do is not weblogging. Just playing a musical instrument where you can play for the enjoyment of it and you can play for others to listen to, but they are different activities.

That being said if you do have an audience, then treat them well and they will treat you well.

—Lindsay Marshall, *http://catless.ncl.ac.uk/Lindsay/weblog/latest.html*

As Dave Winer says, it's the two-way-web. Blogging really enables me to have a conversation with an audience, with feedback via comments and mail.

In February of 2002, I decided I'd like my blog audience to be able to contact me more directly. I considered publishing my instant messaging ID, but I didn't want to constrain my audience to using the same system as me; I also didn't want to have to maintain too many persistent IM buddy relationships.

I solved the issue by building a small browser based chat window and embedding it right in my blog. People can come and visit my blog, and if I'm online, chat directly with me. I like to say that where my web site used to be a brochure about me, it's now a tradeshow booth. You can come through and browse the articles, and if I'm there, talk to me directly.

During the development process, I met a ton of people who came to chat with me and help to guide the development itself. Since then, I've met hundreds of bloggers and browsers, and it's done wonders to get me closer in touch with the community.

—Brent Ashley, *http://brentashley.blogchat.com*

To the new blogger wanting to gather a general audience: be mindful of your readers. By mindful, I mean that the visual display of text shouldn't scare anyone off. Don't tyP3 L1K3 th15!! Keep the text readable with contrasting (but not distracting) colors, use adequate sized fonts, make sure lines don't scrunch together, and try to exercise proper punctuation practices. You don't want to annoy/confuse newcomers. Or if you do, that's fine: just remember that visitors will usually scramble to find a nicer looking page immediately without ever looking back.

Writing style is another matter. Anything goes, but it never hurts to be somewhat engaging. Try to treat each new entry as an improvement in clarifying your voice: the more individuality you put in—avoid lumping detail after detail in endless lists, rants, outpourings, etc.—the greater the chance that readers will get to know you and wait on the edge of their seats for your next story or bit of wisdom.

Even after all is said and done, your readership may never grow big. No worries. You have to do this for yourself first. All that other junk is for if you want to put on a good show for the little window you're opening into your life.

Myself, I put up an online journal to record and share my thoughts. It's interesting (and embarrassing) to see my mentality just a few months before, the stretches of days of whining, moping, etc. Aside from the memories, I think it's helped to improve my writing a bit. A handful of folks have also taken interest in what I have to say; to their credit, I think they're just bored.

—Kaiser Shahid, *http://www.phrogger.com/kaiser/*

My genealogy blog has provided some neat experiences. I've found a number of cousins I wouldn't have normally found through the blog. By publishing the names of my ancestors and the villages they came from, I've made contact with relatives all over America and in Poland as well. One woman in Poznan, Poland, searched the Web for the name of the small village she came from, found it on my blog, realized that she knew my grandmother's late sister who had moved to the village after World War II, and contacted me with a note from that sister's daughters, my mother's first cousins, who the family had lost contact with some years ago. The blog makes fantastic search engine fodder.

—Ralph Brandi, *http://www.thereisnocat.com/*

After reading—and reading—about weblogs for a number of months, I decided the best way to learn about this fascinating subset of the Internet was simply to start a blog myself. One of the first things I realized was how a handful of companies—people, really—had developed amazingly sophisticated yet simple tools to enable personal publishing for so many. The second thing I realized was that the blogging community truly is a community in all the best senses of the word. When I needed help, it was there. When I had questions, they were answered. Not to mention encouragement, virtual pats on the back, advice...and meaningful, challenging interaction.

Blogging also has helped me to rediscover my voice again, both personally and professionally. Putting yourself (your opinions, thoughts, ideas, etc.) out there every day will do that to you. And learning the technologies (CSS, template-driven web sites, RSS, XML, various APIs, third-party tool integration, etc.) couldn't have come at a more opportune time. I had been feeling ho-hum about most things Internet, but the world of weblogs has reinvigorated my sense of enthusiasm for the medium.

—Ed Murray, *http://www.edmurray.org*

Shortly after the Sept 11 attack in NY, I blogged about how angry I was with the "Islamic militants," and how I would give support to USA, regardless of its stand. And all of a sudden, my blog was invaded by Muslims who were angry with me for supporting the US. Such an experience was more of a chiller than neat. It made me realize that the Web is not as decentralized nor empty as it seemed. While I seldom let my online persona interfere with my person offline, the type of response I got from people who'd read my blog actually strengthened my support for the US, to the extent that I started wearing a US flag bandana and carried a bag similarly decorated to school. At the end of the day, I learnt that a certain extent of self-censorship is inevitable. Unless, your blog is like totally anonymous, it'd be wiser to practice some sort of self-censorship, especially when the blogging community in your state is small.

Blogging advice:

Don't tell your boyfriend/girlfriend about your blog, unless you keep absolutely nothing from each other. I've gotten into trouble countless times when my boyfriend reads about something "off-limit" in my blog, like the time I commented that I was picked to do a project with the cutest guy in class, he went off his rockers.

—Lyndy, *http://lyndy.org*

I consume, digest, and excrete information for a living. Whether I'm writing science fiction, editorials, columns, or tech books, whether I'm speaking from a podium or yammering down the phone at some poor reporter, my success depends on my ability to cite and connect disparate factoids at just the right moment.

As a committed infovore, I need to eat roughly six times my weight in information every day or my brain starts to starve and atrophy. I gather information from many sources: print, radio, television, conversation, the Web, RSS feeds, email, chance, and serendipity. I used to bookmark this stuff, but I just ended up with a million bookmarks that I never revisited and could never find anything in.

Theoretically, you can annotate your bookmarks, entering free-form reminders to yourself so that you can remember why you bookmarked this page or that one. I don't know about you, but I never actually got around to doing this—it's one of those get-to-it-later eat-your-vegetables best-practice housekeeping tasks like defragging your hard drive or squeegeeing your windshield that you know you should do but never get around to.

Until I started blogging. Blogging gave my knowledge-grazing direction and reward. Writing a blog entry about a useful and/or interesting subject forces me to extract the salient features of the link into a two- or three-sentence elevator pitch to my readers, whose decision to follow a link is predicated on my ability to convey its interestingness to them. This exercise fixes the subjects in my head the same way that taking notes at a lecture does, putting them in reliable and easily-accessible mental registers.

Blogging also provides an incentive to keep blogging. As Boing Boing's hit-counter rises steadily, growing 10–30 percent every month, I get a continuous, low-grade stream of brain-rewards; rewards that are reinforced by admiring email, cross-links from other blogs that show up in my referrer logs, stories that I broke climbing the ranks on Daypop and Blogdex (and getting picked up by major news outlets). The more I blog, the more reward I generate. Strangers approach me at conferences and tell me how much they liked some particular entry; people whose sites I've pointed to send me grateful email thanking me for bringing their pet projects to the attention of so many people.

Blogging begets blogging. I blog because I'm in the business of locating and connecting interesting things. Operating a popular blog gives people an incentive to approach me with interesting things of their own devising or discovery, for inclusion on Boing Boing. The more I blog, the more of these things I get, as other infovores toss choice morsels over my transom. The feedback loop continues on Boing Boing's message boards, where experts and amateurs debate and discuss the stories I've posted, providing depth and context for free, fixing the most interesting aspects of the most interesting subjects even more prominently in my foremind.

The upshot is that operating Boing Boing has not only given me a central repository of all of the fruits of my labors in the information fields, but it also has increased the volume and quality of the yield. I know more, find more, and understand better than I ever have, all because of Boing Boing.

The nuggets I've mined are at my instant disposal. I can use Blogger's search interface to retrieve the stories I've posted with just a few keywords. While prepping a speech, writing a column, or working on a story, I will usually work with a browser window open to Blogger's Edit Your Blog screen, cursor tabbed into the search field. I flip back and forth between my browser and my editor, entering a few keywords and instantly retrieving the details of some salient point—it's my personal knowledge management system, annotated and augmented by my readers.

Being deprived of my blog right now would be akin to suffering extensive brain-damage. Huge swaths of acquired knowledge would simply vanish. Just as my TiVo frees me from having to watch boring television by watching it for me, my blog frees me up from having to remember the minutae of my life, storing it for me in handy and contextual form.

—Cory Doctorow, *http://www.boingboing.net/*

Check around to see if your city has a blogging community. Some cities have such communities and arrange happy hours or other fun events in the city. One example: *dfwblogs.com* (we rule!).

Since blogging, I've meet and shared a room with a fellow bloggette at SXSW [South by South-West]; got hooked on Googlewhacking, sent and received a gift from the Secret Santa Exchange; met the DFWblogs.com crowd at SXSW; gotten help on a personal level from a bloggette—help that I otherwise might not have gotten if I had not met her; I edited a book because someone found me through my weblog; a fellow bloggette who works for a web design shop received an RFP with a chance to bid from a major drink distributor through her blog; shared pain with fellow bloggers after 9/11; and gotten to know many cool people who have made me laugh, cry, smile, freak out, or just celebrate life.

—Meryl K. Evans, *http://www.meryl.net/blog*

In March of 2000, my husband and I decided to divorce, after nearly 10 years (and one daughter) of being together. While the decision was relieving to me, it seemed to unleash this flood of intellectual activity that I'd held in during my marriage, issues I wasn't even aware existed until then. It seemed the time had come to get it all out so I could make some sense of what I was going through and start completely anew. I had always written in blank journals, but during my marriage I stopped. So, I figured since I wasn't going to be married anymore, I could start back up again. The only thing was, I wasn't entirely convinced I could write about anything that wasn't business-like or technically-useful in nature (I'm a technical writer by trade). I hadn't written anything personal in years—I wasn't sure I ever could again.

So, to re-start my un-technical writing engine, I signed up for a free account on Xanga.com and began practicing, writing reviews of things I liked or found useful. It was great practice, and I got some cool feedback from the other members there and it gave me some hope that perhaps I could write my way out of a paper bag if necessary.

Shortly afterward, as I started getting more comfortable, I decided to use my existing web site (malleron.com) for something other than an extended hard drive. In looking around for diary scripts, I happened upon Blogger and immediately signed up. Of course, I wasn't exactly sure what I wanted to say and procrastinated for weeks before I wrote anything. I worried for days about the consequences of putting my personal thoughts online: what if a co-worker reads it? What if my ex-husband reads it? What if I get fired because of it? What if anyone reads it and gets the wrong idea about me? What if someone reads it, looks up my domain record, and stalks me? What are the risks to my daughter if I do this?

Finally, after what seemed like forever, I posted something to my site. It took me several hours and felt rather painful, but when I saw it published I felt strangely better. For the first year or so, I didn't post very often or regularly. After my divorce was final, however, my posts picked up in both frequency and intensity. I even started getting visitor feedback on my writing, which was at once gratifying and frightening.

When I started a blog, I didn't even know what it was or how it was "supposed" to be used. It just looked like an efficient way to keep a journal online, and I needed something that would challenge me to be truthful with myself about my life so far and where I wanted to go. Having it online seemed the natural thing to do since I was afraid the insulation of an offline journal (which no one else would ever see) would encourage me to avoid the issues I was looking to explore. Plus, I figured if you're going to be your own therapist and bare your soul in public, you may as well be as truthful as you can. Indeed, I had avoided so many issues, lied to myself so often throughout my marriage. I couldn't afford to any longer now that it was just me and my 2-year-old daughter. I needed the public space to force me to examine myself and my life, even when I didn't want to because of all the fear and guilt I carried.

Now that I've been keeping a blog for a couple years, I can't imagine not writing in it or not writing at all, period. Keeping a blog has helped me through a lot in my life— most of which I wish had never happened—as has the positive feedback. I've even made some new friends because of my blog, people I wouldn't have known if I kept all my thoughts in a book in my desk drawer. People who have expanded my awareness and made my roughest times much more bearable.

—Jenny, *http://www.malleron.com*

While working for my previous employer, AGENCY.COM, we launched a weblog (*http://lab.agency.com*) using Movable Type. We were all interested in weblogging and how it made publishing and communicating thoughts, insight, and knowledge easier. Interested in how far the tool and the concept could be taken, we endeavored to be a bit different. We wanted something that featured posts that were more refined and in-depth than the multiple short off the cuff posts that were common in the blogsphere. The *lab.agency.com* site would also feature contribution from multiple authors as opposed to a single individual. I would guess that some would argue this approach isn't blogging at all. I even question it myself.

At the time we started, it was (I think) pretty unique in that it was run by a commercial entity who is paid for its thinking.

I think it was a success, but marginally so.

You're always a little bit better for trying something, even if it doesn't succeed as you have planned because you always have the knowledge of why it didn't work to avoid issues next time. Here is some of the wisdom I gained on weblogging that I can impart from my experience with this project:

- Frequency of updates is important to effectively communicating through a weblog. In choosing to exclusively publish in-depth and, therefore, long-format entries, the communal dialogue of the medium is diminished as less attractive and less interesting. I liken this type of posting to a conference presentation rather then a birds-of-a-feather (BOF). Another effect of our focus on in-depth pieces is that the time and effort required to compose an entry put quite a burden on contributors particularly given other responsibilites. I personally found myself looking at a backlog of posts I wanted to do. Sometimes by the time I got around to finishing or even starting a post it wasn't relevant. In retrospect, I think brief and rapid posts in which our views would take shape and change over time would have been more effective.

- A group weblog requires coordination and focus. When it came to topic matter the site had loose requirements. Being a diverse group of individuals from quite different backgrounds and different belief systems, the site seemed a bit scattershot and struggled to have an identity in my opinion. The freedom of one author with free reign to the weblog's content work because the personality and interests of that author are defined. Combining a group of personalities with a loose (or no) focus is a different matter. It becomes too difficult for one person to filter and follow along. Coupled with our low frequency of posts, no real personality or focus emerged.

- Weblogging must come from personal motivation and passion—not just another line item on a typically too long list of responsibilities. There were some less than inspired posts made because someone was getting poked and prodded to make one. Others simply didn't make any despite being prime candidates to participate. This is why I believe that while the concept of a knowledge weblog (or k-log) is a good and valid assertion, a mangerial dictate will not derive much value out of the effort to use use weblogs on knowledge or project management. The reality is they are unlikely to be successful anytime soon without a cultural shift that will take years to achieve at best. While the difficult situation of the company contributed to the loss of motivation, in retrospect, contributors should have been completely voluntary and given their own personal weblogs to operate.

The site got off to a good start when "soft launched" but slowly began to loose interest for the reasons I stated above. By the time it was officially (hard) launched (*http://biz.yahoo.com/prnews/020424/nyw046_1.html*), it was struggling under its own weight and the pall of impending reductions and reorganization in the company tempered much of the enthusiasm.

I'm not discouraged at all in my first experience with participating in weblogging. I believe in it perhaps maybe even more so than before. In fact I'm setting up my own to continue publishing my thoughts and insights while I look for new employment. It's a great way to stay sharp. I've also found it to be a good way to get prospective employers to get a better sense of my abilities and knowledge of the space. Perhaps it will help me land a new job and that would be a really interesting story worth publishing. ;)

—Timothy Appnel, *http://tima.mplode.com*

Keeping a blog updated daily is taking on quite a bit. It sounds simple, just type out a few lines about your day, your thoughts of the day or what you found on the Web that day. Doesn't sound complicated. But it can be. I don't feel like writing every day. Some days I don't feel like even turning on the computer except for a quick game or nine. So, my blog quickly gets stale. Still, I haven't totally abandoned it.

A blog is fun too. You can do so much with them. You only have to please yourself really so design away. Add those fantasy graphics you wouldn't want to use on your personal site. Add that font you love even though no one else has it downloaded. Go wild, find a jungle cat skin background and make that the focus of your blog.

—ThatGrrl, *http://www.thatgrrl.com/*

Some essential blogging tips:

In order to keep your blogs really fresh, invite a group of your friends/colleagues and give them blogging access. That way, you'll have several reporters blogging information, and you won't end up killing yourself, trying to keep your blog populated with good information.

If you use Blogger, upgrade to Blogger Pro. You can have your team post to the blog from email, create and syndicate your blog as an RSS feed, and a whole lot more!

Adding the ability to post comments on your blog extends interactivity and usefulness to the blog itself. Blogs are about community and information, and commenting is a real way to gauge your viewer's blogging efforts.

Blogging is one of the quickest ways to update your site. Syndicating others' blogs into your own site is another. There is a wealth of information out there—tap into it!

—Eric E, Dolecki, *http://www.ericd.net*

While I rode into the bloggiing community on the coattails of my son (www.theone-truebix.com), who was blogging before there were official blogs, I have come into my own among some major bloggers, and the process is keeping me sane. I retired from my job more than a year ago to care for my 86 year old mother (something I swore I would never do, but, well, connections are connections after all). Making that decision, however, disconnected me from the creatively and intellectually active life that I've always had. Blogging re-wired my personal connections and resurrected my identity as a writer and a catalyst for ideological exploration. It's not that blogging has enabled me to find my voice; as a published poet who used to also give reading, I've always had a very strong voice. Blogging has given my voice an even larger world to reach. While I'm tempted to say that it's unfortunate that I haven't encountered many other bloggers bear my age (62) with similar interests, the truth is that I am energized, excited, and inspired by the amazing young minds I continue to meld with. In a truly magical way, they have given me my dream: Cronedom. "Wise Woman" status. And I say that with only a partial "smirk." (I have done some "virtual rituals" that have been as much fun as the old 1960s happenings—and ultimately more productive to boot.) Through the magic on the blognet, I've been able to tough the lives of people I never would have met otherwise, and in many ways, I know some of them better than I know people who have been in my "real" life for years. And at some point, when life frees me up to do so, I will go "on the road" and get a hug in person some of those bloggers whose virtual touches have transformed my unexpected and isolating situations into an extended family party. I am still on a quest for "older-wiser" bloggers. If you know of any, send them my way.

—Elaine Frankonis

I have met people because of my weblog, even I got my present job because of it! I try to use it as an "alternative communication media." I don't write every day. I usually write something about a subject I think will be interesting, maybe from the news, maybe one thought about life, and then let people comment about it or share different opinions and use the blog as a little "debate space." Them when the comments slow down, I write again, another subject, and the process starts again. Sometimes I also write about myself or a movie too.

—Javi Loureiro (Barcelona, Spain), *http://www.sieyin.com*

First, if you are using a blog because it's important to you (whether that's in a metaphysical sense or a business sense) you should make sure that you have more than one way to post. I'm a Blogger Pro member, but I also keep a bare-bones API site in my bookmarks (*www.teknik.net/misfit*)for times when I'm on the road with my PDA (which doesn't support the right IE functions) or when the Pro publishing engine is out of whack.

Second, realize that your blog doesn't have to be your whole site. In my case, I have the blog with my images "tucked away" so that someone visiting for the first time isn't immediately hit with a five minute wait.

Finally, remember that your blog should be about your voice and your thoughts. Many blogs seem to be more about "Me too" than "About me."

—Ewan Grantham, *http://www.a1161.com/blog.html*

I have been interested for some time in becoming more of a producer than a consumer: I want to give back in some way. I find mailing lists and newsgroups are OK for some interchanges and seach engines can help locate stuff, but sometimes it helps to find a site that gives the information you seek some context. You can find related informationat the fog density you feel comfortable , or ask the author a question.

So I have a place to collect my random musings and HOWTOs, and like a snowball, it gets larger and larger with each entry. A couple of hundred visits a day after just a couple of months makes me think some of this is useful. Rather than bother people with email, I can let them find stuff via Google and still feel like I'm being useful.

As for MT, a friend showed me his site and told me how easy it was to setup: took me less than an hour and it's been easy. Like all good tools, it lets you focus on what you're doing, not how to use the tool. I have done very little in terms of customization (Mena made all that unnecessary: thanks!), and it looks great.

—Paul Beard *http://paulbeard.no-ip.org/movabletype*

Blog for fun. If it stops being fun, you're doing it wrong.

Don't worry about what everyone else does on their blog. Do what you want. It's your blog, it should reflect you.

Keep the front page down to 7 days or 50 KB, whichever is smaller.

Don't bother writing your own blogging tool unless you're in it for the long haul. After writing my own tool and using it for a few months, I still had a long list of features to implement. Instead of taking another month to implement all of them, I got then in about 15 minutes by installing Movable Type.

—Dan Hersam, *http://dan.hersam.com*

Since Movable Type lets you set up multiple blogs from the same installation, I set up a second one in a password protected part of my web site. Combined with the "Post to MT" bookmarklet, it's a very convenient way for me to record and organize personal bookmarks and notes as I'm surfing along on one of the 4 different computers I use daily. I can go back later to review and format the information for my public site.

—Laura Blalock, *http://www.imaginaryworld.net*

Do not blog unless you are ready for your details to be unleashed to the world! Remember that your readers are other bloggers, who link, quote, forward, gossip, and more about every word you write it, generally but hours after you have published it yourself. Also, Google catches stuff for quite a while, so once it's published, it's difficult to get rid of.

Blogging enables you to easily publish and release your stream of consciousness thoughts, essentially giving you instant gratification. However, it is helpful for yourself and readers to start with a quote, bulletpoints that summarize your day, etc. This helps to ground them and also is a great way to make yourself think of what the net of it was. It is also cool to quote someone else, because it downgradesthe blog from being 100% self-absorbed to 90%.

—Joyce Guan, *http://www.clownagama.com*

Use a content managment system (Blogger, Movable Type, or the like) if you're new to blogging or web design. It will let you focus on quality content.

Layout is not THAT important. People read blogs to learn about the blogger, not to see their cool design skills (although they're definitely nice to see :)).

Don't make a post just because you haven't made one on a specific day. That's no way to develop quality content, and it's almost always obvious.

Blogging for yourself can be liberating—use your blog as an online diary of your thoughts. Keep the URL secret if you want, but blogging is a great outlet for stress and other problems of the everyday world.

Don't be scared of blogging/bloggers. Jump in and have fun!

Don't worry about posting about every single thing that happens in your life. Strike a balance between enough detail to get the interesting things and too much detail to separate the good stuff from the bad.

—Greg Leffler, *http://greg.louisville.ky.us*

When we talk about weblogs, we're talking about a way of organizing information, independent of its topic. What we write about does not define us as bloggers; it's how we write about it (frequently, ad nauseaum, peppered with links).

Weblogs simply provide the framework, as haiku imposes order on words. The structure of the documents we're creating enable us to build our social networks on top of it—the distributed conversations, the blogrolling lists, and the friendships that begin online and are solidified over a "bloggers dinner" in the real world.

As bloggers, we're in the middle of, and enjoying, an evolution of communication. The traits of weblogs mentioned above will likely change and advance as our tools improve and our technology matures. What's important is that we've embraced a medium free of the physical limitations of pages, intrusions of editors, and delays of tedious publishing systems. As with free speech itself, what we say isn't as important as the system that enables us to say it.

—Meg Hourihan, *http://www.megnut.com*

Index

We'd like to hear your suggestions for improving our indexes. Send email to *index@oreilly.com*.

About the Authors

Cory Doctorow (*www.craphound.com*) is the coeditor of *Boing Boing: A Directory of Wonderful Things* (*boingboing.net*), and is the outreach coordinator for the Electric Frontier Foundation (*www.eff.org*). Cory is a prolific and award-winning science fiction writer; his first novel, *Down and Out in Magic Kingdom*, will be published by Tor Books in late 2002. He is a regular contributor to *Wired* magazine and a columnist for the O'Reilly Network.

Rael Dornfest is a researcher at O'Reilly & Associates, Inc., focusing on technologies just beyond the pale. He assesses, experiments, programs, and writes for the O'Reilly Network and O'Reilly publications. Rael is program chair for the O'Reilly Emerging Technology Conference and O'Reilly Mac OS X Conference, chair of the RSS-DEV Working Group, and developer of Meerkat: An Open Wire Service (*meerkat.oreillynet.com*). In his copious free time, Rael develops bits and bobs of freeware (most notably, Blosxom) and maintains his raelity bytes weblog (*www.oreillynet.com/~rael*).

J. Scott Johnson is the president and founder of The FuzzyGroup, Inc. (*www.fuzzygroup.net*), a software, services, and web development company. He is also a regular blogger (*www.fuzzyblog.com*), software engineer, and author of the popular Marketing 101 series of blog articles. Earlier in his career, he was vice president of engineering for Mascot Network, where he led the development and deployment of Internet portals for over 300,000 college students; chief technology strategist for Dataware Technologies, where he led the development of Enterprise Knowledge Management Systems; and president/founder of NTERGAD, where he created the award-winning HyperWriter family of products.

Shelley Powers is an author and independent consultant currently living in St. Louis. She's authored and coauthored several other O'Reilly books, including *Developing ASP Components* and *Unix Power Tools*, Third Edition. In addition to her writing, Shelley is also a technology architect and senior software developer. She maintains a set of web sites under the Burningbird Network (*burningbird.net*), including the Burningbird weblog (*weblog.burningbird.net*).

Benjamin Trott is a programmer and cocreater of Movable Type. With Mena G. Trott, he is a partner and cofounder of Six Apart. He develops all the backend code for Movable Type, contributes regularly to the Comprehensive Perl Archive Network (CPAN), and has written for Perl.com. Benjamin likes cryptography and Serge Gainsbourg, and he dreams about universal wireless, so he can travel to France.

Mena G. Trott is a designer and cocreator of Movable Type. She has partnered with Benjamin Trott to form Six Apart, a company developed to promote personal publishing on the Web through innovative tools. Mena enjoys making things aesthetically pleasing as well as functionally intuitive. When she's not developing Movable Type, she writes her own weblog, *dollarshort.org*. Mena loves West Highland white terriers, French pop music, Disneyland, and ice cream.

Colophon

Our look is the result of reader comments, our own experimentation, and feedback from distribution channels. Distinctive covers complement our distinctive approach to technical topics, breathing personality and life into potentially dry subjects.

The animals on the cover of *Essential Blogging* are flat-headed cats. Also known as little Malayan red cats, flat-headed cats are found in tropical forests in Thailand, Malaysia, Borneo, and Sumatra.

Obviously, the most distinctive feature found on the flat-headed cat is its head, which is flat and enhanced by its unusually small ears. Also, its eye sockets are completely encircled by bone, increasing the width of the head.

The flat-headed cat is nocturnal, and its diet consists mainly of fish and frogs. Because of its well-developed premolars and webbed feet, the flat-headed cat is highly adaptable to its fishing environment—more so than even the fishing cat.

Sarah Sherman was the production editor and copyeditor, and Linley Dolby was the proofreader for *Essential Blogging*. Linley Dolby, Mary Anne Weeks Mayo, and Claire Cloutier provided quality control. Johnna Van Hoose Dinse wrote the index.

Ellie Volckhausen designed the cover of this book, based on a series design by Edie Freedman. The cover image is a 19th-century engraving from the Dover Pictorial Archive. Emma Colby produced the cover layout with QuarkXPress 4.1 using Adobe's ITC Garamond font.

Melanie Wang designed the interior layout, based on a series design by David Futato. This book was converted to FrameMaker 5.5.6 with a format conversion tool created by Erik Ray, Jason McIntosh, Neil Walls, and Mike Sierra that uses Perl and XML technologies. The text font is Linotype Birka; the heading font is Adobe Myriad Condensed; and the code font is LucasFont's TheSans Mono Condensed. The illustrations that appear in the book were produced by Robert Romano and Jessamyn Read using Macromedia FreeHand 9 and Adobe Photoshop 6. The tip and warning icons were drawn by Christopher Bing. This colophon was written by Sarah Sherman.

Other Titles Available from O'Reilly

Web Administration

Web Privacy with P3P

By Lorrie Faith Cranor
1st Edition September 2002 (est.)
384 pages (est.), ISBN 0-596-00371-4

Many people other than web developers will be interested in this new book. Privacy consultants, corporate decision-makers, lawyers, public policy-makers, developers of P3P software products, and any individual interested in online privacy issues will want to understand the P3P protocol and how web sites can be configured to comply with it. Because the chair of W3C's P3P Specification Working Group wrote the book, *Web Privacy with P3P* goes right to source.

Web Security, Privacy & Commerce, 2nd Edition

By Simson Garfinkel with Gene Spafford
2nd Edition November 2001
792 pages, ISBN 0-596-00045-6

Web Security, Privacy & Commerce cuts through the front-page sensationalism and examines the major issues facing e-commerce. It reveals what the real risks are and how to minimize them. Dramatically expanded from the first edition, it includes new information about PKI, privacy, and e-commerce and examines what works or doesn't work on today's web. Destined to be the classic reference on web security risks and the techniques and technologies that protect users, organizations, systems, and networks.

Running Weblogs with Slash

By chromatic, Brian Aker & David Krieger
1st Edition January 2002
288 pages, ISBN 0-596-00100-2

Running Weblogs with Slash is written for system administrators who may not have the time or the background to learn all about Slash by reading the source code. The book collects the knowledge currently distributed throughout the Slash source code, Slashcode web site, and mailing lists, and organizes it into a coherent package. As a bonus, the book shares how various Slash administrators have customized their sites.

Apache: The Definitive Guide, 3rd Edition

By Ben Laurie & Peter Laurie
3rd Edition December 2002 (est.)
476 pages (est.), Includes CD-ROM
ISBN 0-596-00203-3

This complete guide to the Apache web server discusses how to obtain, set up, and secure the software on both Unix and Windows systems. The updated 3rd edition covers both Apache 1.3 and Apache 2.0, the latest release of the software, and contains new material on mod_perl, PHP, Cocoon, Tomcat, and other new technologies that are associated with this dominant web server software.

Web Performance Tuning, 2nd Edition

By Patrick Killelea
2nd Edition, March 2002
480 pages, ISBN 0-596-00172-X

Web Performance Tuning covers web server software and how to get optimal performance from a browser; tuning the hardware; and maximizing the capacity of the network itself. Readers start with concrete advice for improving crippled performance and move on to a conceptual background of the principles of computing performance. Finally, examining web transactions in detail, the author points out the weak links in the chain and shows how to strengthen them.

Perl for Web Site Management

By John Callender
1st Edition October 2001
528 pages, ISBN 1-56592-647-1

Perl for Web Site Management shows readers how to use Perl to help do everyday web tasks. Assuming no prior programming experience, this book teaches how to write CGI scripts, incorporate search engines, convert multiple text files into HTML, monitor log files, and track users as they navigate to a site. Whether the reader is a web programmer, web administrator, a designer—or simply a dabbler, this book provides a practical, hands-on introduction to Perl.

O'REILLY®

To order: *800-998-9938* • *order@oreilly.com* • *www.oreilly.com*
Online editions of most O'Reilly titles are available by subscription at *safari.oreilly.com*
Also available at most retail and online bookstores.

Web Administration

Server Load Balancing

By Tony Bourke
1st Edition August 2001
192 pages, ISBN 0-596-00050-2

Load balancing distributes traffic efficiently among network servers so that no individual server is overburdened. This vendor-neutral guide to the concepts and terminology of load balancing offers practical guidance to planning and implementing the technology in most environments. It includes a configuration guide with diagrams and sample configurations for installing, configuring, and maintaining products from the four major server load balancing vendors.

Web Caching

By Duane Wessels
1st Edition June 2001
318 pages, ISBN 1-56592-536-X

A properly designed web cache, by reducing network traffic and improving access times to popular web sites, is a boon to network administrators and web users alike. This book hands you all the technical information you need to design, deploy, and operate an effective web caching service. It also covers the important political aspects of web caching, including privacy and security issues.

Incident Response: Planning & Management

By Kenneth R. van Wyk &
Richard Forno
1st Edition August 2001
234 pages, ISBN 0-596-00130-4

Incident Response has the technical and administrative information organizations need for planning how to handle computer-related incidents. The book describes and compares a variety of problem-solving approaches, and outlines techniques and procedures for an incident response team to use. In addition, *Incident Response* describes several types of tools for investigating incidents and lists extensive online resources.

Building Internet Firewalls, 2nd Edition

By Elizabeth D. Zwicky, Simon Cooper
& D. Brent Chapman
2nd Edition June 2000
894 pages, ISBN 1-56592-871-7

Completely revised and much expanded, this second edition of the highly respected and best-selling *Building Internet Firewalls* now covers Unix, Linux, and Windows NT. It's a practical and detailed guide that provides step-by-step explanations of how to design and install firewalls, and how to configure Internet services to work with a firewall. It covers a wide range of services and protocols. It also contains a complete list of resources, including the location of many publicly available firewalls construction tools.

HTTP Pocket Reference

By Clinton Wong
1st Edition May 2000
80 pages, ISBN 1-56592-862-8

All web programmers, administrators, and application developers need to be familiar with HTTP in order to work effectively. The *HTTP Pocket Reference* provides a solid conceptual foundation of HTTP, and also serves as a quick reference to each of the headers and status codes that compose an HTTP transaction. For those who need to get "beyond the browser," this book is the place to start.

O'REILLY®

To order: *800-998-9938* • *order@oreilly.com* • *www.oreilly.com*
Online editions of most O'Reilly titles are available by subscription at *safari.oreilly.com*
Also available at most retail and online bookstores.

How to stay in touch with O'Reilly

1. Visit our award-winning web site

http://www.oreilly.com/

★ "Top 100 Sites on the Web"—PC Magazine
★ CIO Magazine's Web Business 50 Awards

Our web site contains a library of comprehensive product information (including book excerpts and tables of contents), downloadable software, background articles, interviews with technology leaders, links to relevant sites, book cover art, and more. File us in your bookmarks or favorites!

2. Join our email mailing lists

Sign up to get email announcements of new books and conferences, special offers, and O'Reilly Network technology newsletters at:

http://www.elists.oreilly.com

It's easy to customize your free elists subscription so you'll get exactly the O'Reilly news you want.

3. Get examples from our books

To find example files for a book, go to:

http://www.oreilly.com/catalog

select the book, and follow the "Examples" link.

4. Work with us

Check out our web site for current employment opportunities:

http://jobs.oreilly.com/

5. Register your book

Register your book at:

http://register.oreilly.com

6. Contact us

O'Reilly & Associates, Inc.
1005 Gravenstein Hwy North
Sebastopol, CA 95472 USA
TEL: 707-827-7000 or 800-998-9938
　　　　(6am to 5pm PST)
FAX: 707-829-0104

order@oreilly.com
For answers to problems regarding your order or our products. To place a book order online visit:

http://www.oreilly.com/order_new/

catalog@oreilly.com
To request a copy of our latest catalog.

booktech@oreilly.com
For book content technical questions or corrections.

corporate@oreilly.com
For educational, library, and corporate sales.

proposals@oreilly.com
To submit new book proposals to our editors and product managers.

international@oreilly.com
For information about our international distributors or translation queries. For a list of our distributors outside of North America check out:

http://international.oreilly.com/distributors.html

O'REILLY®

To order: *800-998-9938 • order@oreilly.com • www.oreilly.com*
Online editions of most O'Reilly titles are available by subscription at *safari.oreilly.com*
Also available at most retail and online bookstores.